PRINCE of PERSIA

Created by
Jordan Mechner

Written by
A. B. Sina

Artwork by
LeUyen Pham & Alex Puvilland

Color by
Hilary Sycamore

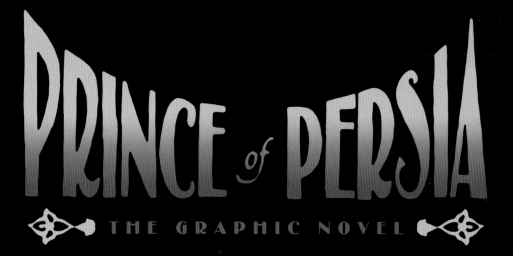

PRINCE of PERSIA
THE GRAPHIC NOVEL

:01

First Second
New York & London

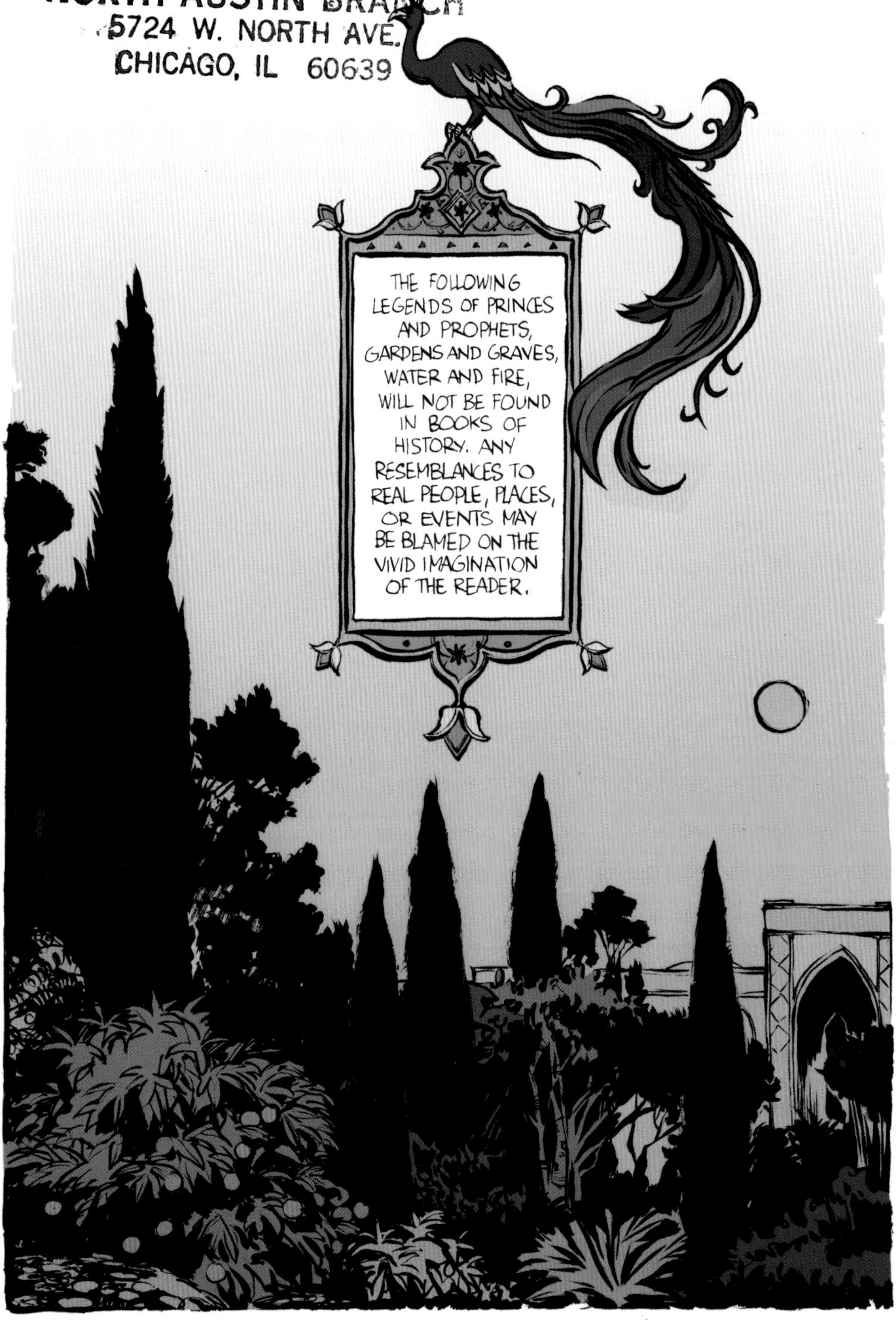
THE FOLLOWING LEGENDS OF PRINCES AND PROPHETS, GARDENS AND GRAVES, WATER AND FIRE, WILL NOT BE FOUND IN BOOKS OF HISTORY. ANY RESEMBLANCES TO REAL PEOPLE, PLACES, OR EVENTS MAY BE BLAMED ON THE VIVID IMAGINATION OF THE READER.

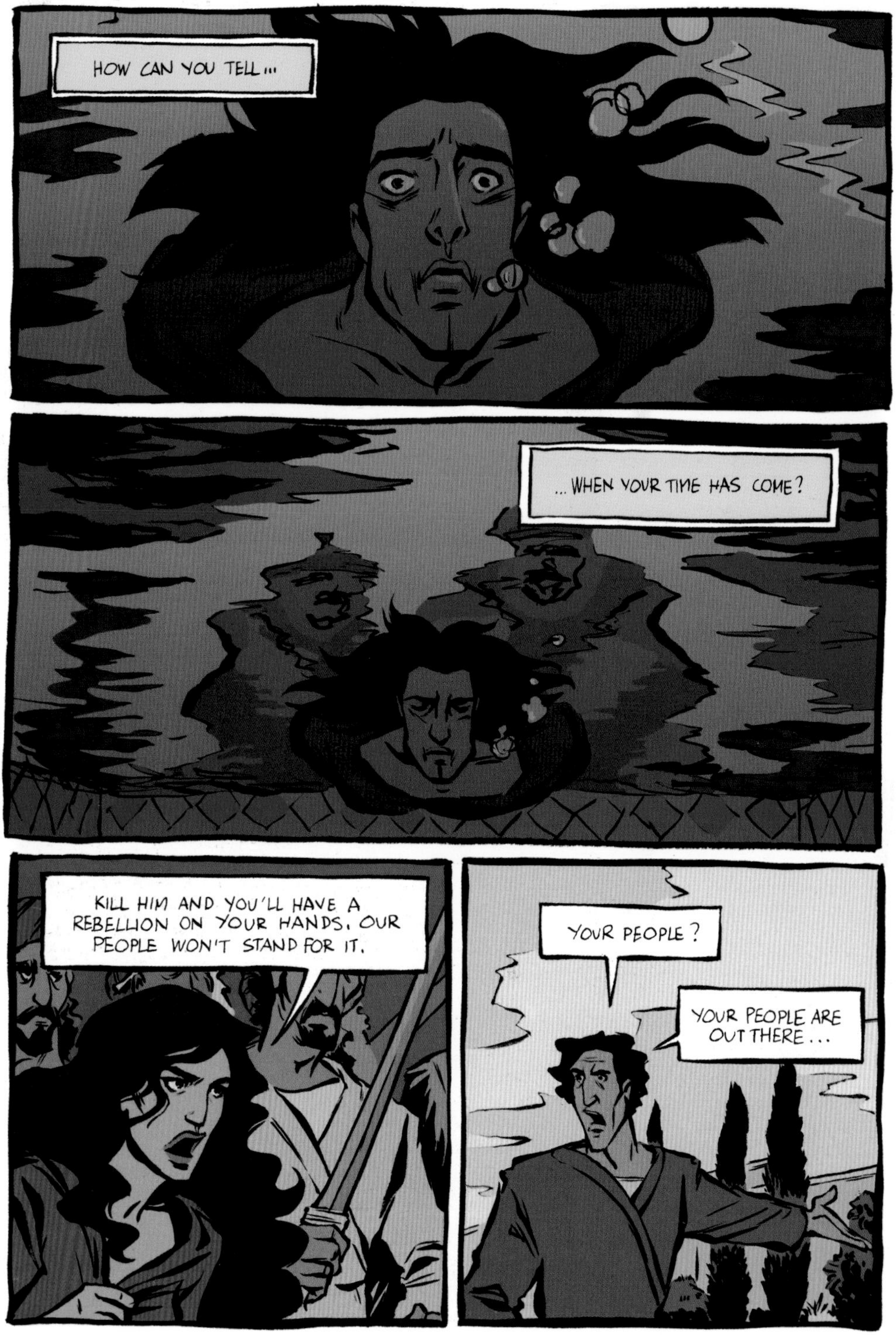
HOW CAN YOU TELL...
...WHEN YOUR TIME HAS COME?
KILL HIM AND YOU'LL HAVE A REBELLION ON YOUR HANDS. OUR PEOPLE WON'T STAND FOR IT.
YOUR PEOPLE?
YOUR PEOPLE ARE OUT THERE...

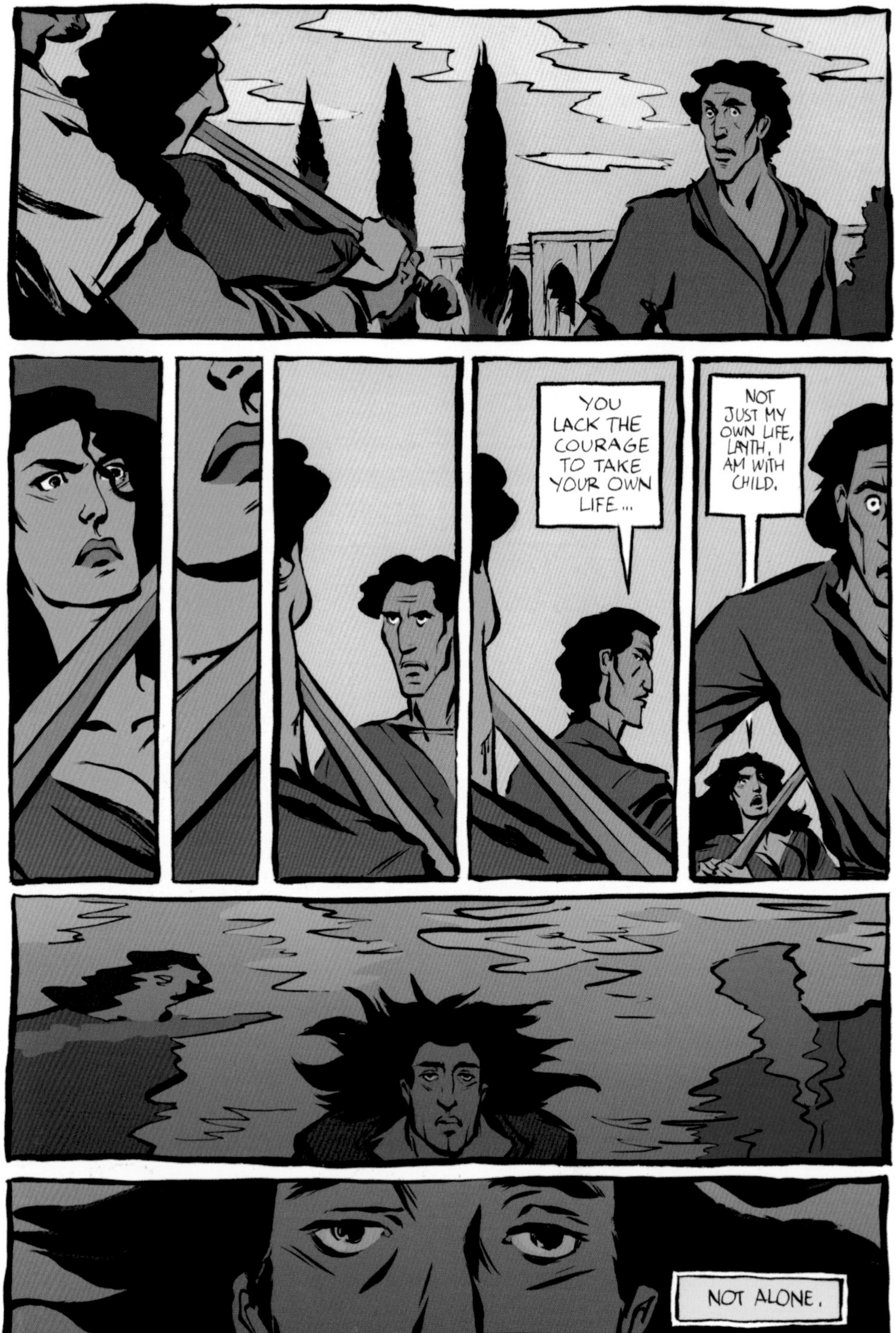
YOU LACK THE COURAGE TO TAKE YOUR OWN LIFE...
NOT JUST MY OWN LIFE, LAYTH, I AM WITH CHILD.
NOT ALONE.

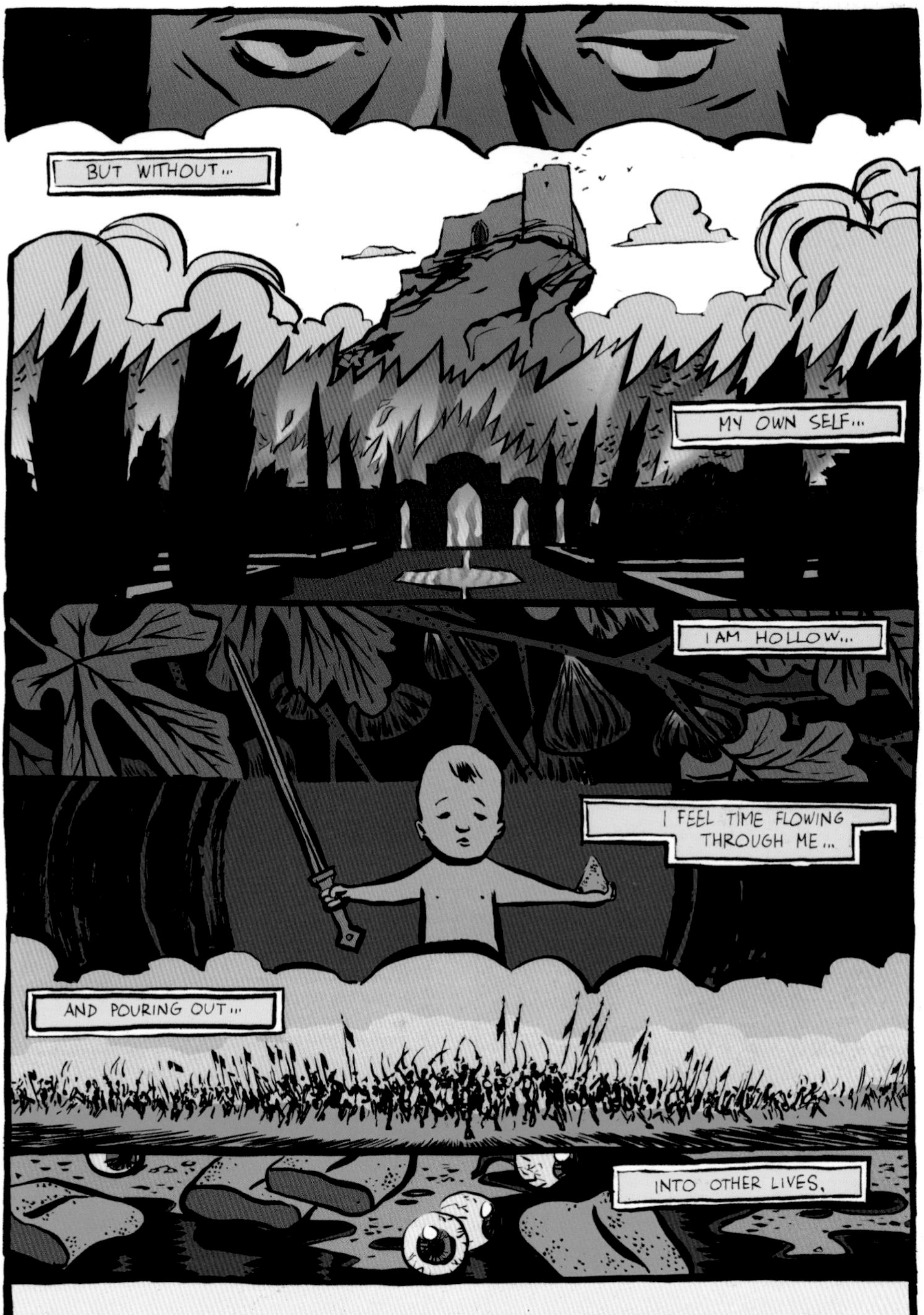
BUT WITHOUT...
MY OWN SELF...
I AM HOLLOW...
I FEEL TIME FLOWING THROUGH ME...
AND POURING OUT...
INTO OTHER LIVES,

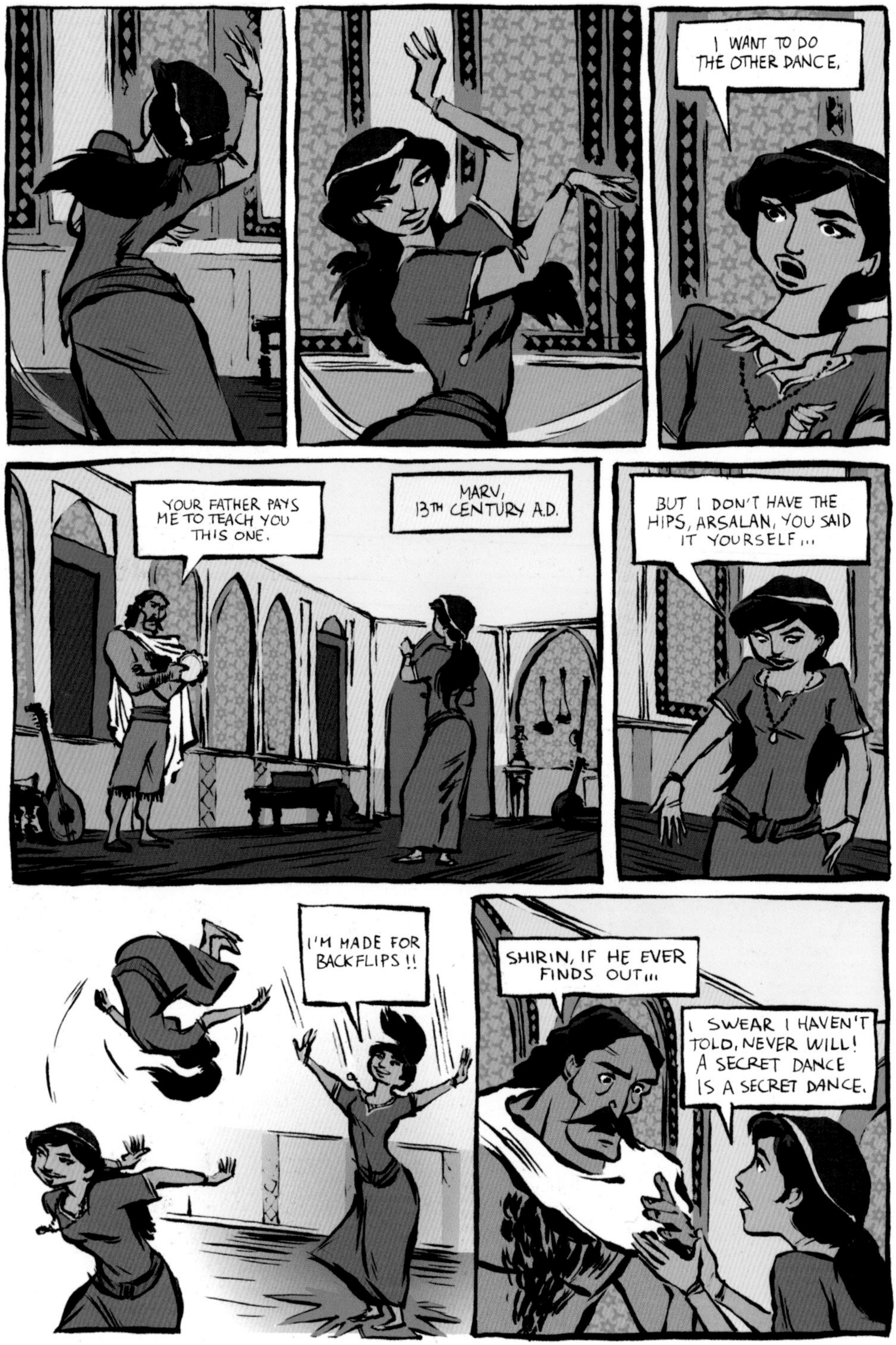
I WANT TO DO THE OTHER DANCE.
YOUR FATHER PAYS ME TO TEACH YOU THIS ONE.
MARV, 13TH CENTURY A.D.
BUT I DON'T HAVE THE HIPS, ARSALAN, YOU SAID IT YOURSELF...
I'M MADE FOR BACKFLIPS!!
SHIRIN, IF HE EVER FINDS OUT...
I SWEAR I HAVEN'T TOLD, NEVER WILL! A SECRET DANCE IS A SECRET DANCE.

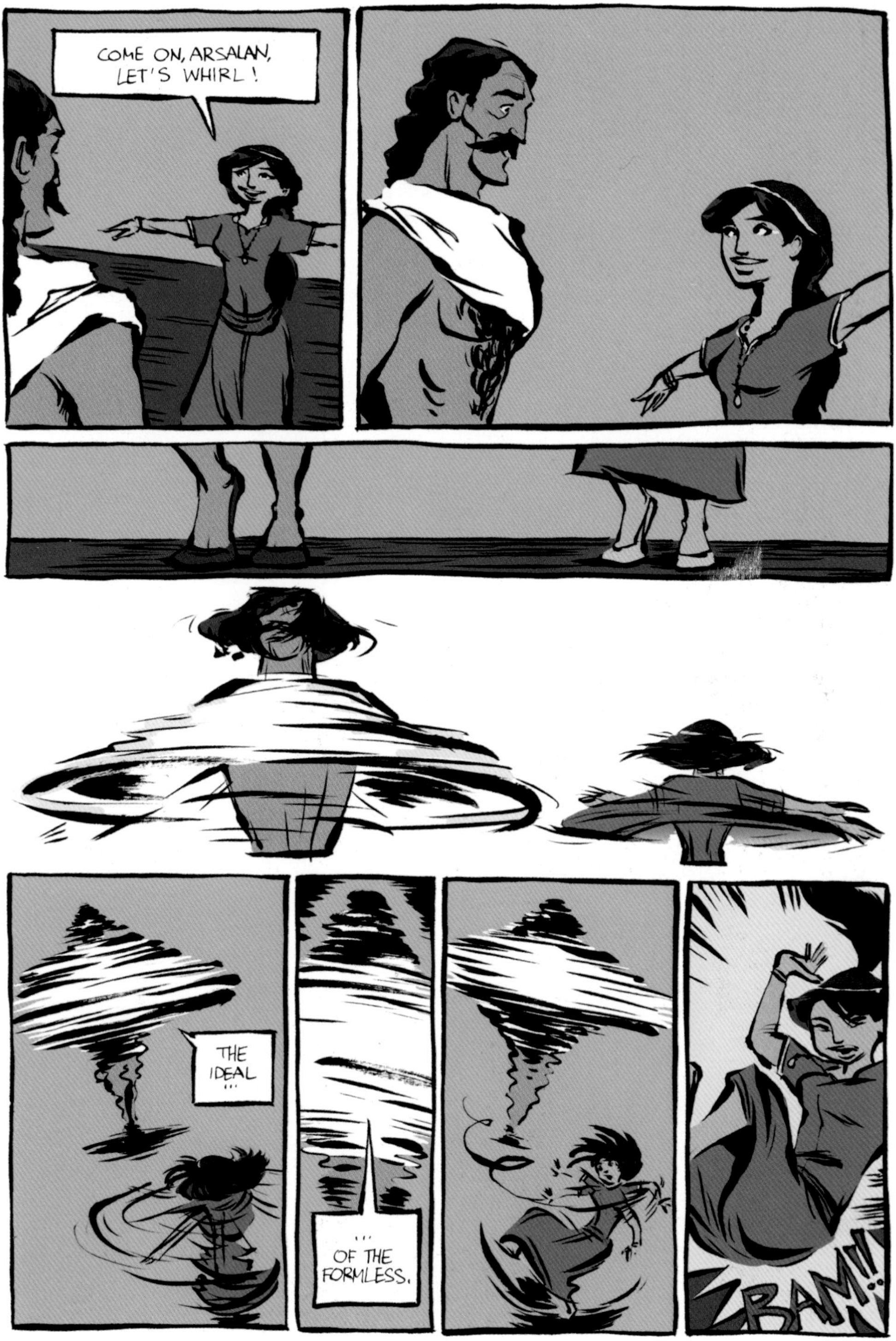
COME ON, ARSALAN, LET'S WHIRL!
THE IDEAL ...
... OF THE FORMLESS.
BAM!!

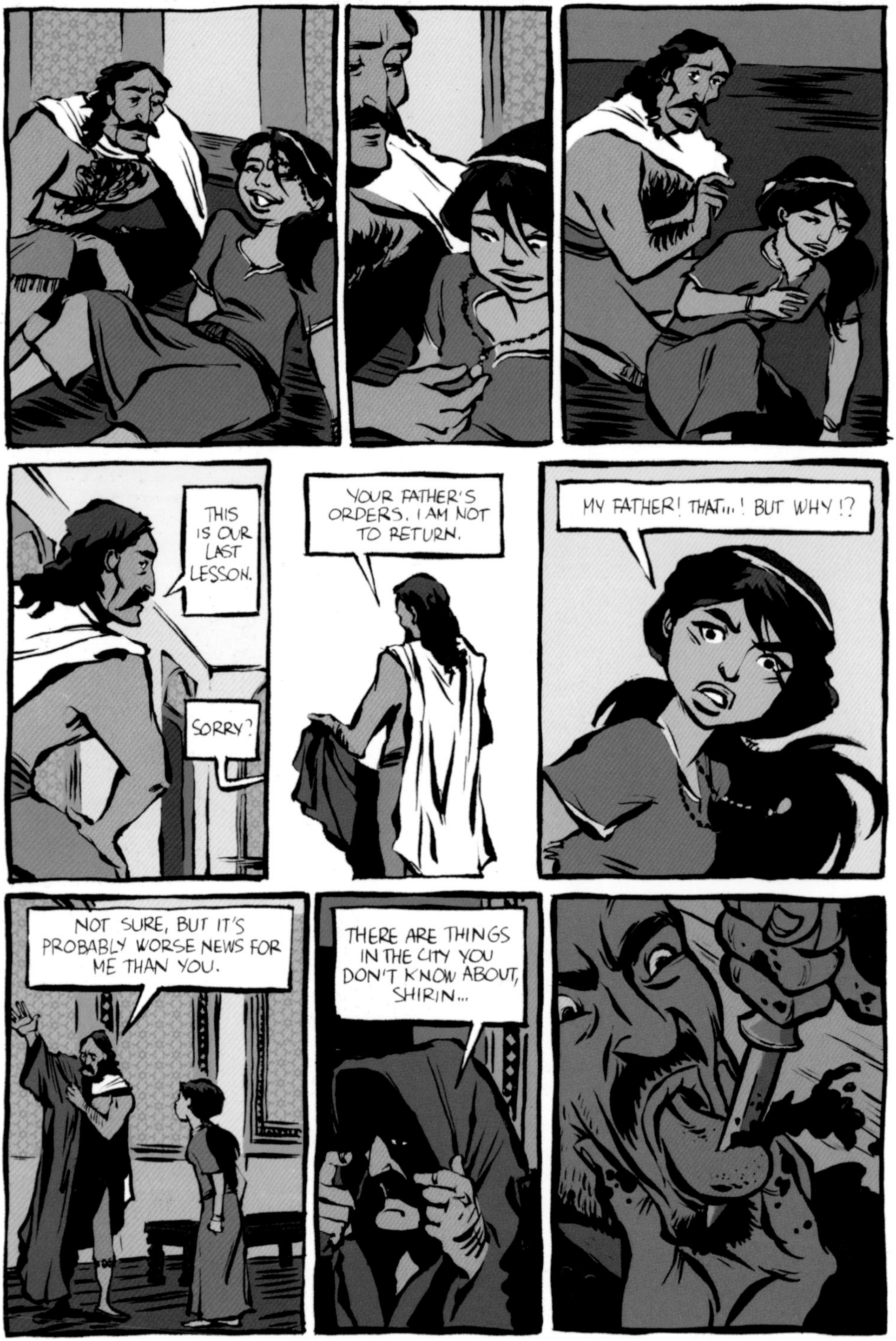
THIS IS OUR LAST LESSON.
SORRY?
YOUR FATHER'S ORDERS. I AM NOT TO RETURN.
MY FATHER! THAT...! BUT WHY!?
NOT SURE, BUT IT'S PROBABLY WORSE NEWS FOR ME THAN YOU.
THERE ARE THINGS IN THE CITY YOU DON'T KNOW ABOUT, SHIRIN...

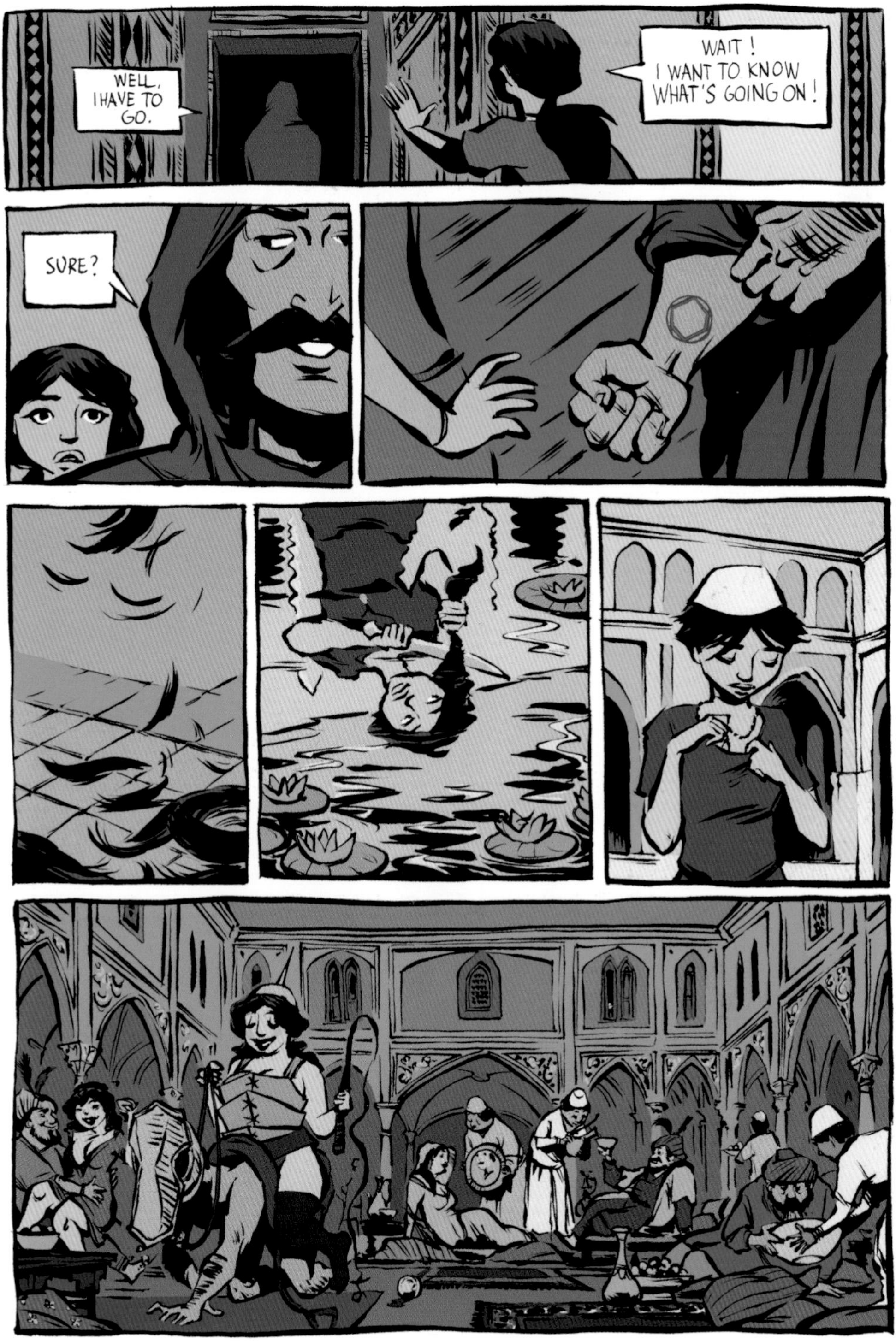
WELL, I HAVE TO GO.
WAIT ! I WANT TO KNOW WHAT'S GOING ON !
SURE?

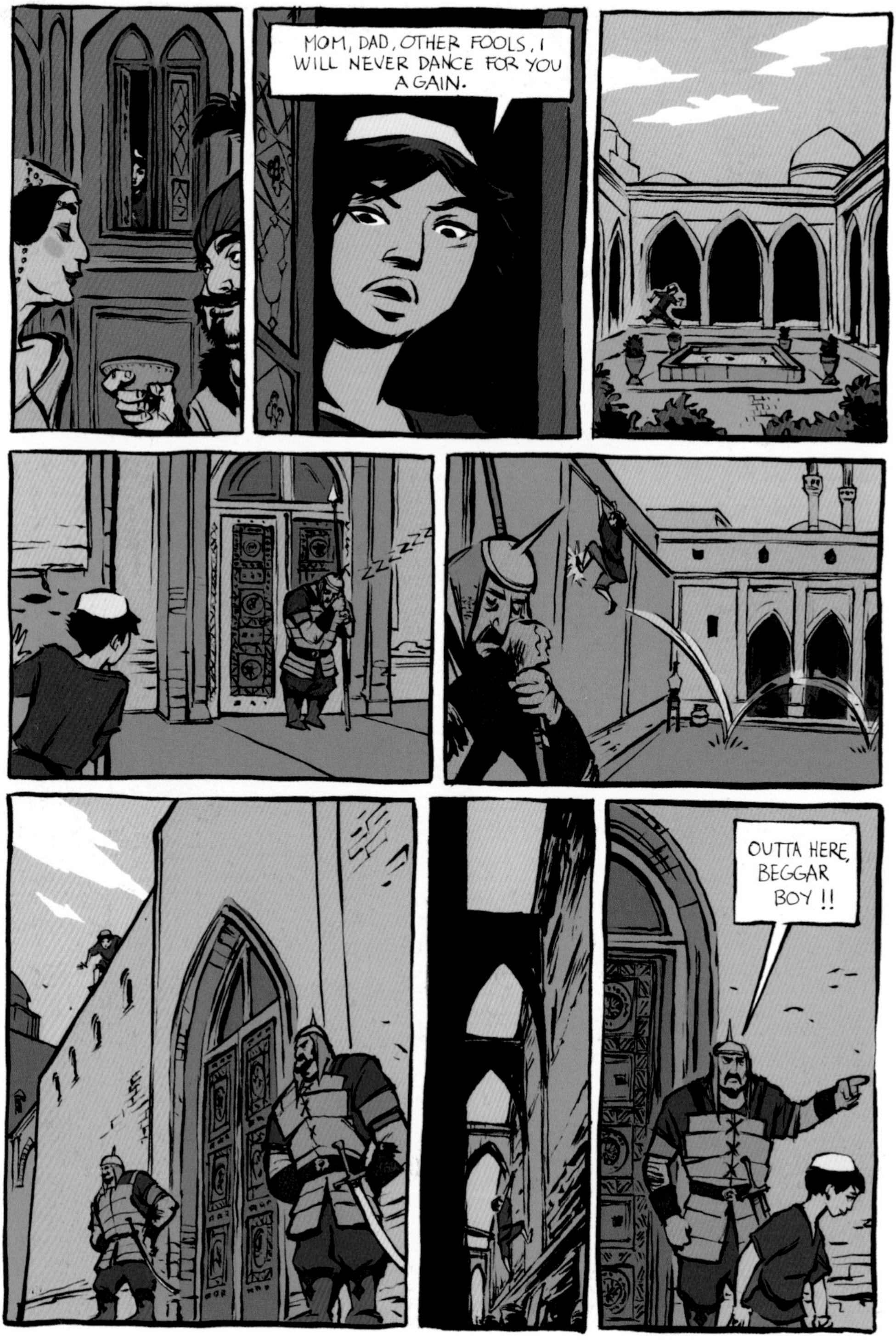
MOM, DAD, OTHER FOOLS, I WILL NEVER DANCE FOR YOU AGAIN.
ZZZZZZ
OUTTA HERE, BEGGAR BOY!!

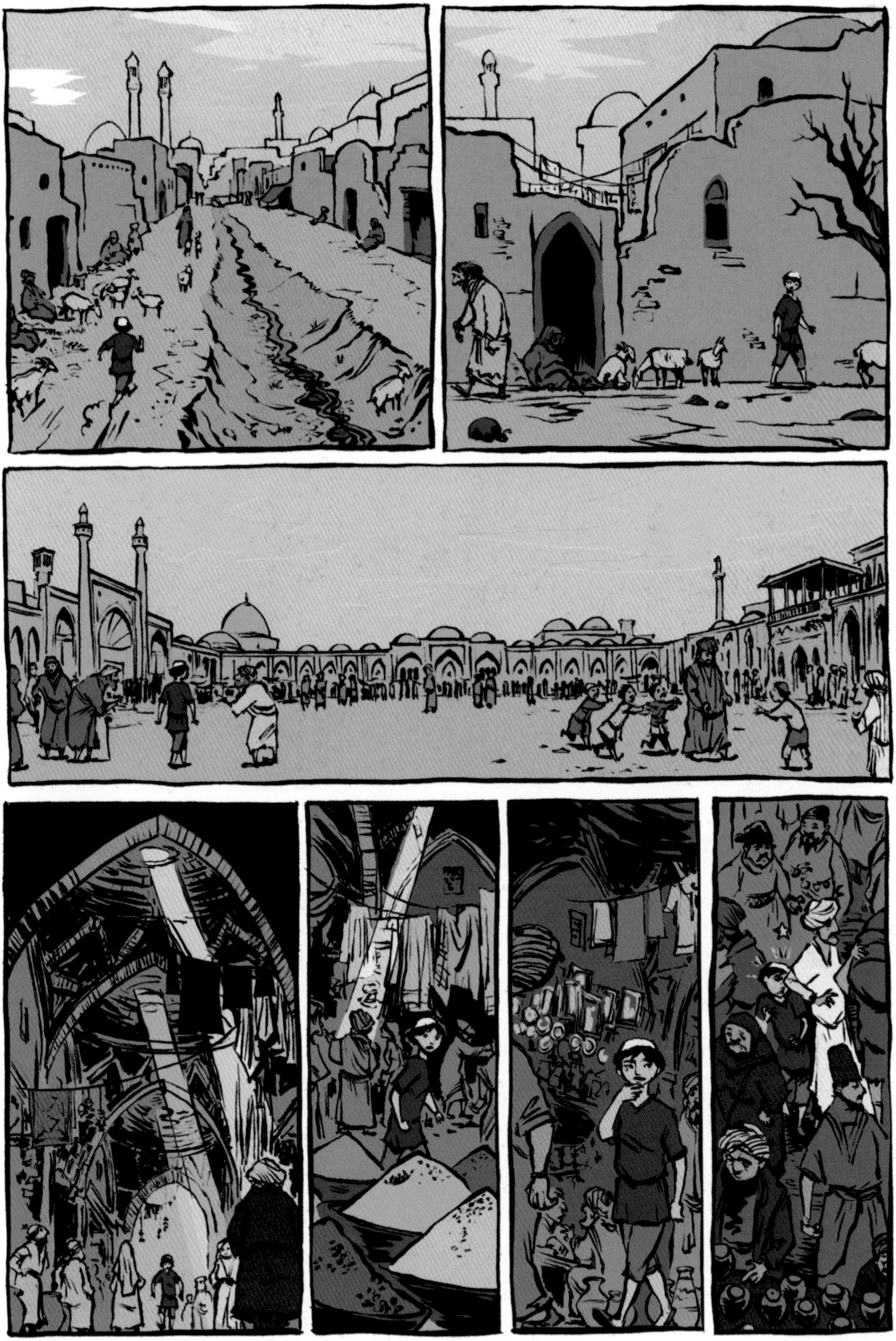

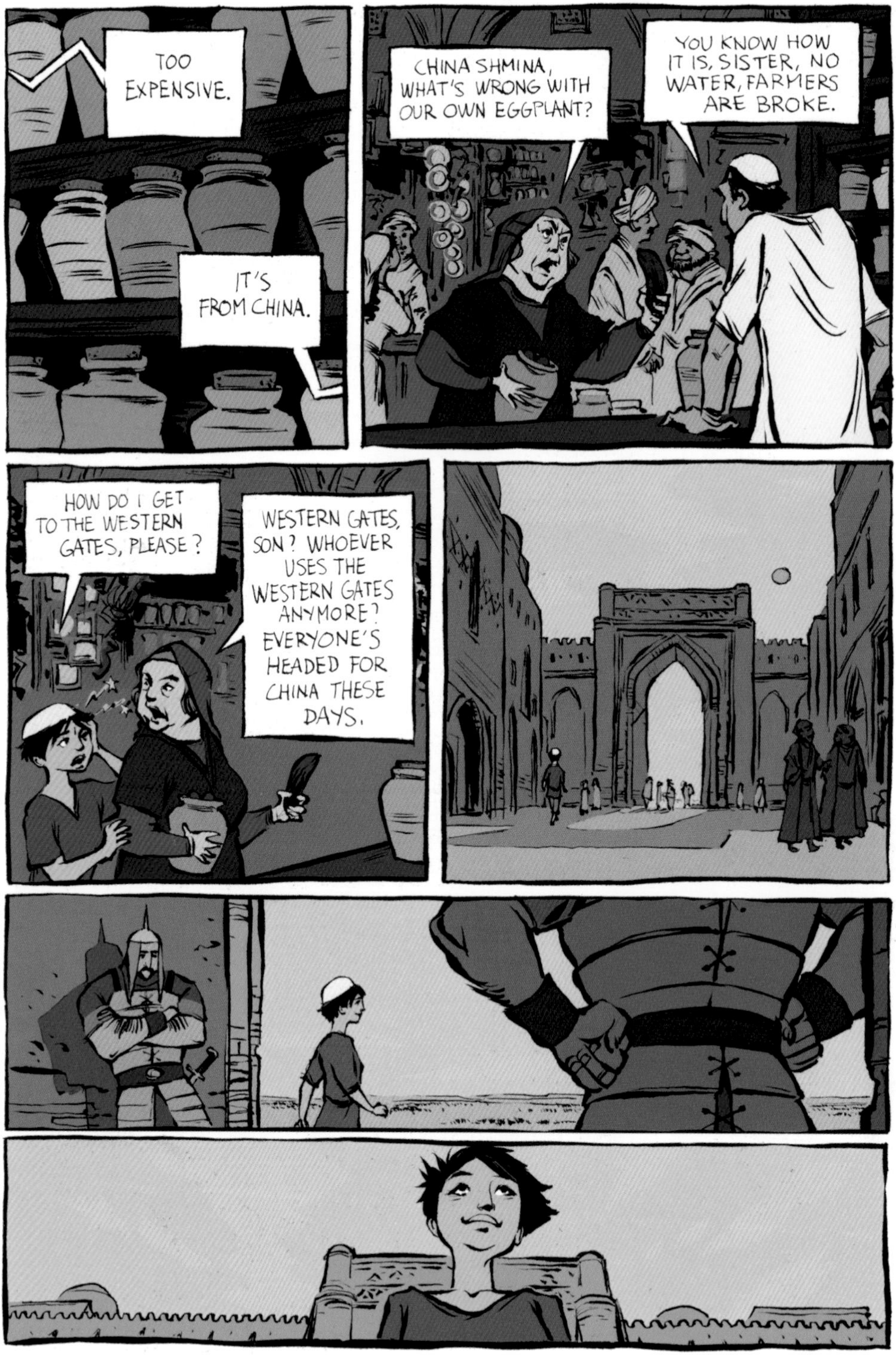
TOO EXPENSIVE.
IT'S FROM CHINA.
CHINA SHMINA, WHAT'S WRONG WITH OUR OWN EGGPLANT?
YOU KNOW HOW IT IS, SISTER, NO WATER, FARMERS ARE BROKE.
HOW DO I GET TO THE WESTERN GATES, PLEASE?
WESTERN GATES, SON? WHOEVER USES THE WESTERN GATES ANYMORE? EVERYONE'S HEADED FOR CHINA THESE DAYS.

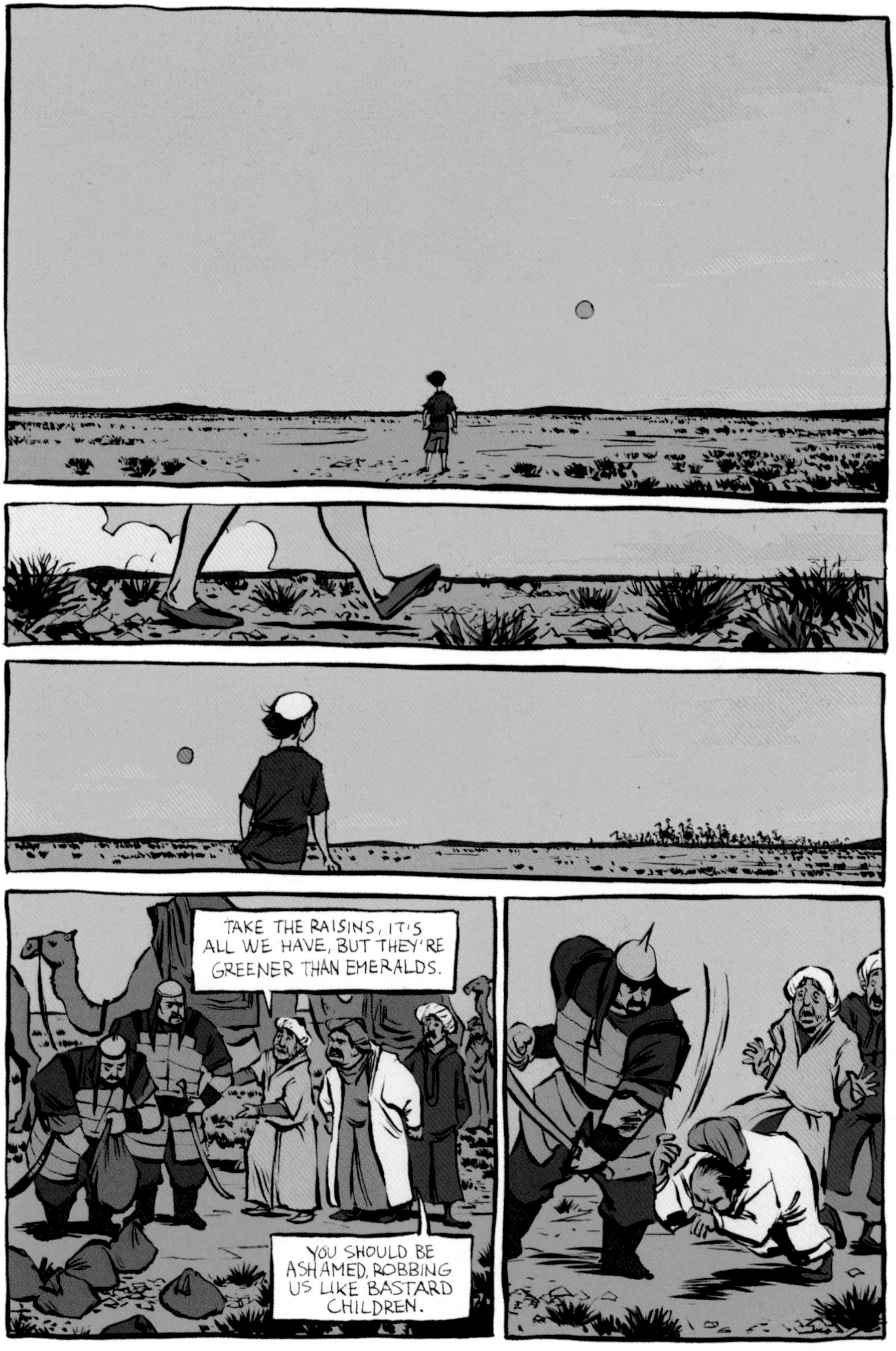
TAKE THE RAISINS, IT'S ALL WE HAVE, BUT THEY'RE GREENER THAN EMERALDS.
YOU SHOULD BE ASHAMED, ROBBING US LIKE BASTARD CHILDREN.

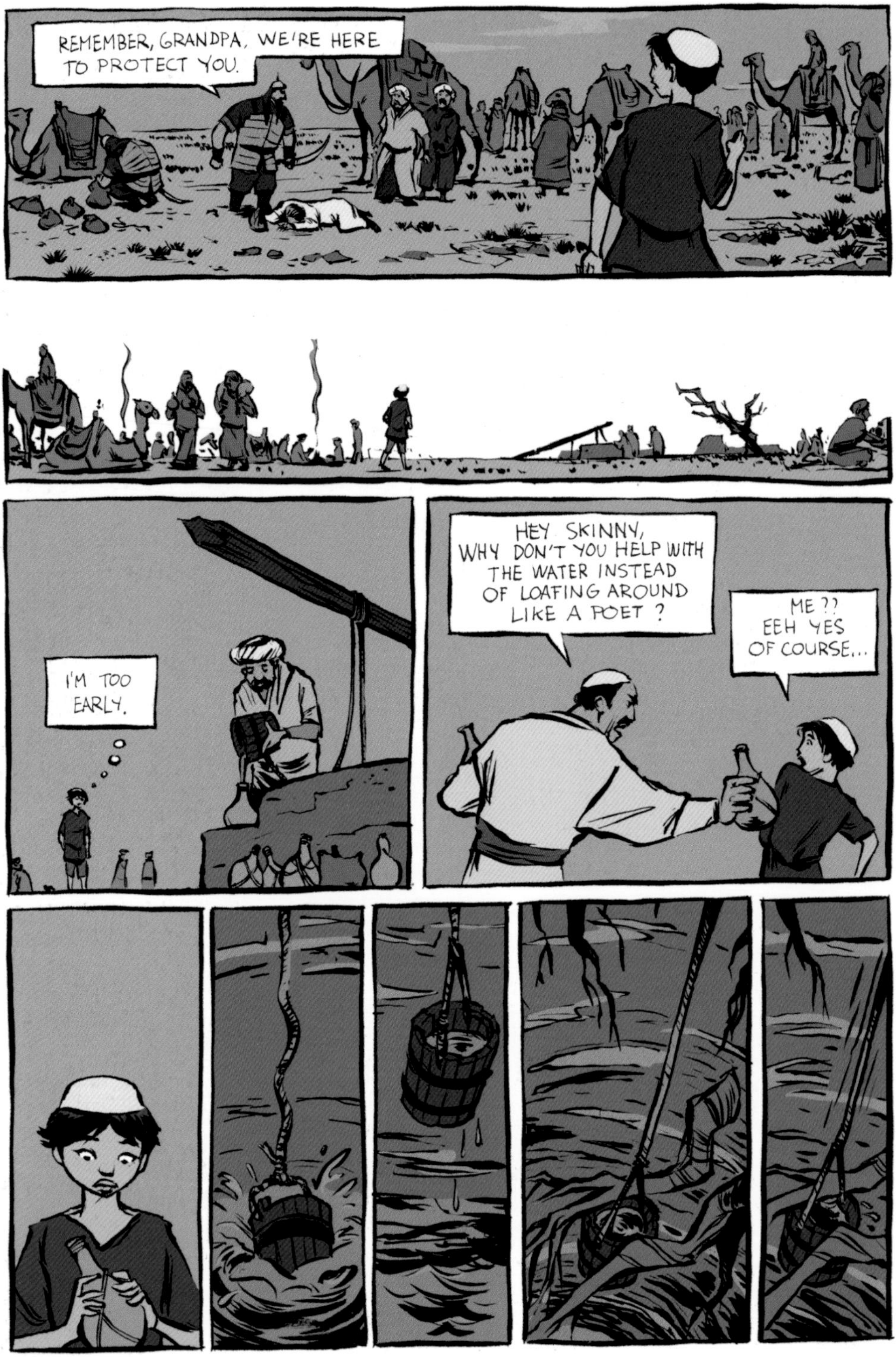
REMEMBER, GRANDPA, WE'RE HERE TO PROTECT YOU.
I'M TOO EARLY.
HEY SKINNY, WHY DON'T YOU HELP WITH THE WATER INSTEAD OF LOAFING AROUND LIKE A POET ?
ME ?? EEH YES OF COURSE...

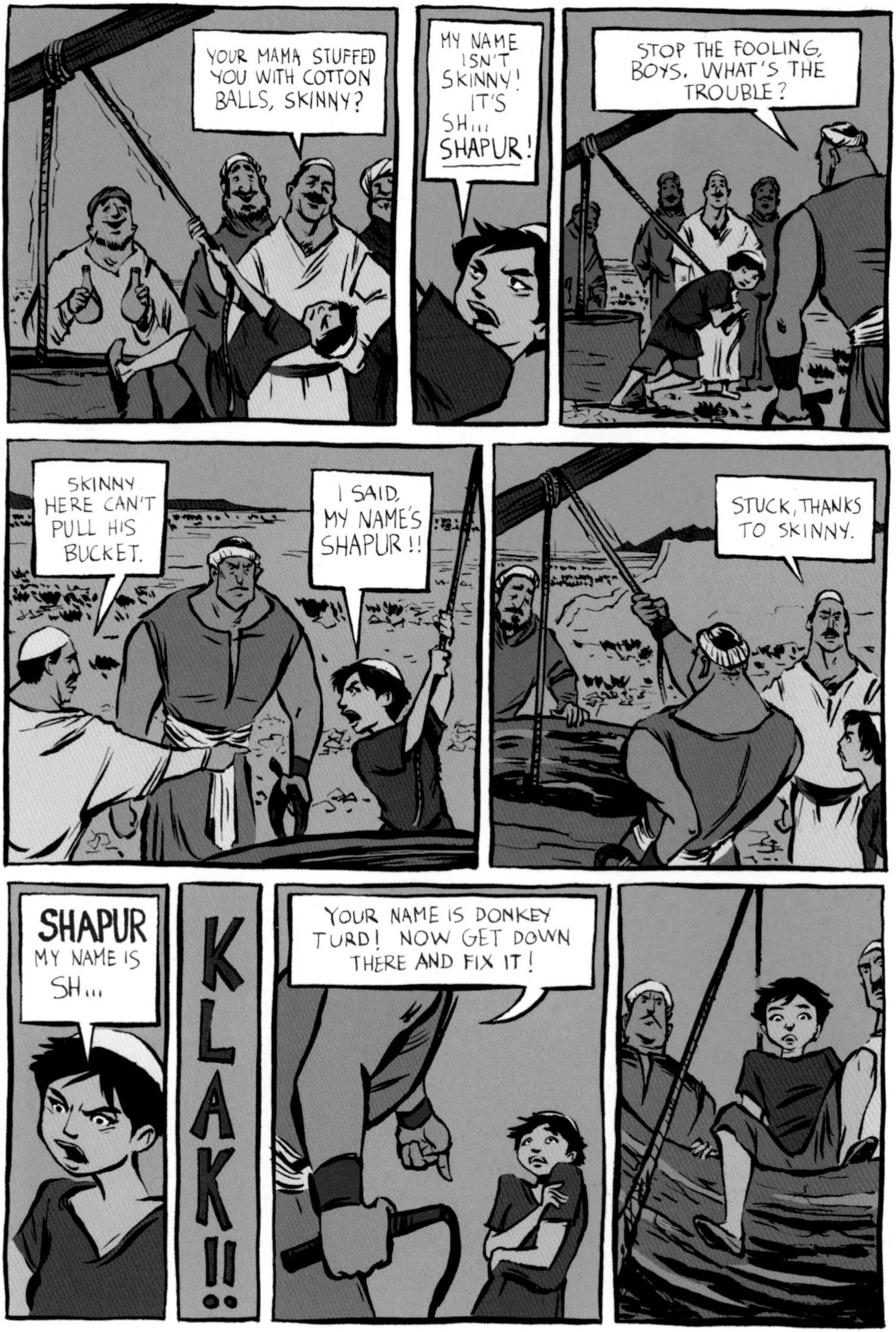
YOUR MAMA STUFFED YOU WITH COTTON BALLS, SKINNY?
MY NAME ISN'T SKINNY! IT'S SH... SHAPUR!
STOP THE FOOLING, BOYS. WHAT'S THE TROUBLE?
SKINNY HERE CAN'T PULL HIS BUCKET.
I SAID, MY NAME'S SHAPUR!!
STUCK, THANKS TO SKINNY.
MY NAME IS SH... SHAPUR
KLAK!!
YOUR NAME IS DONKEY TURD! NOW GET DOWN THERE AND FIX IT!

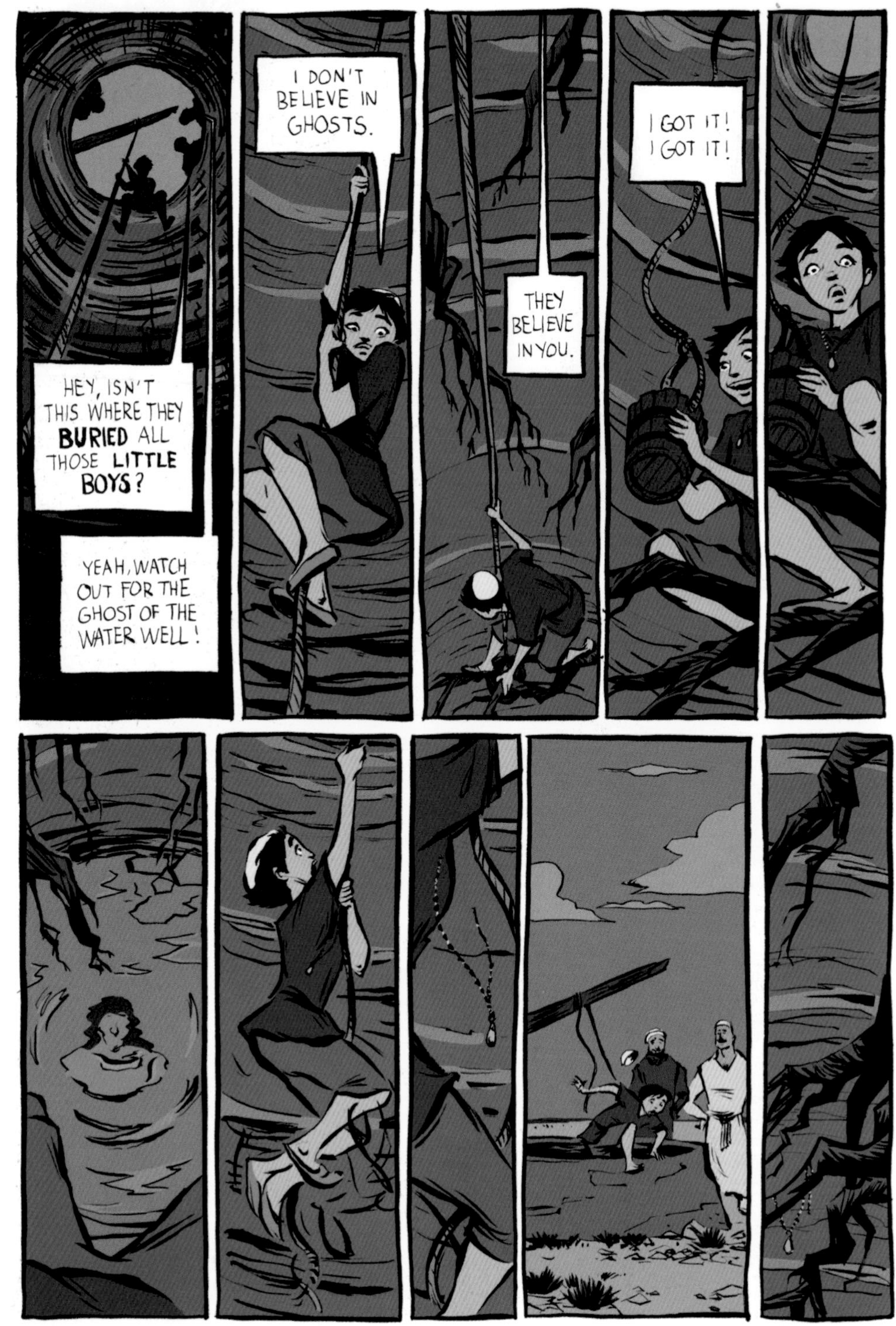
HEY, ISN'T THIS WHERE THEY **BURIED** ALL THOSE **LITTLE BOYS**?
YEAH, WATCH OUT FOR THE GHOST OF THE WATER WELL!
I DON'T BELIEVE IN GHOSTS.
THEY BELIEVE IN YOU.
I GOT IT! I GOT IT!

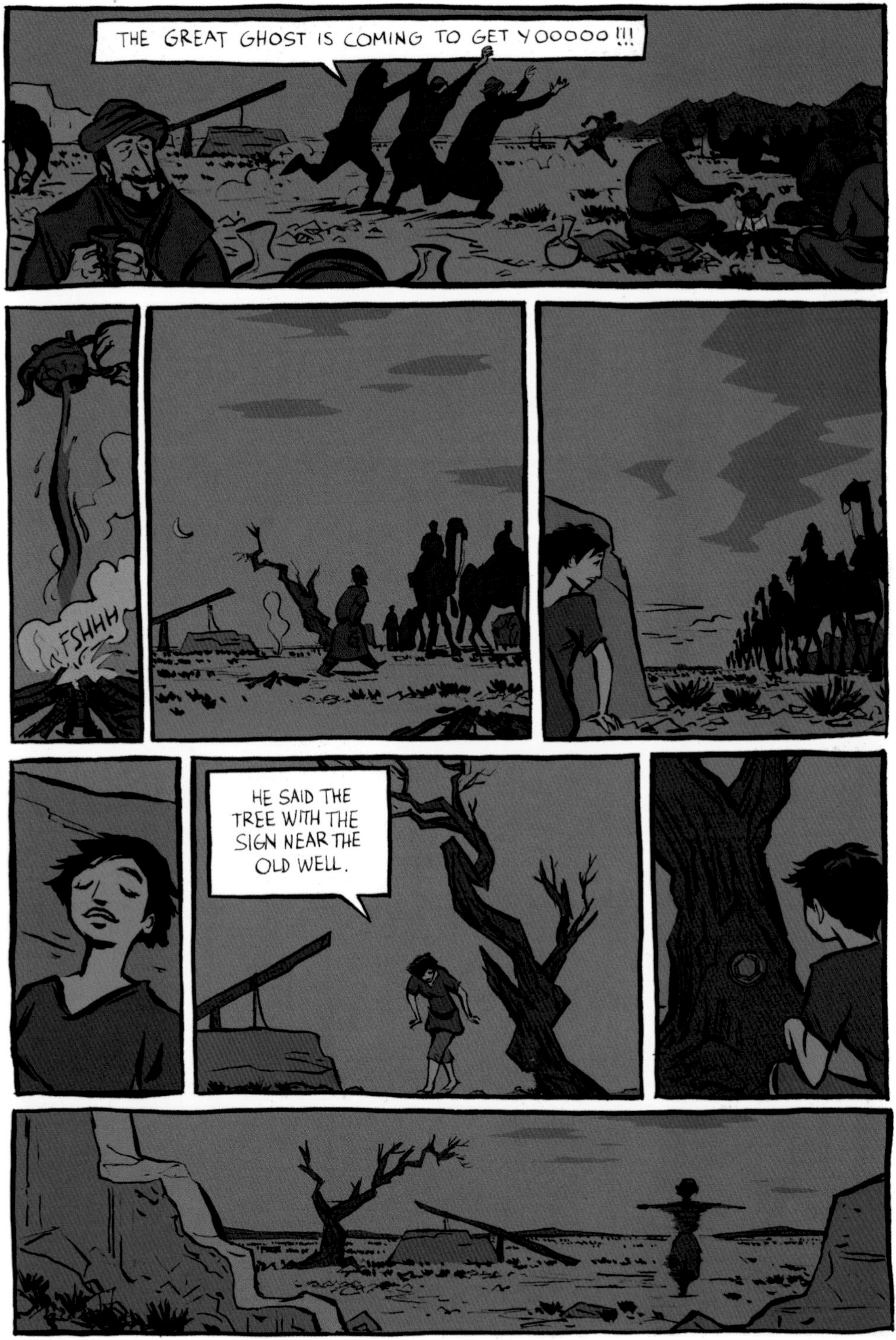
THE GREAT GHOST IS COMING TO GET YOOOOO!!!
FSHHH
HE SAID THE TREE WITH THE SIGN NEAR THE OLD WELL.

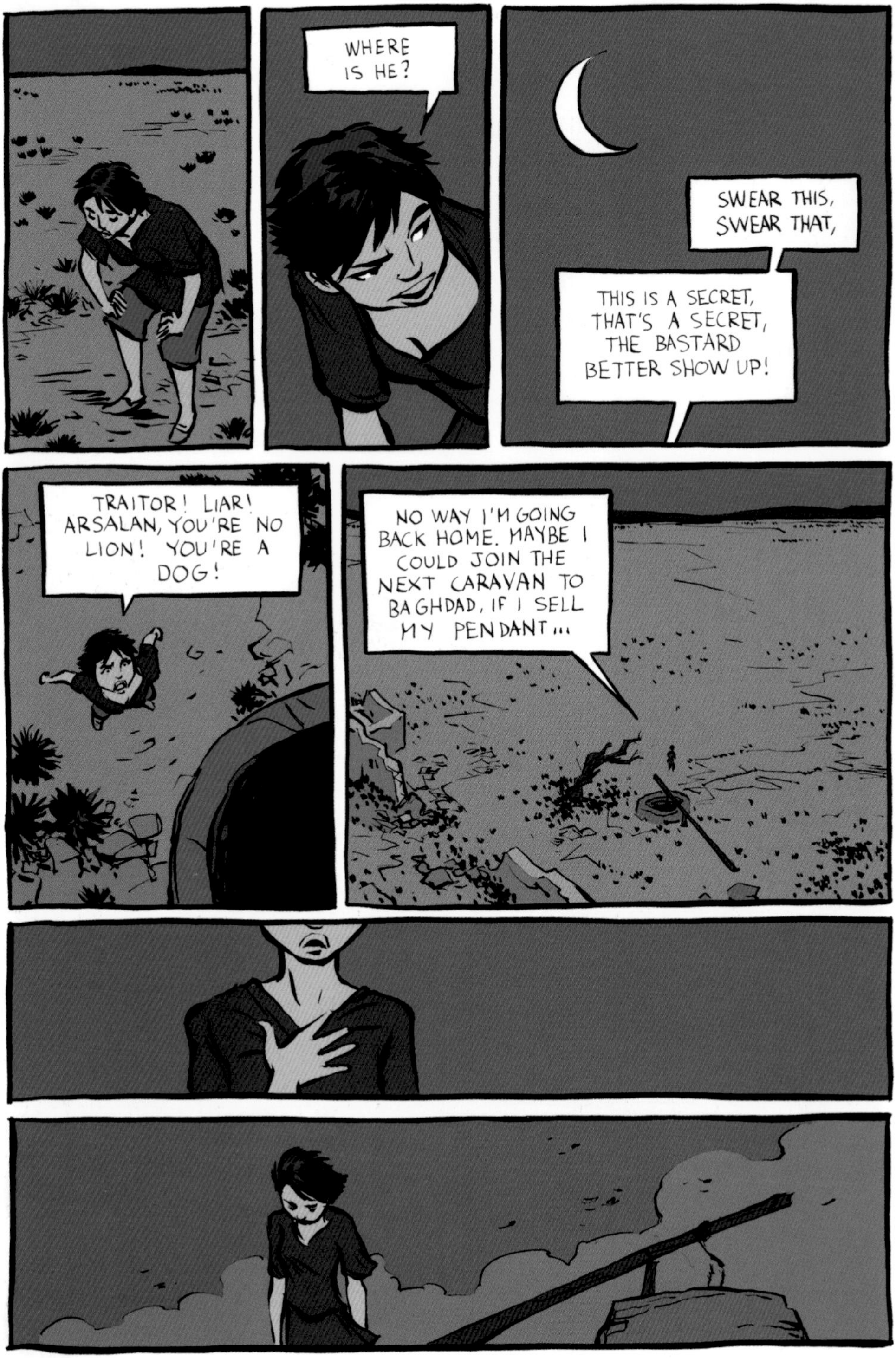
WHERE IS HE?
SWEAR THIS, SWEAR THAT,
THIS IS A SECRET, THAT'S A SECRET, THE BASTARD BETTER SHOW UP!
TRAITOR! LIAR! ARSALAN, YOU'RE NO LION! YOU'RE A DOG!
NO WAY I'M GOING BACK HOME. MAYBE I COULD JOIN THE NEXT CARAVAN TO BAGHDAD, IF I SELL MY PENDANT...

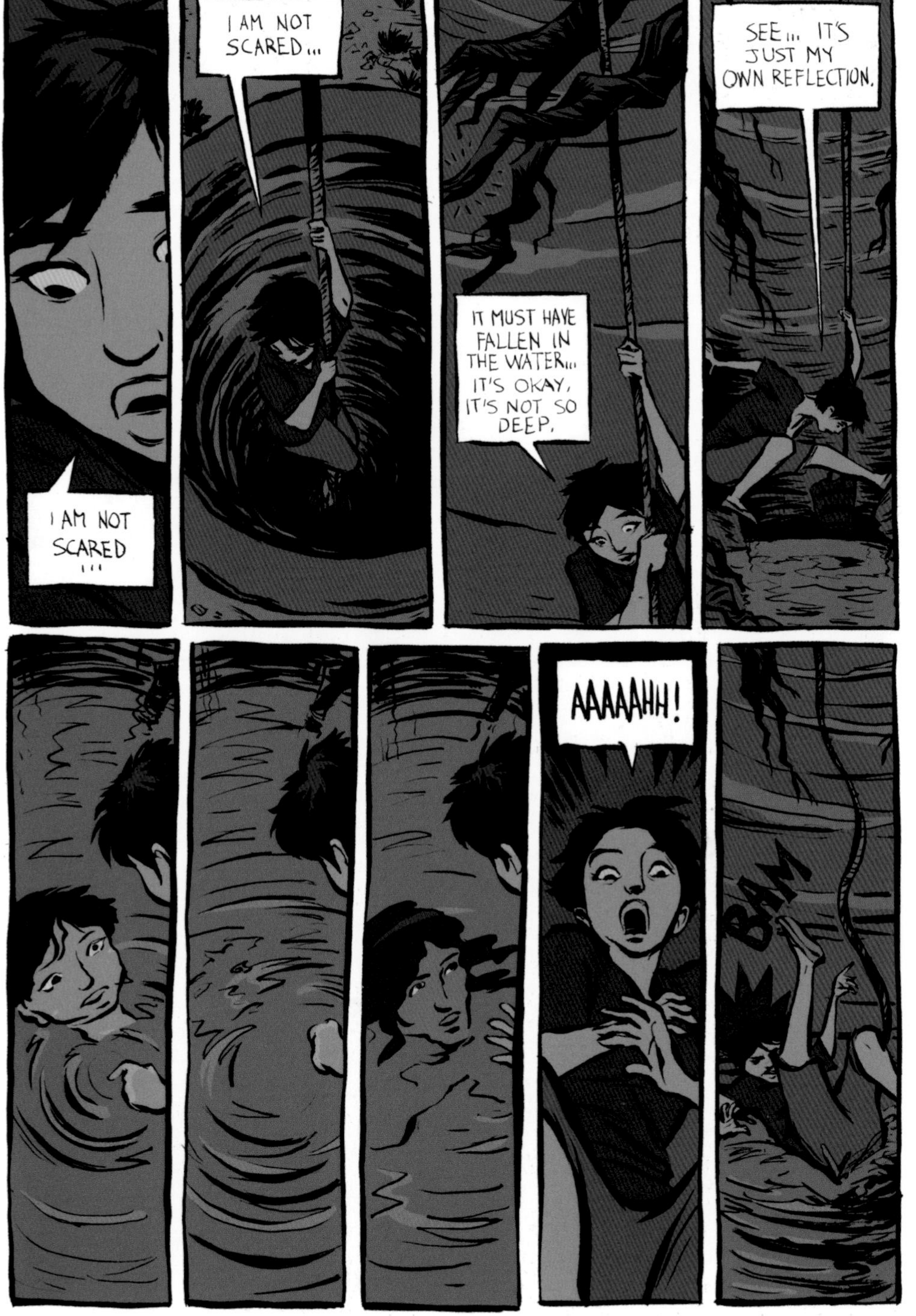
I AM NOT SCARED ...
I AM NOT SCARED ...
IT MUST HAVE FALLEN IN THE WATER... IT'S OKAY, IT'S NOT SO DEEP.
SEE... IT'S JUST MY OWN REFLECTION.
AAAAAHH!
BAM

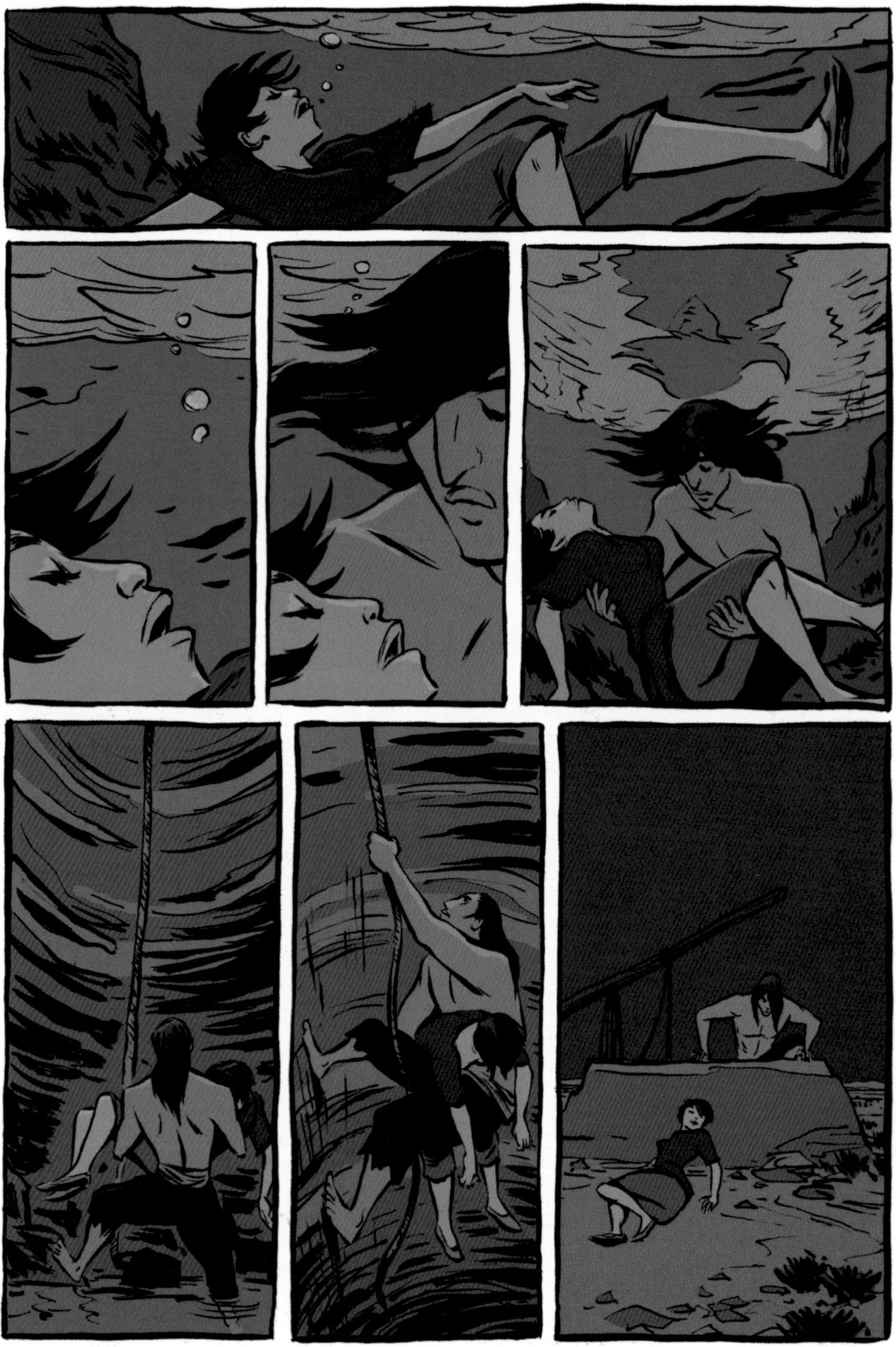

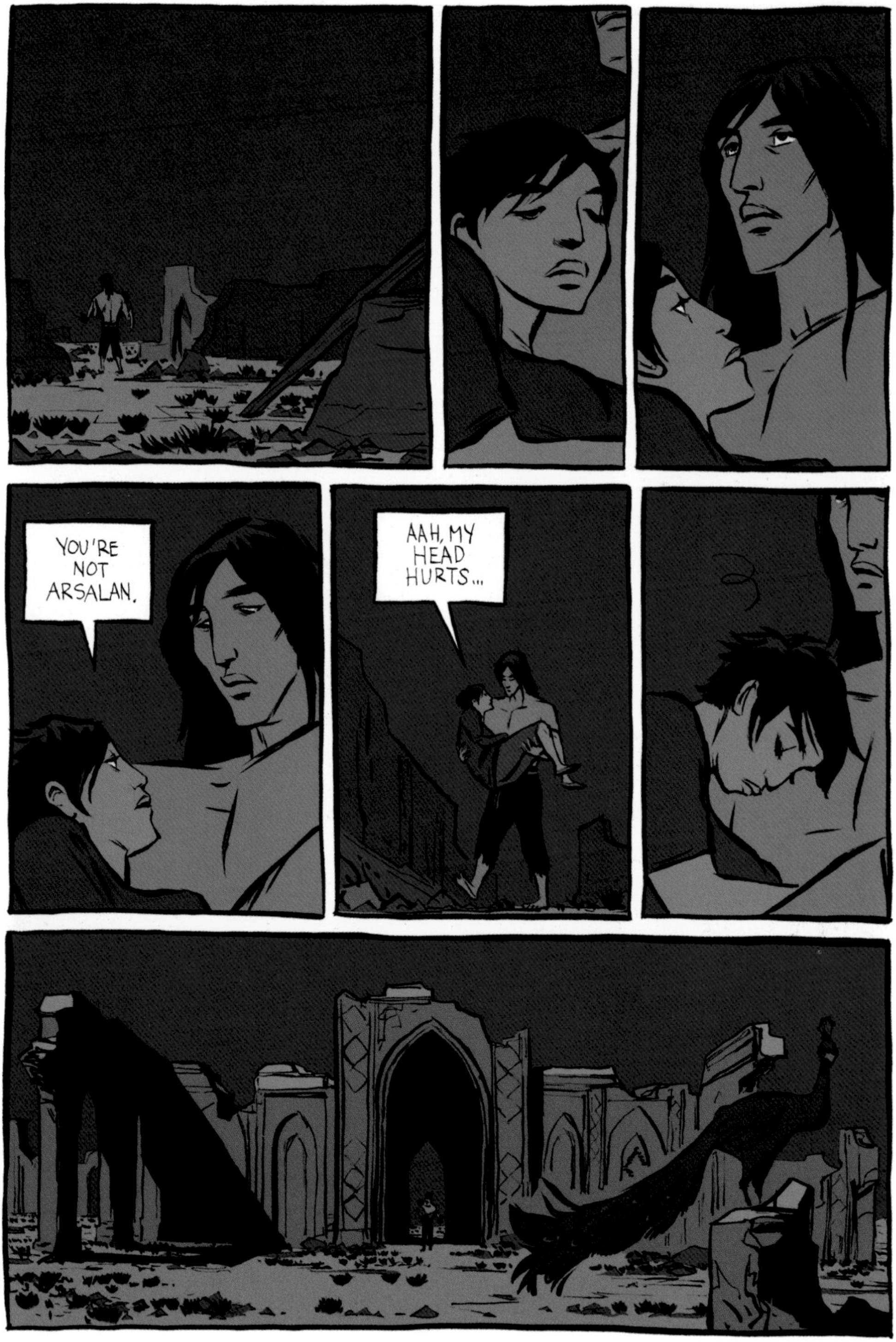
YOU'RE NOT ARSALAN.
AAH, MY HEAD HURTS...

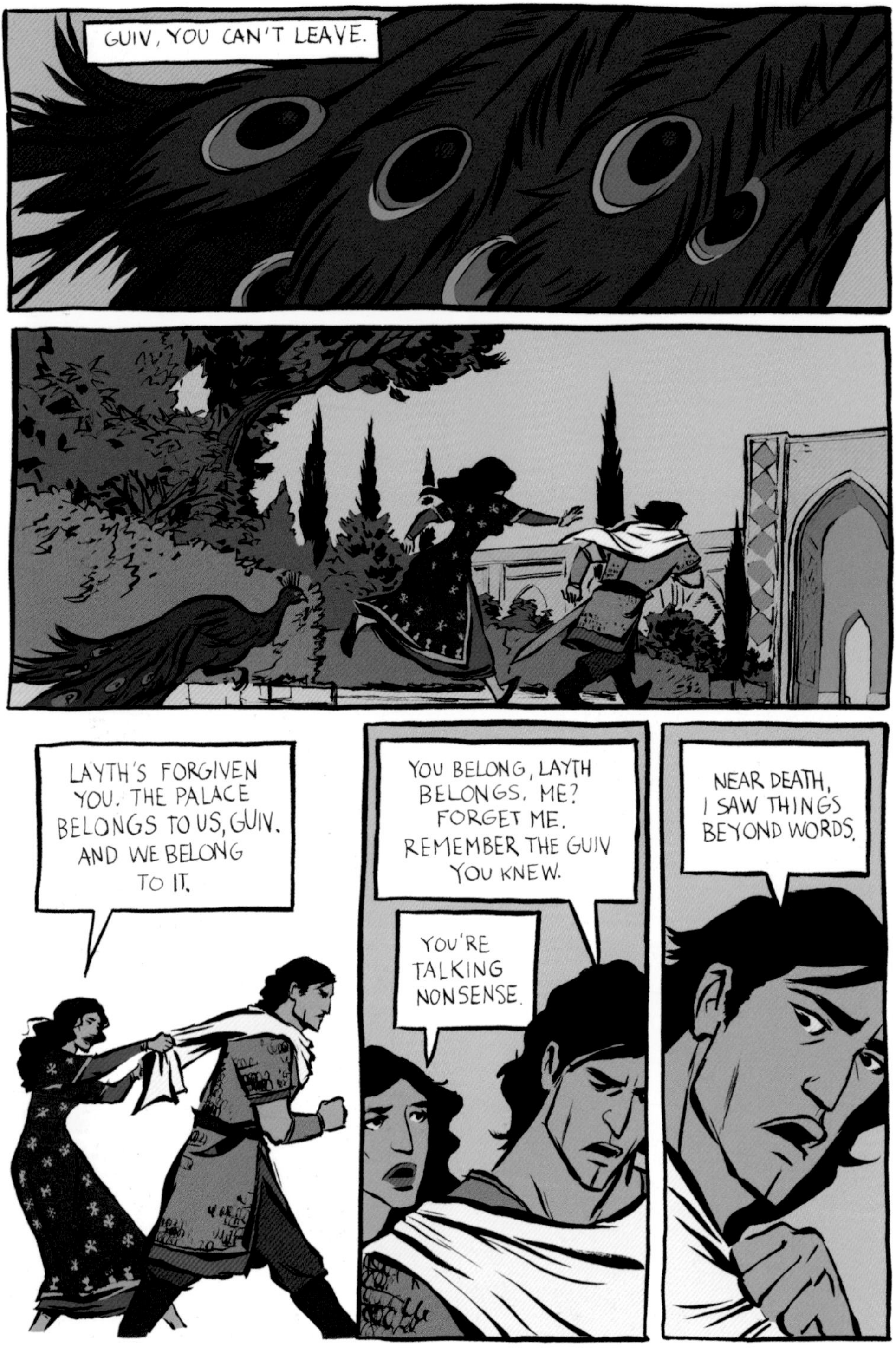
GUIV, YOU CAN'T LEAVE.
LAYTH'S FORGIVEN YOU. THE PALACE BELONGS TO US, GUIV. AND WE BELONG TO IT.
YOU BELONG, LAYTH BELONGS. ME? FORGET ME. REMEMBER THE GUIV YOU KNEW.
YOU'RE TALKING NONSENSE.
NEAR DEATH, I SAW THINGS BEYOND WORDS.

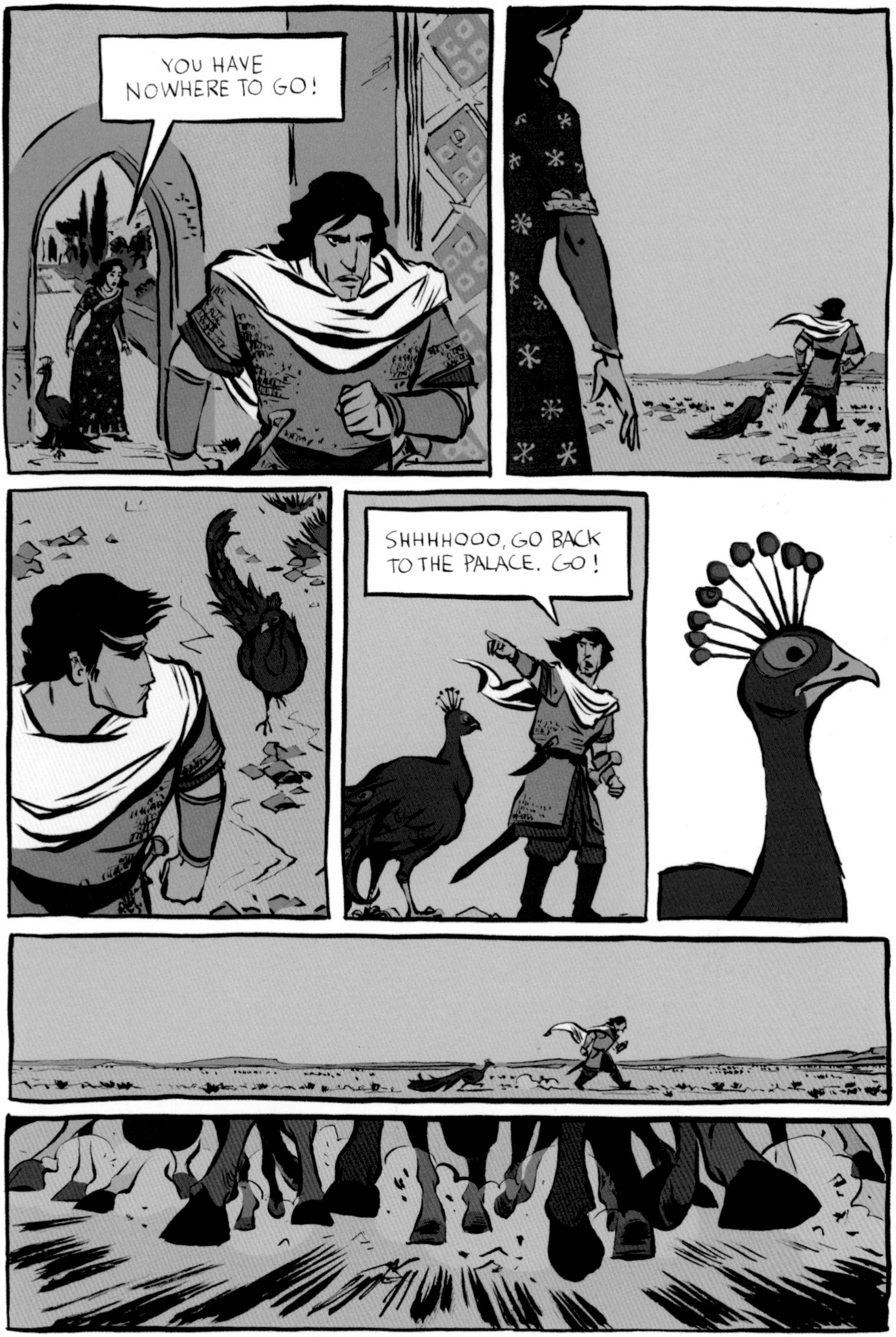
YOU HAVE NOWHERE TO GO!
SHHHHOOO, GO BACK TO THE PALACE. GO!

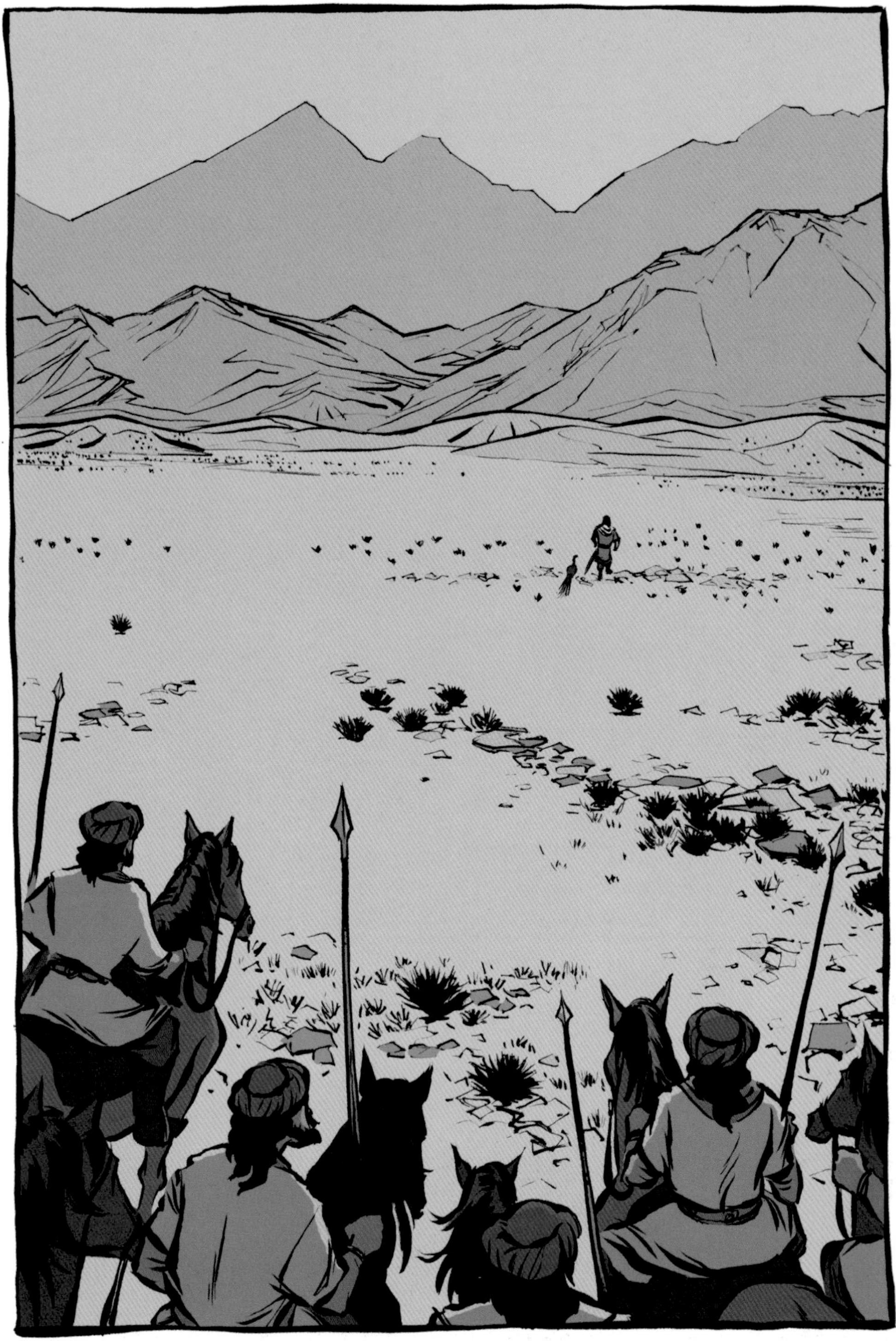

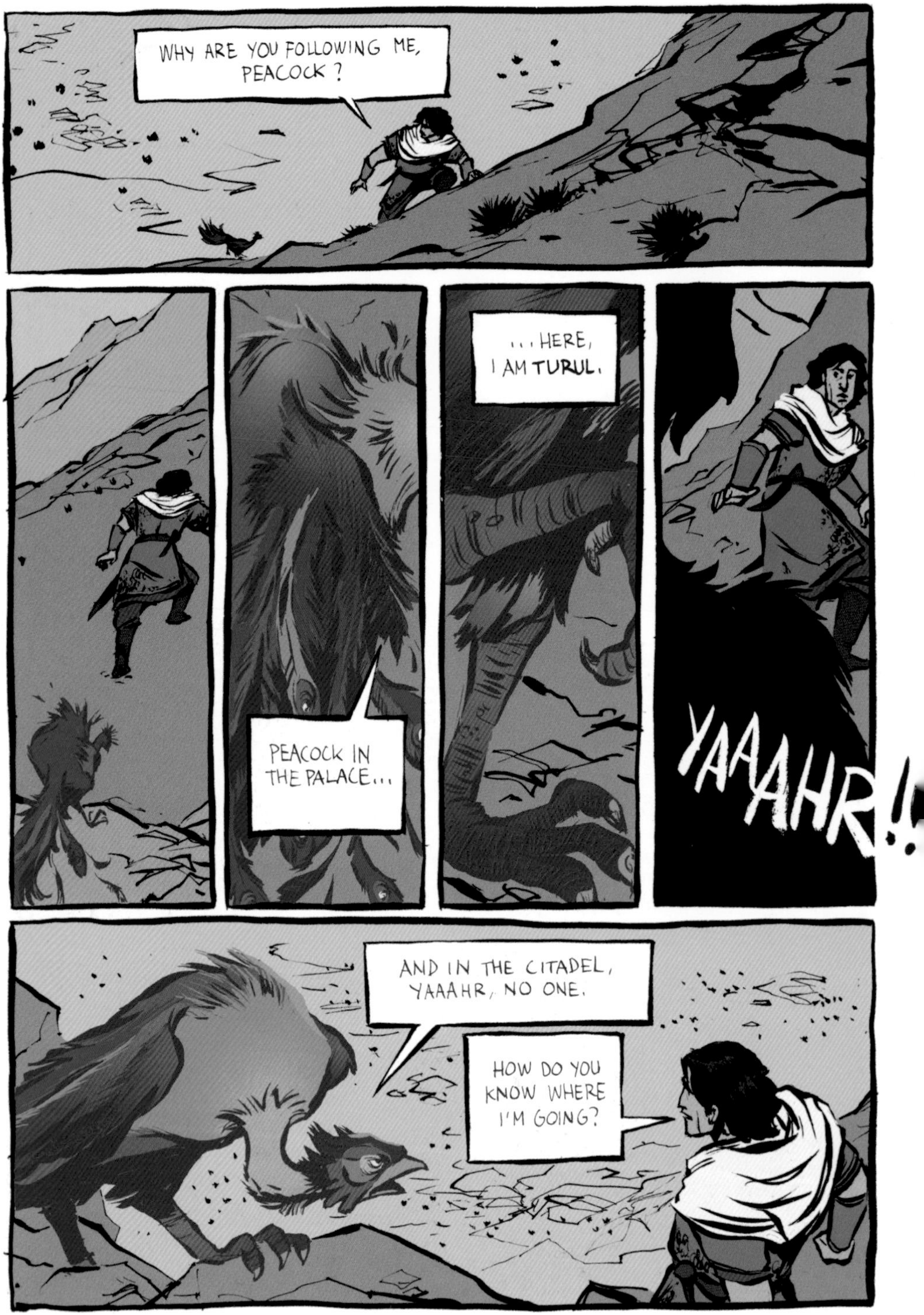
WHY ARE YOU FOLLOWING ME, PEACOCK ?
PEACOCK IN THE PALACE...
...HERE, I AM TURUL.
YAAAAHR!!
AND IN THE CITADEL, YAAAHR, NO ONE.
HOW DO YOU KNOW WHERE I'M GOING?

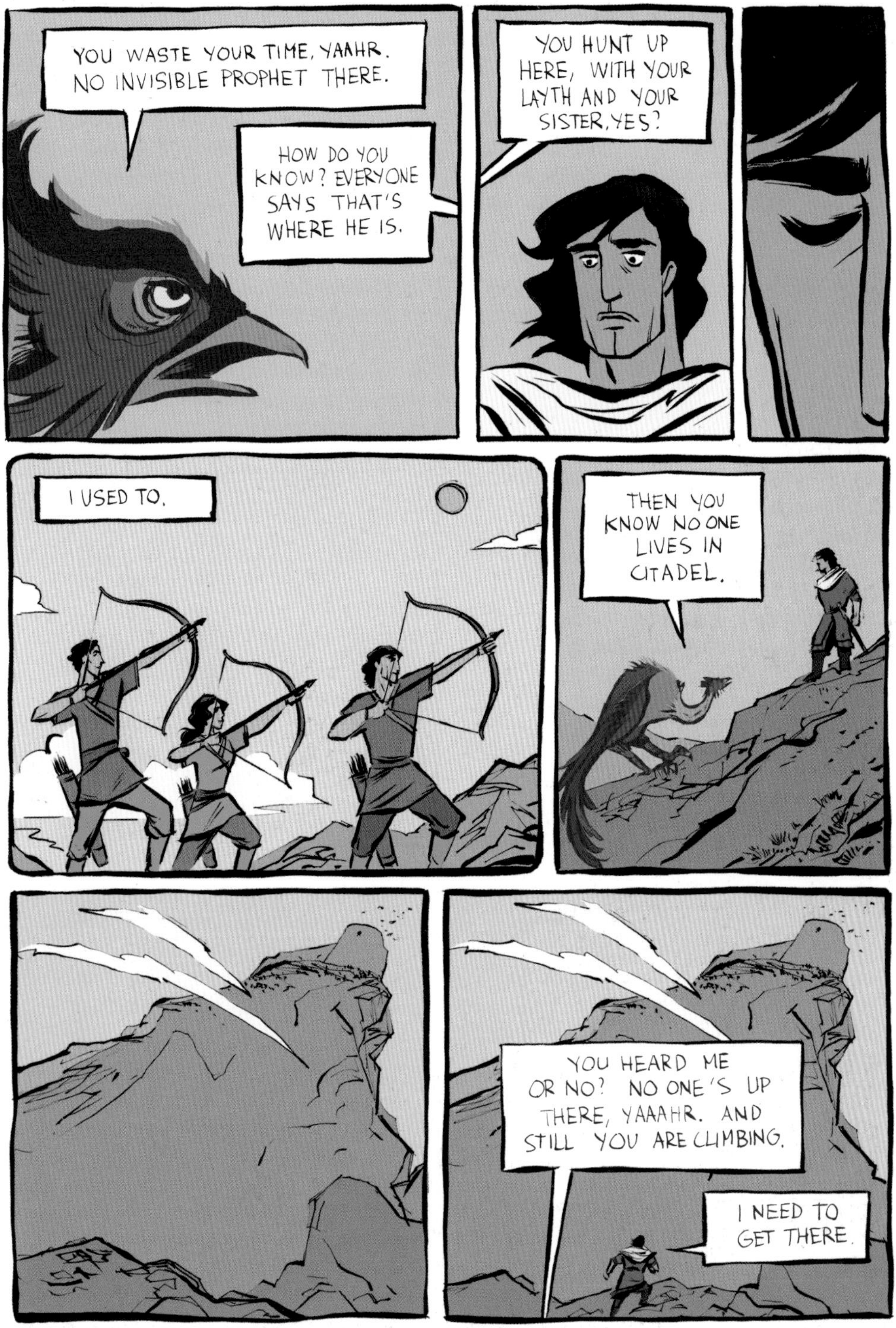
YOU WASTE YOUR TIME, YAAHR. NO INVISIBLE PROPHET THERE.
HOW DO YOU KNOW? EVERYONE SAYS THAT'S WHERE HE IS.
YOU HUNT UP HERE, WITH YOUR LAYTH AND YOUR SISTER, YES?
I USED TO.
THEN YOU KNOW NO ONE LIVES IN CITADEL.
YOU HEARD ME OR NO? NO ONE'S UP THERE, YAAAHR. AND STILL YOU ARE CLIMBING.
I NEED TO GET THERE.

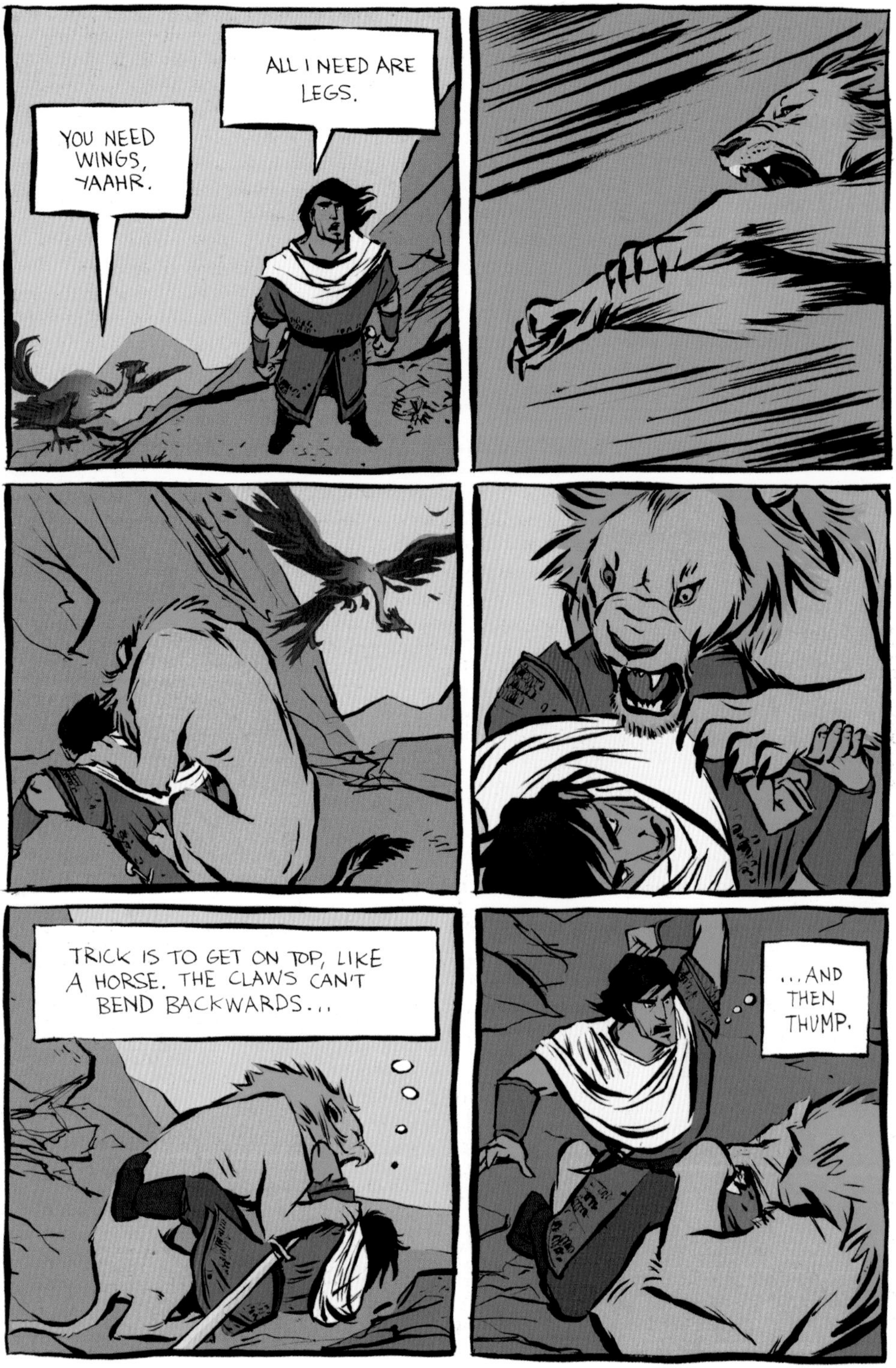
YOU NEED WINGS, YAAHR.
ALL I NEED ARE LEGS.
TRICK IS TO GET ON TOP, LIKE A HORSE. THE CLAWS CAN'T BEND BACKWARDS...
...AND THEN THUMP.

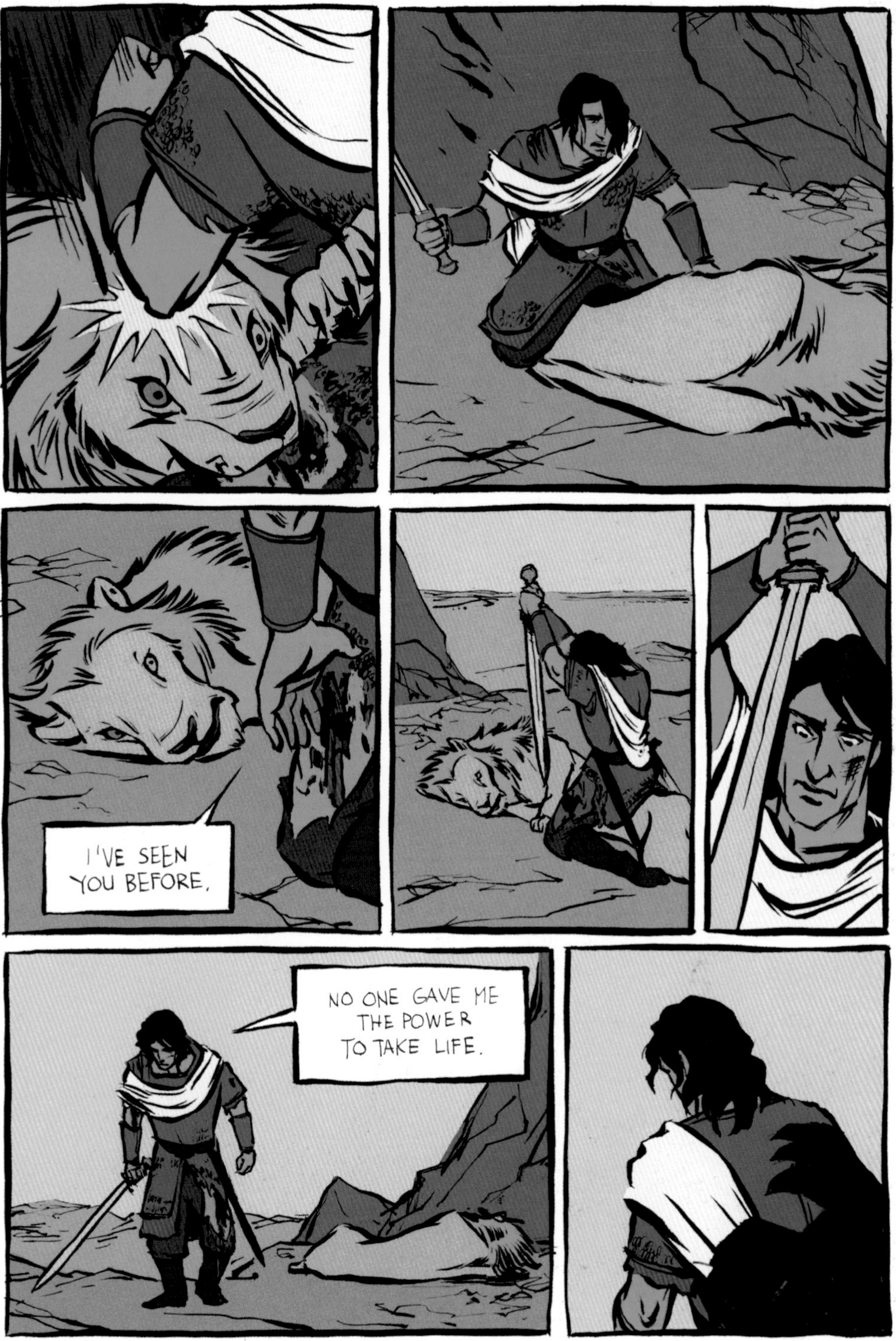
I'VE SEEN YOU BEFORE.
NO ONE GAVE ME THE POWER TO TAKE LIFE.

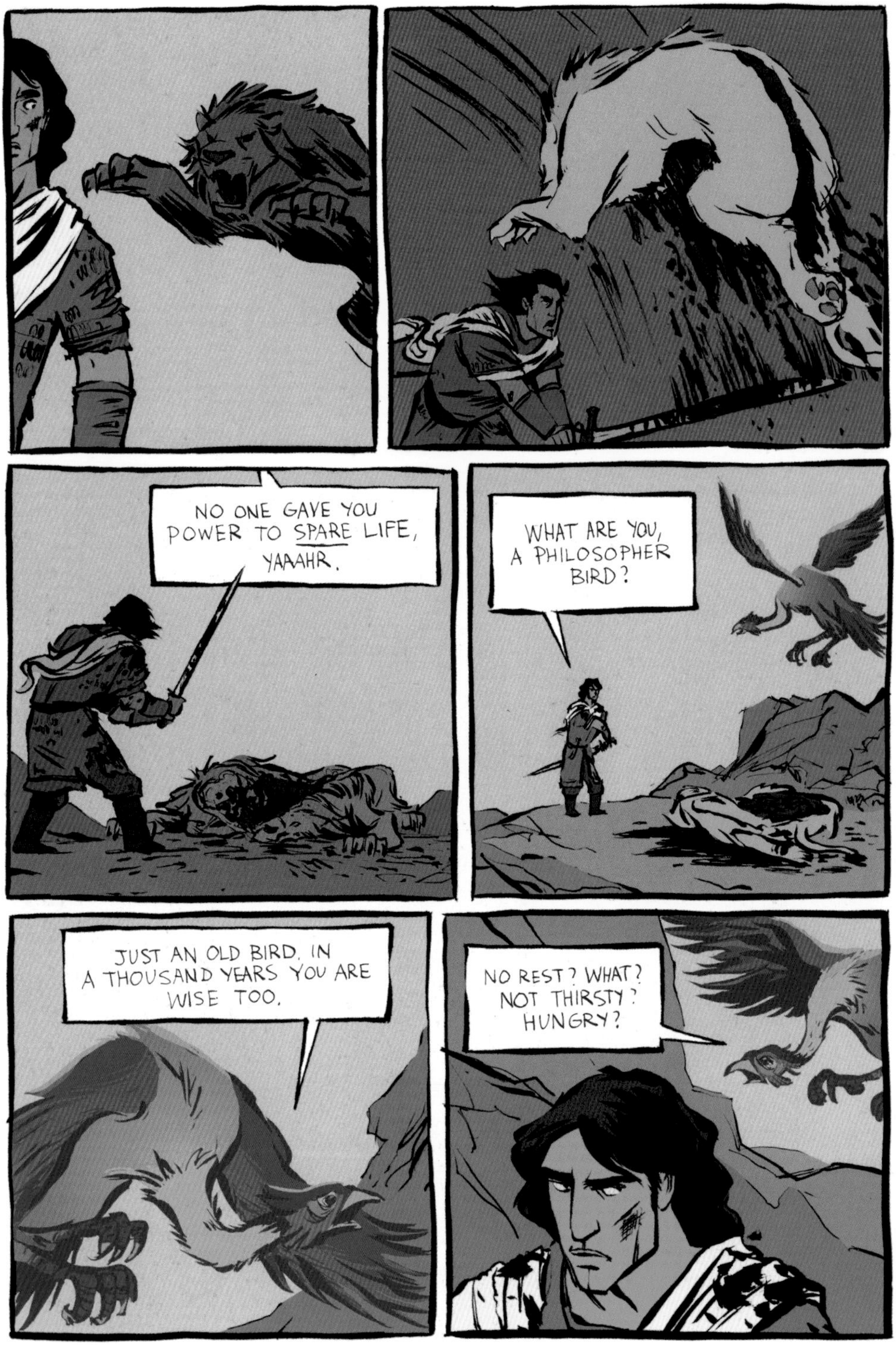
NO ONE GAVE YOU POWER TO SPARE LIFE, YAAAHR.
WHAT ARE YOU, A PHILOSOPHER BIRD?
JUST AN OLD BIRD. IN A THOUSAND YEARS YOU ARE WISE TOO.
NO REST? WHAT? NOT THIRSTY? HUNGRY?

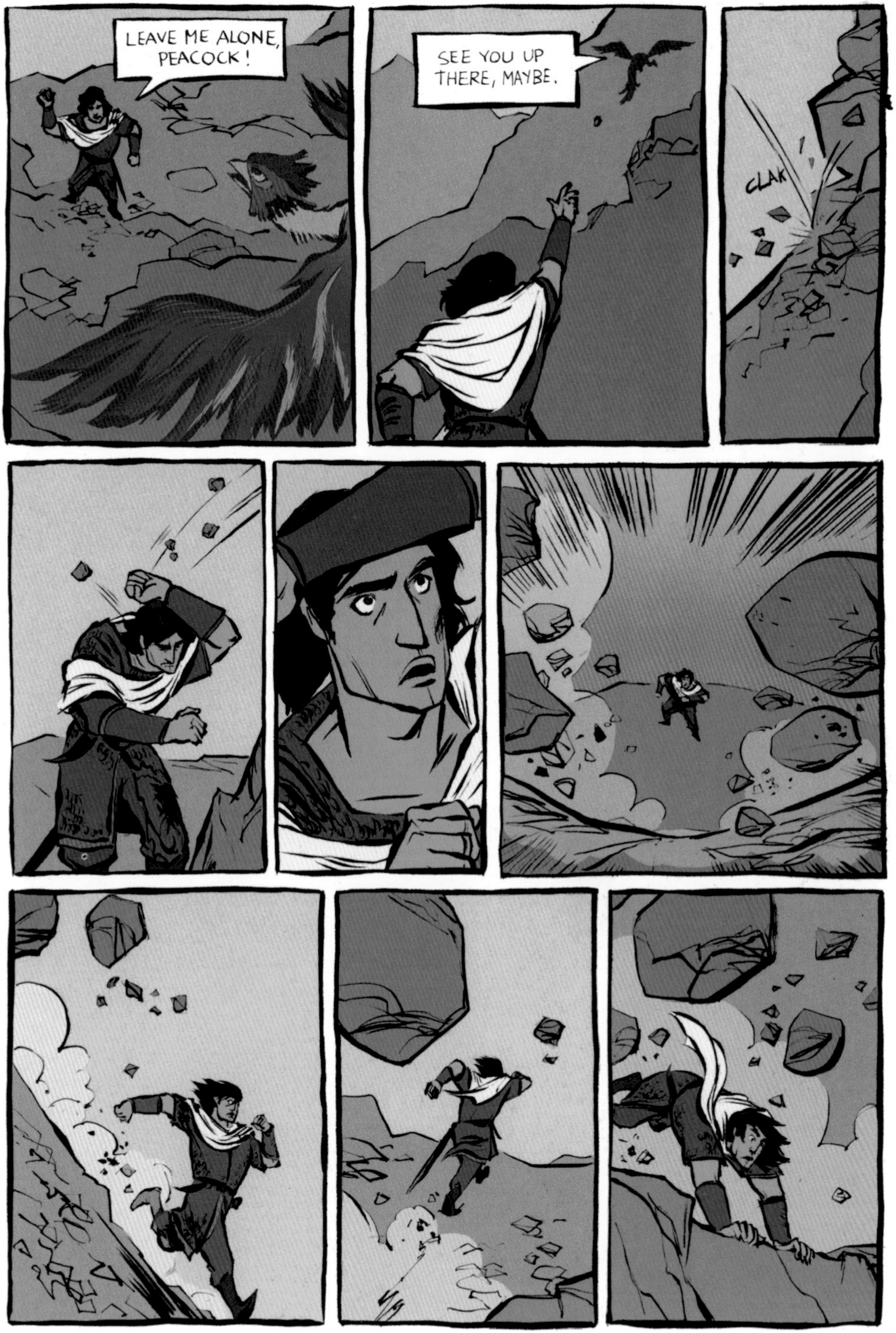
LEAVE ME ALONE, PEACOCK!
SEE YOU UP THERE, MAYBE.
CLAK

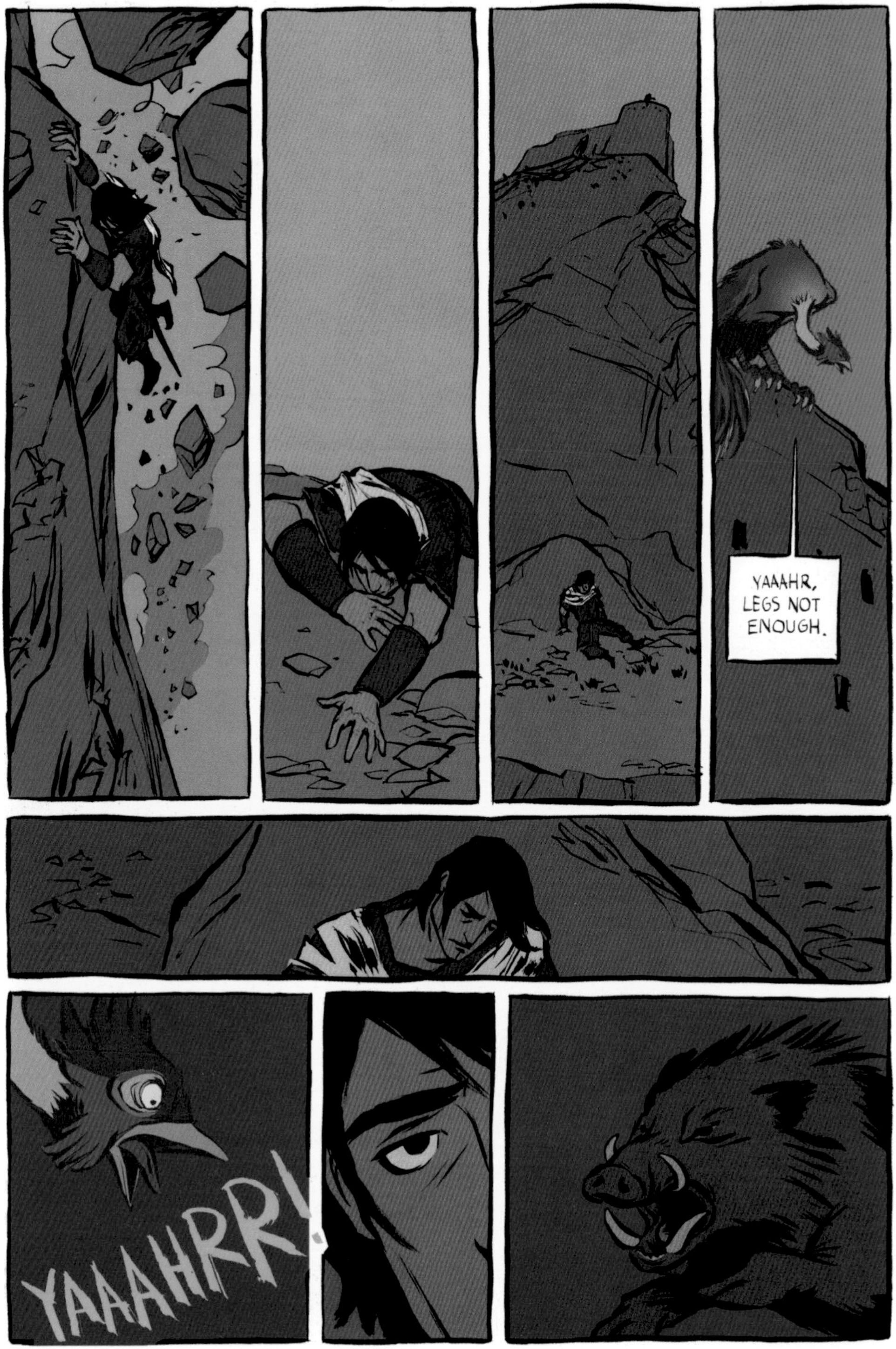
YAAAHR, LEGS NOT ENOUGH.
YAAAHRR!

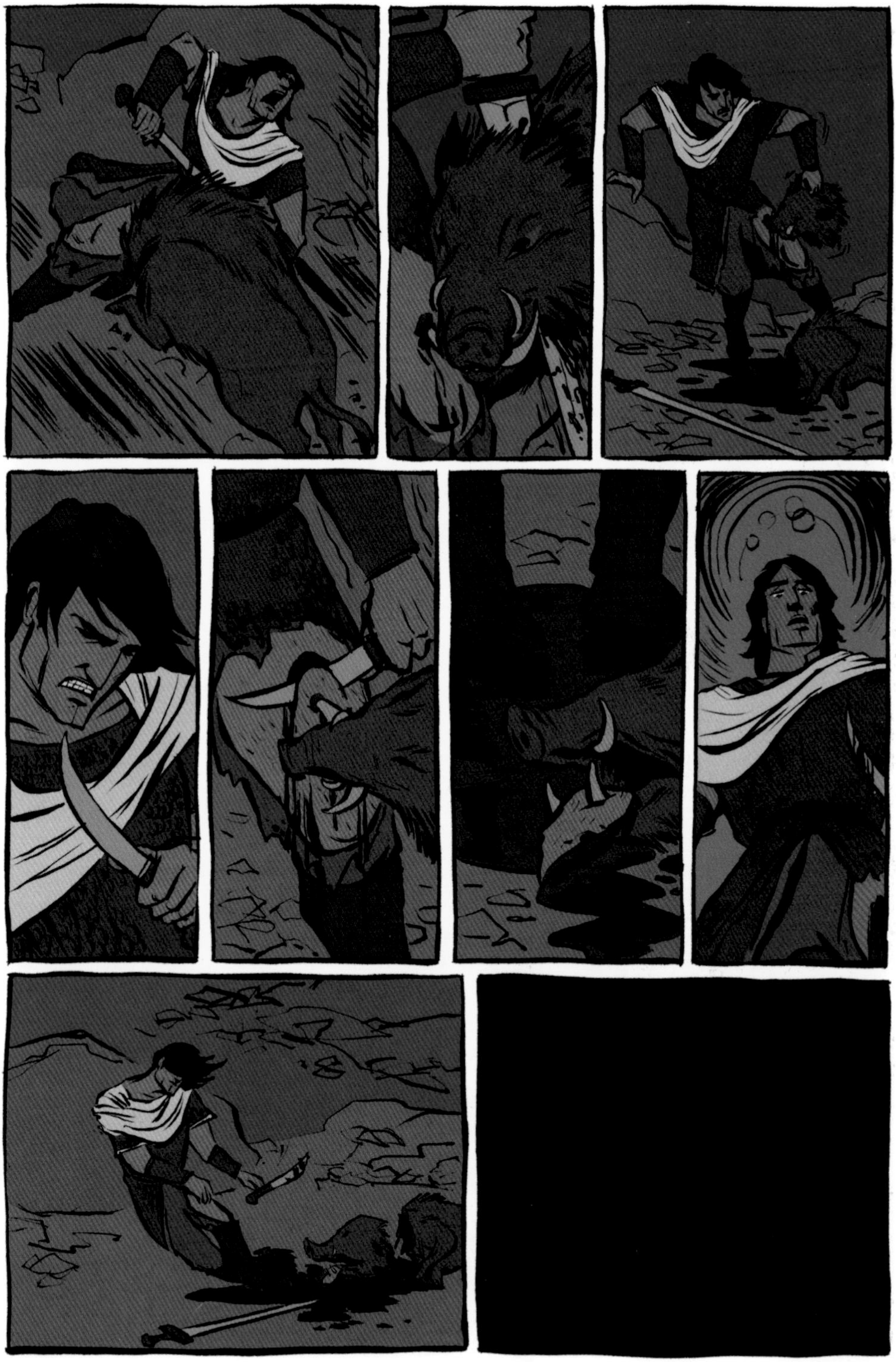

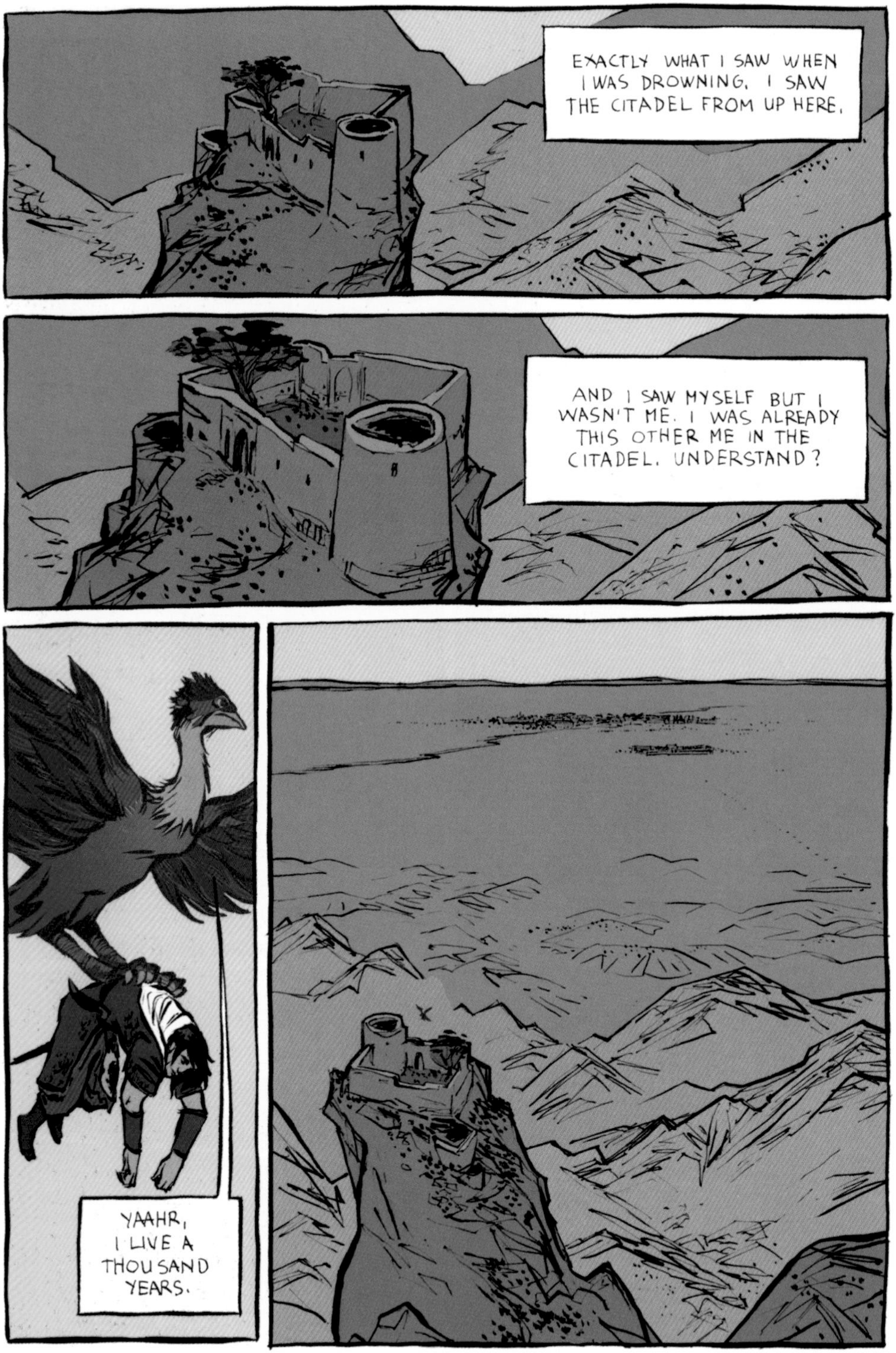
EXACTLY WHAT I SAW WHEN I WAS DROWNING. I SAW THE CITADEL FROM UP HERE.
AND I SAW MYSELF BUT I WASN'T ME. I WAS ALREADY THIS OTHER ME IN THE CITADEL. UNDERSTAND?
YAAHR, I LIVE A THOUSAND YEARS.

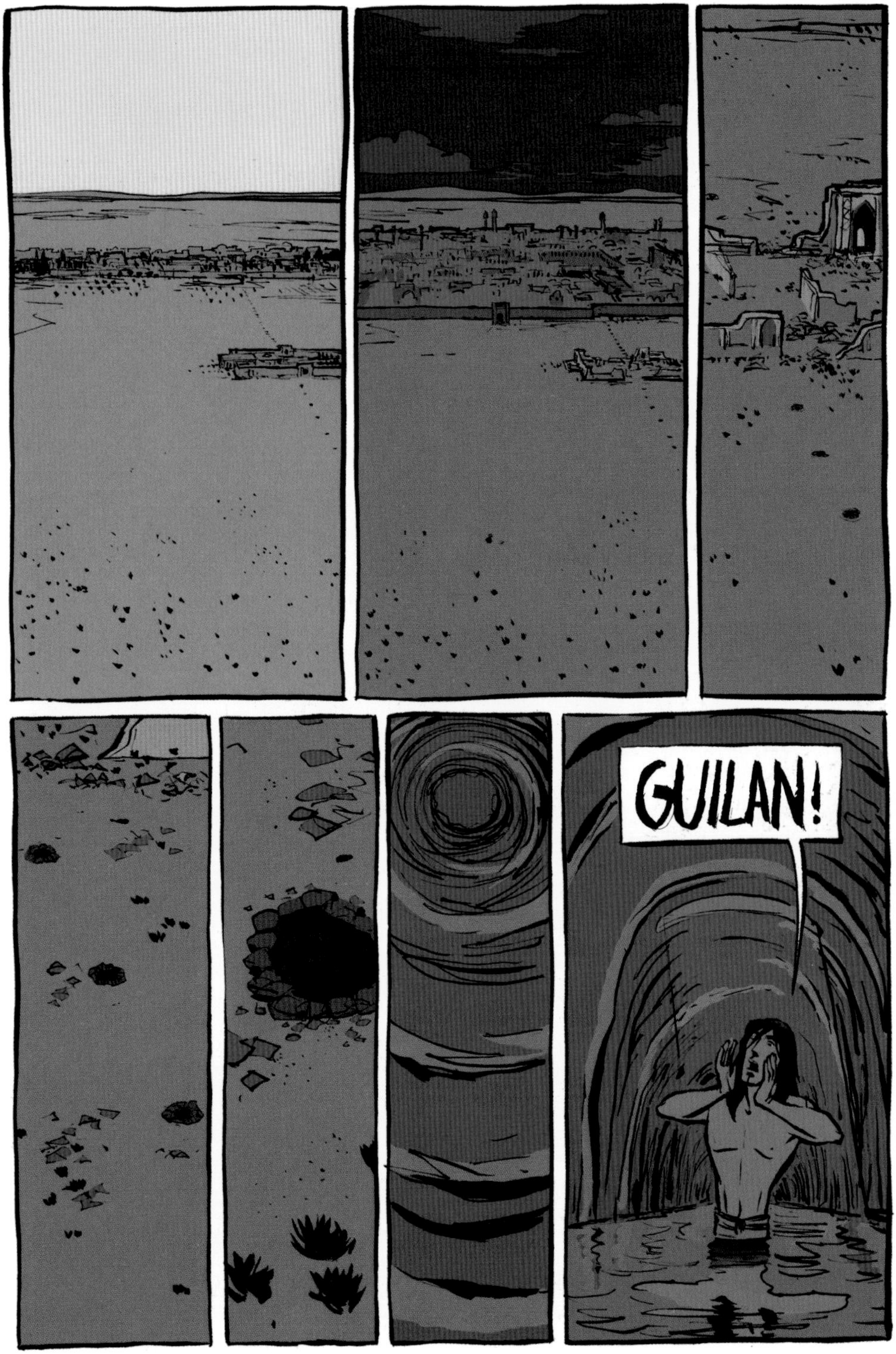
GUILAN!

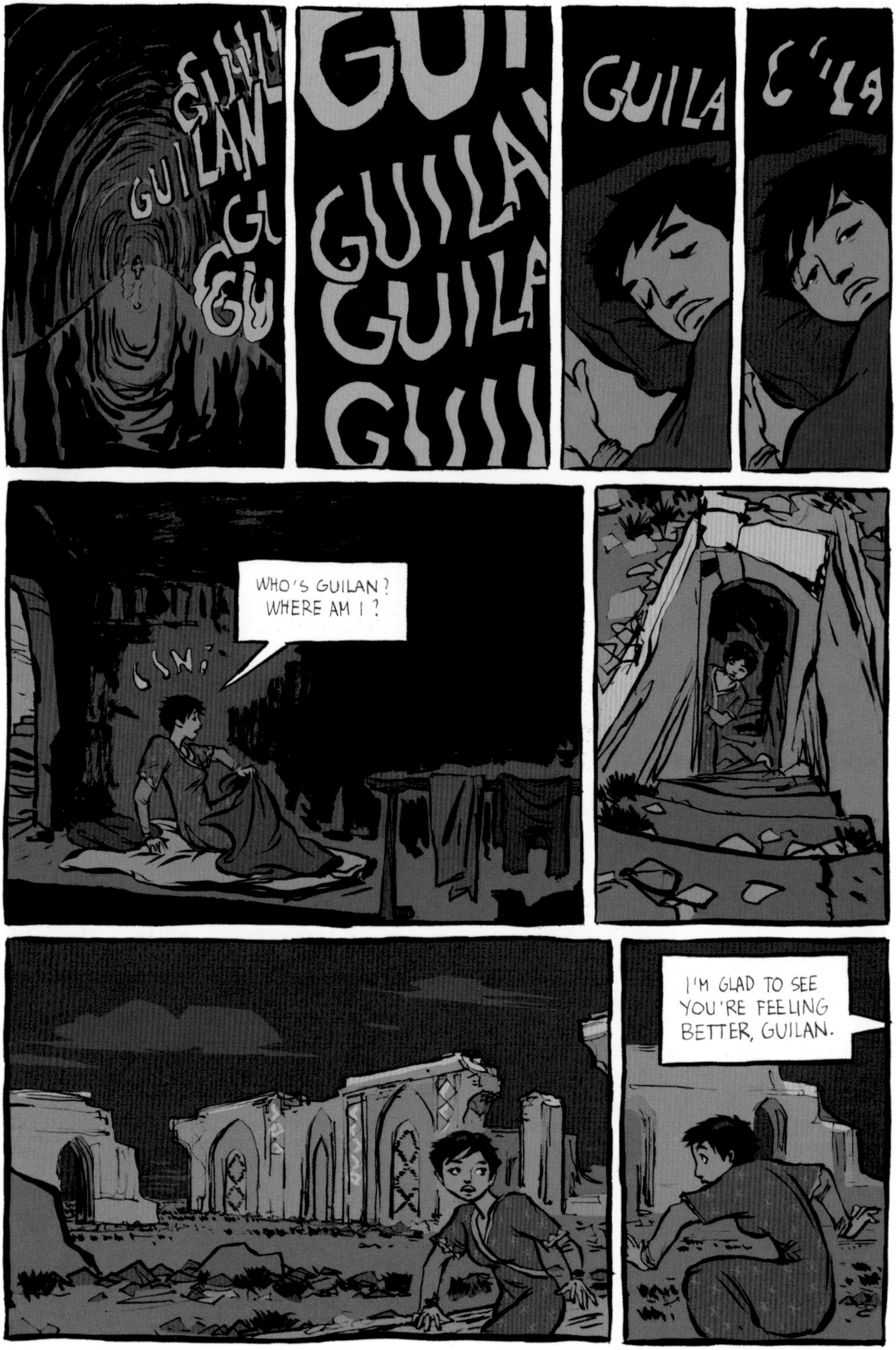
GUILAN
GU
GU
GUI
GUILA
GUILA
GUILA
WHO'S GUILAN? WHERE AM I?
I'M GLAD TO SEE YOU'RE FEELING BETTER, GUILAN.

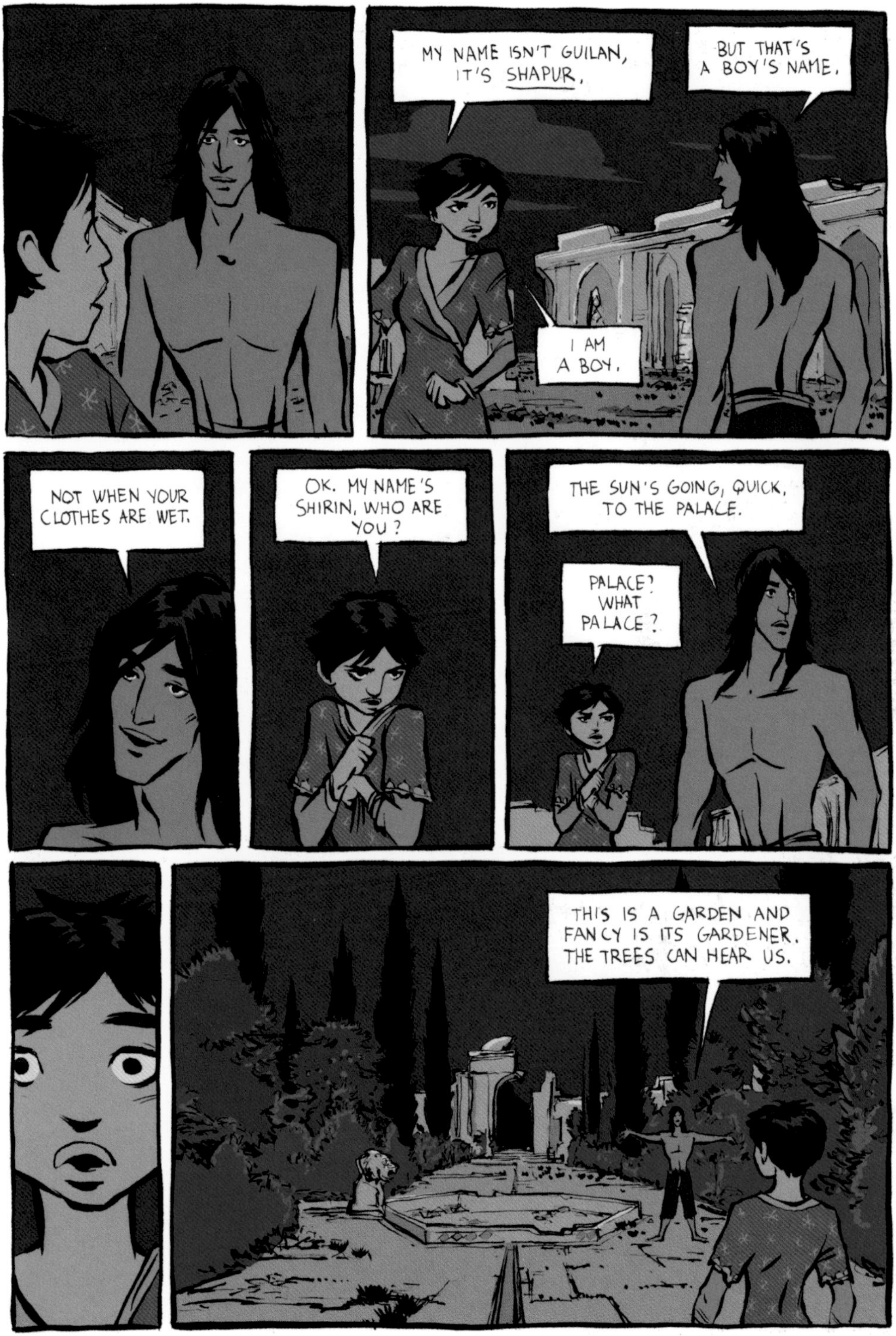
MY NAME ISN'T GUILAN, IT'S SHAPUR.
BUT THAT'S A BOY'S NAME.
I AM A BOY.
NOT WHEN YOUR CLOTHES ARE WET.
OK. MY NAME'S SHIRIN, WHO ARE YOU?
THE SUN'S GOING, QUICK, TO THE PALACE.
PALACE? WHAT PALACE?
THIS IS A GARDEN AND FANCY IS ITS GARDENER. THE TREES CAN HEAR US.

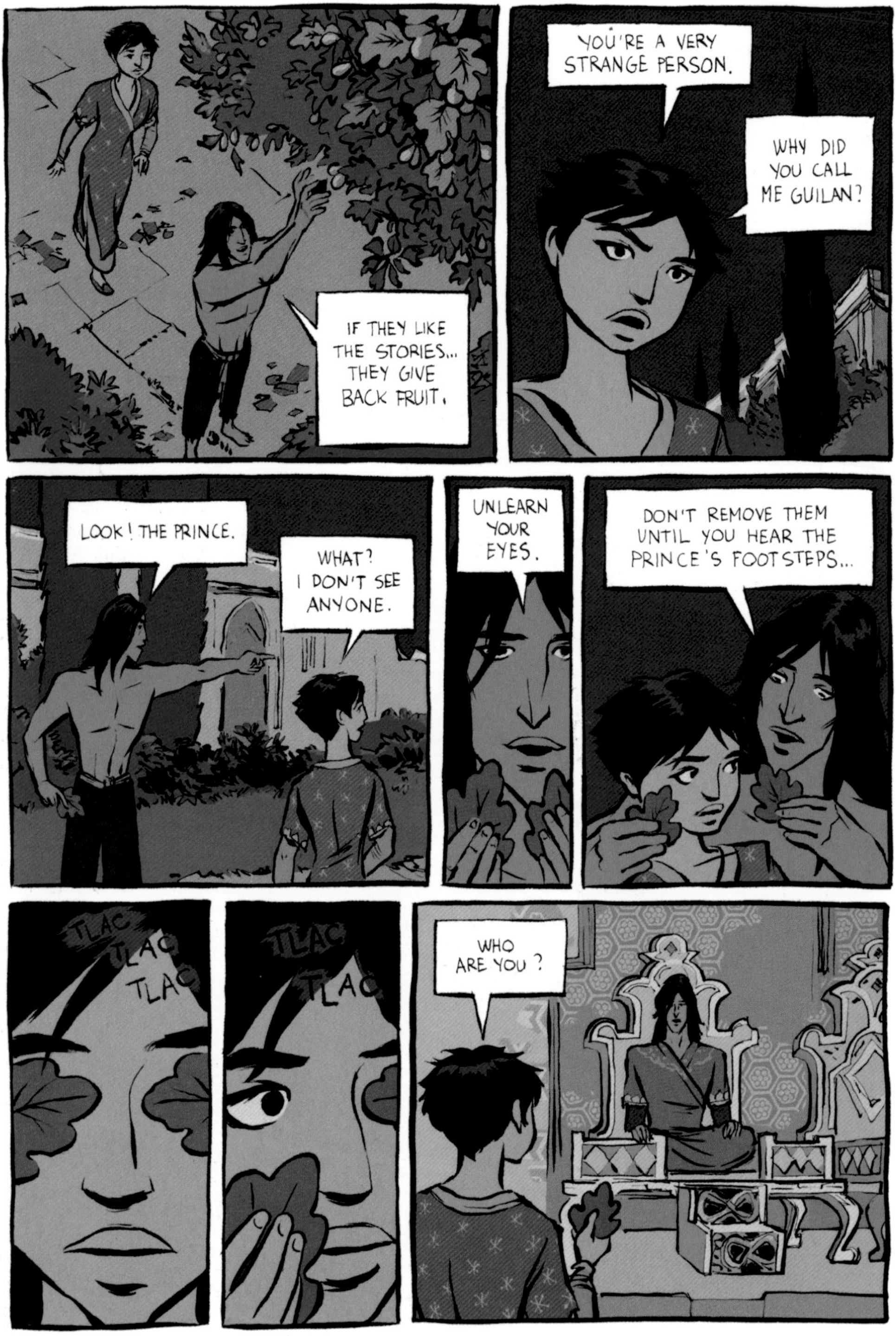
IF THEY LIKE THE STORIES... THEY GIVE BACK FRUIT.
YOU'RE A VERY STRANGE PERSON.
WHY DID YOU CALL ME GUILAN?
LOOK! THE PRINCE.
WHAT? I DON'T SEE ANYONE.
UNLEARN YOUR EYES.
DON'T REMOVE THEM UNTIL YOU HEAR THE PRINCE'S FOOTSTEPS...
TLAC TLAC TLAC
TLAC TLAC
WHO ARE YOU?

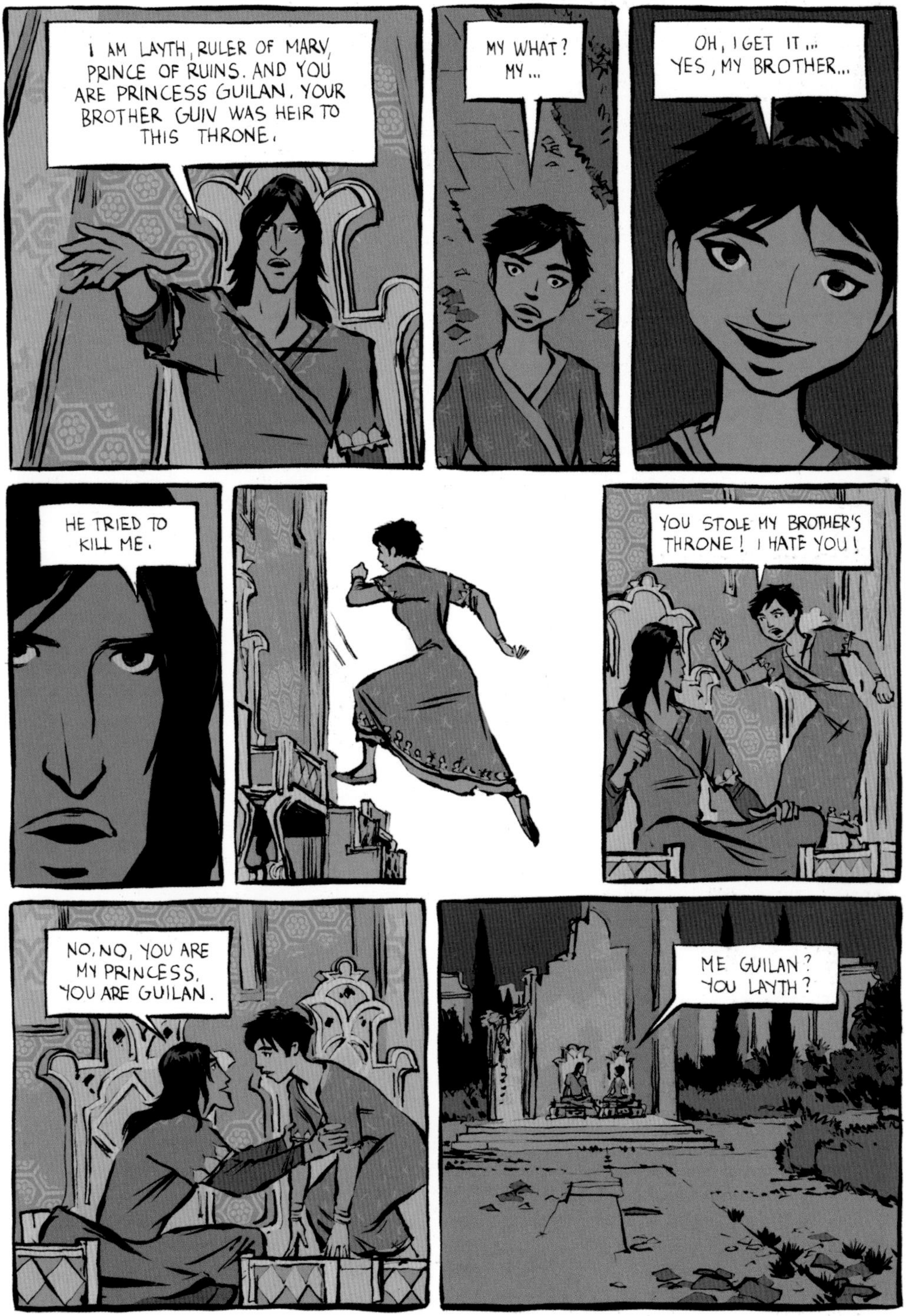
I AM LAYTH, RULER OF MARV, PRINCE OF RUINS. AND YOU ARE PRINCESS GUILAN. YOUR BROTHER GUIV WAS HEIR TO THIS THRONE.
MY WHAT? MY...
OH, I GET IT... YES, MY BROTHER...
HE TRIED TO KILL ME.
YOU STOLE MY BROTHER'S THRONE! I HATE YOU!
NO, NO, YOU ARE MY PRINCESS. YOU ARE GUILAN.
ME GUILAN? YOU LAYTH?

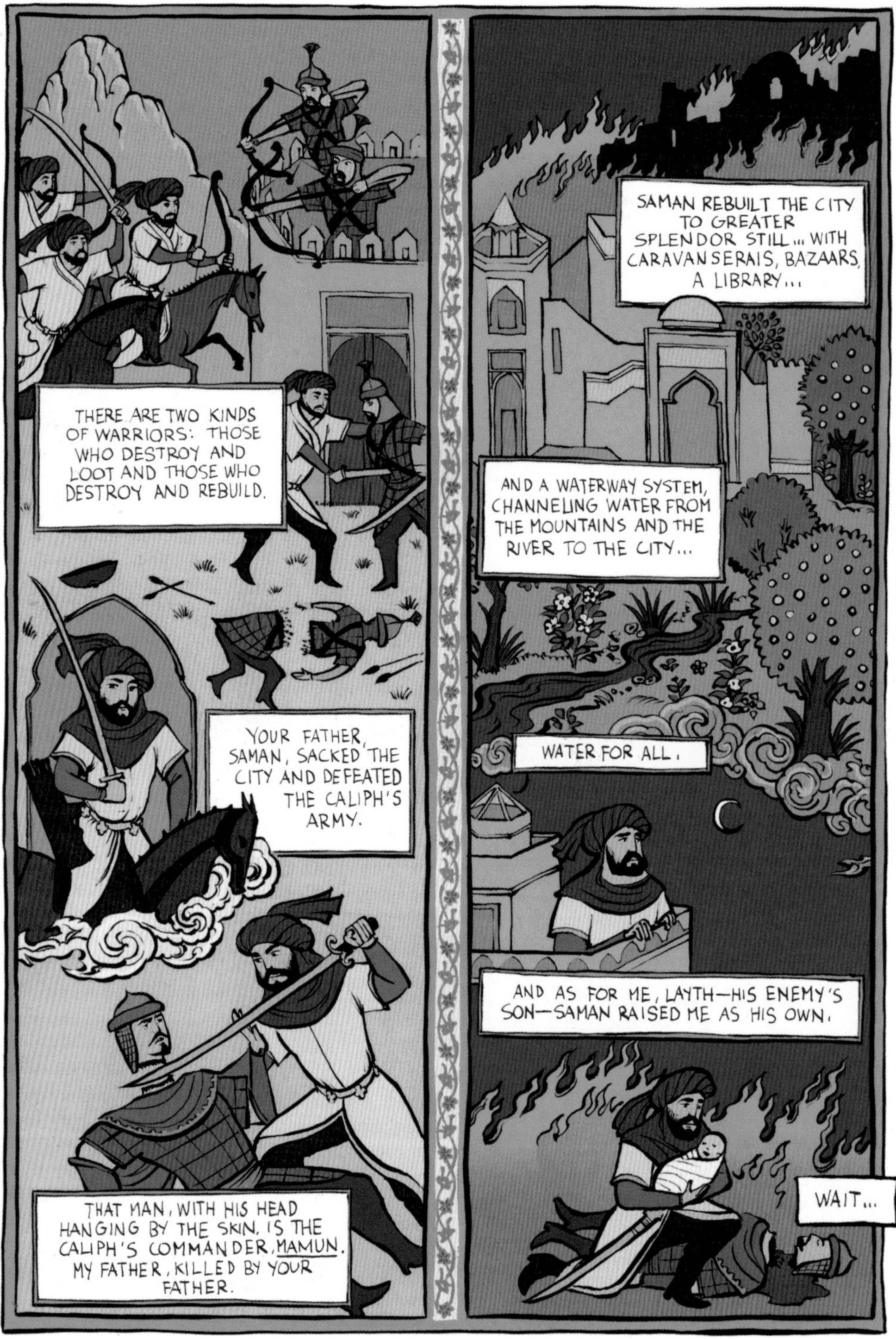
THERE ARE TWO KINDS OF WARRIORS: THOSE WHO DESTROY AND LOOT AND THOSE WHO DESTROY AND REBUILD.
YOUR FATHER, SAMAN, SACKED THE CITY AND DEFEATED THE CALIPH'S ARMY.
THAT MAN, WITH HIS HEAD HANGING BY THE SKIN, IS THE CALIPH'S COMMANDER, MAMUN. MY FATHER, KILLED BY YOUR FATHER.
SAMAN REBUILT THE CITY TO GREATER SPLENDOR STILL... WITH CARAVANSERAIS, BAZAARS, A LIBRARY...
AND A WATERWAY SYSTEM, CHANNELING WATER FROM THE MOUNTAINS AND THE RIVER TO THE CITY...
WATER FOR ALL.
AND AS FOR ME, LAYTH—HIS ENEMY'S SON—SAMAN RAISED ME AS HIS OWN.
WAIT...

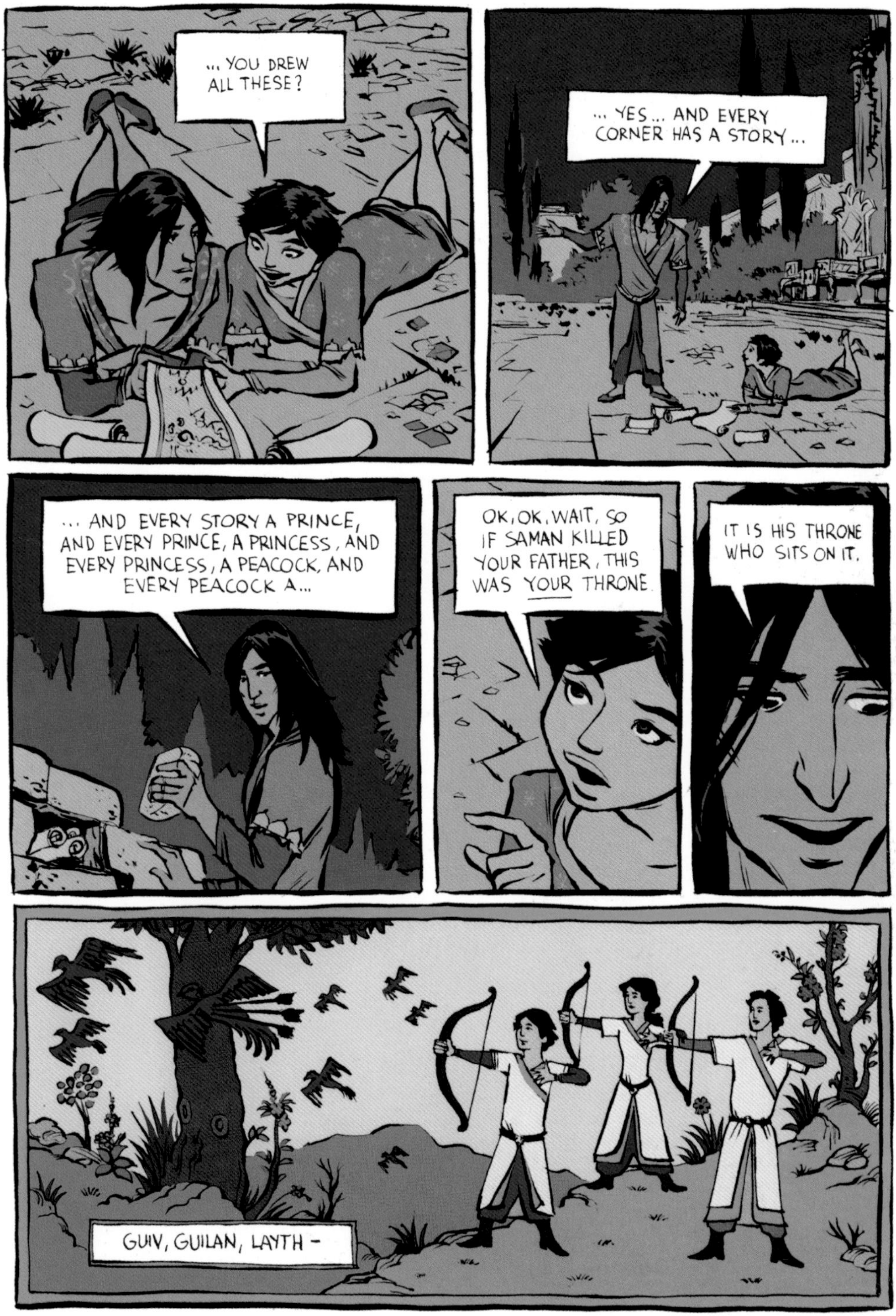
... YOU DREW ALL THESE?
... YES... AND EVERY CORNER HAS A STORY...
... AND EVERY STORY A PRINCE, AND EVERY PRINCE, A PRINCESS, AND EVERY PRINCESS, A PEACOCK, AND EVERY PEACOCK A...
OK, OK, WAIT, SO IF SAMAN KILLED YOUR FATHER, THIS WAS YOUR THRONE.
IT IS HIS THRONE WHO SITS ON IT.
GUIV, GUILAN, LAYTH -

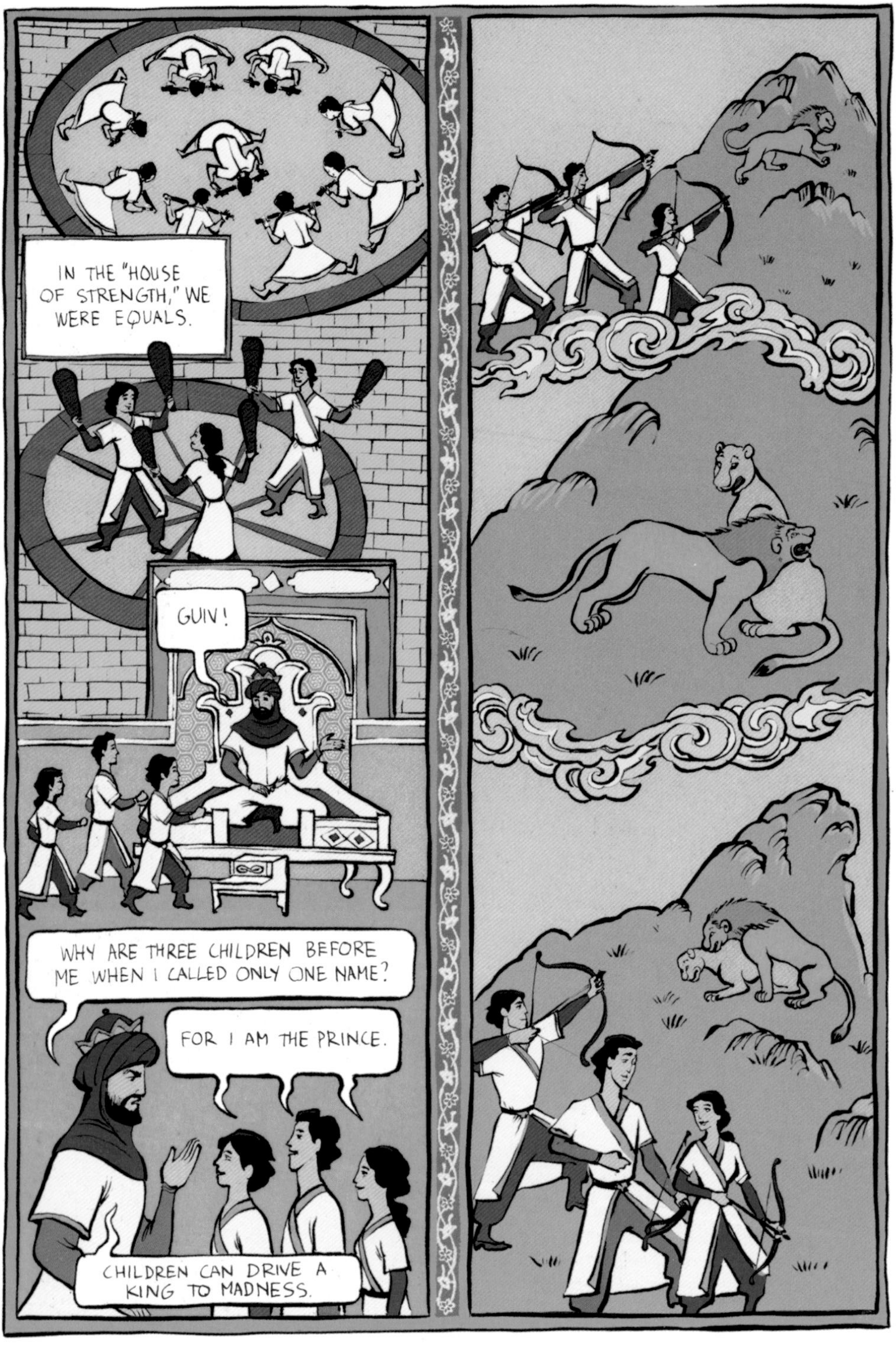
IN THE "HOUSE OF STRENGTH," WE WERE EQUALS.
GUIV!
WHY ARE THREE CHILDREN BEFORE ME WHEN I CALLED ONLY ONE NAME?
FOR I AM THE PRINCE.
CHILDREN CAN DRIVE A KING TO MADNESS.

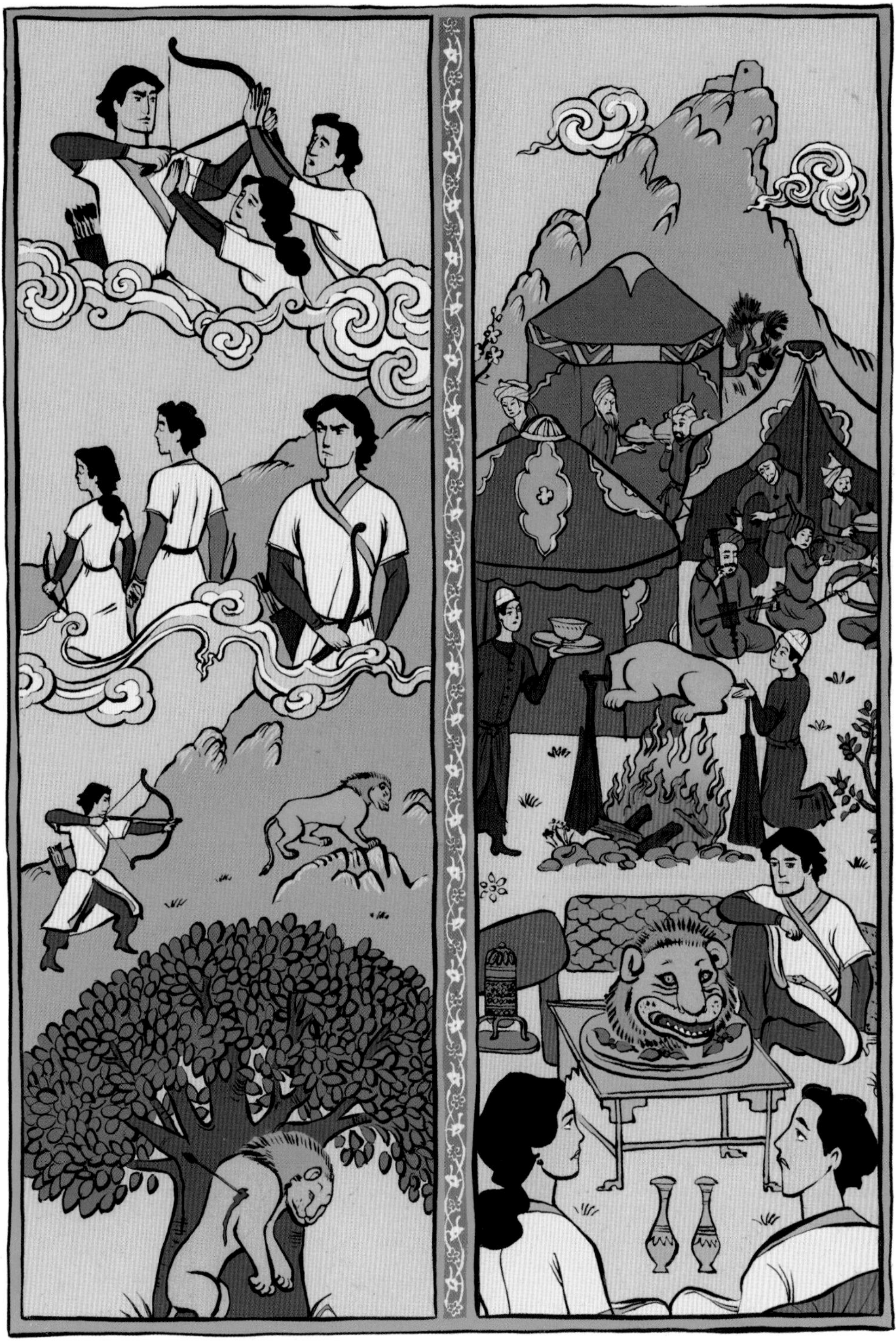

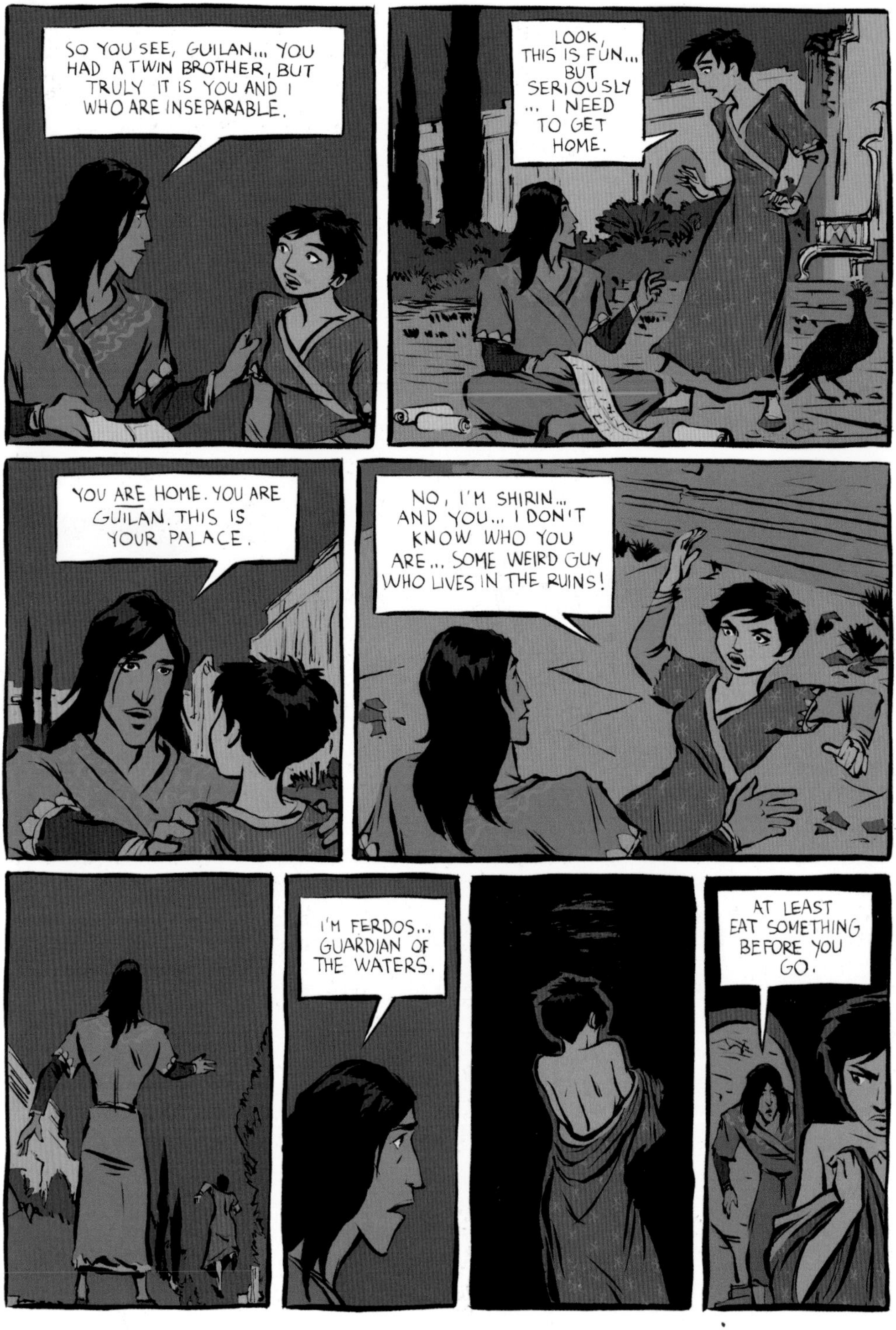
SO YOU SEE, GUILAN... YOU HAD A TWIN BROTHER, BUT TRULY IT IS YOU AND I WHO ARE INSEPARABLE.
LOOK, THIS IS FUN... BUT SERIOUSLY ... I NEED TO GET HOME.
YOU ARE HOME. YOU ARE GUILAN. THIS IS YOUR PALACE.
NO, I'M SHIRIN... AND YOU... I DON'T KNOW WHO YOU ARE... SOME WEIRD GUY WHO LIVES IN THE RUINS!
I'M FERDOS... GUARDIAN OF THE WATERS.
AT LEAST EAT SOMETHING BEFORE YOU GO.

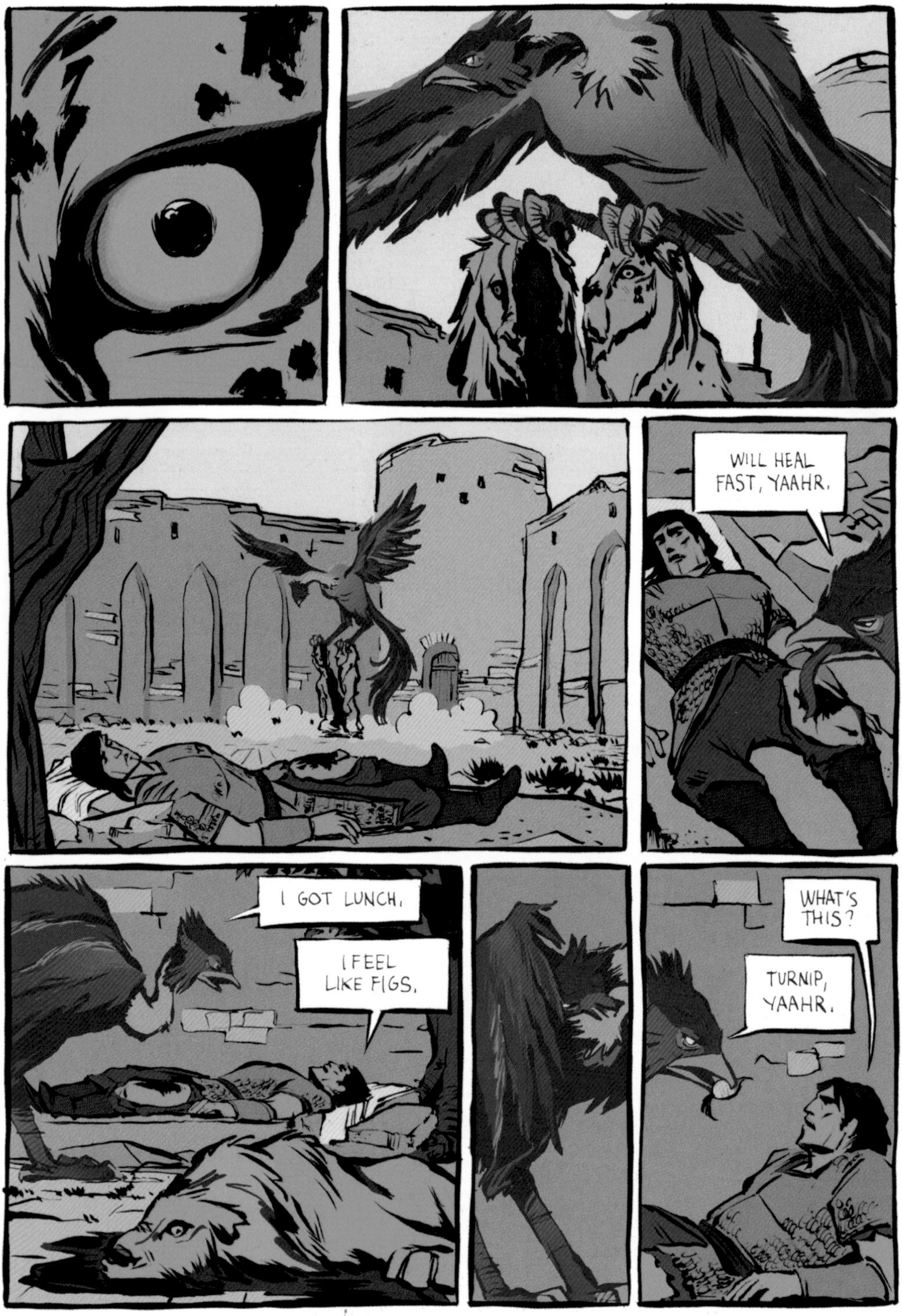

WILL HEAL FAST, YAAHR.
I GOT LUNCH.
I FEEL LIKE FIGS.
WHAT'S THIS?
TURNIP, YAAHR.

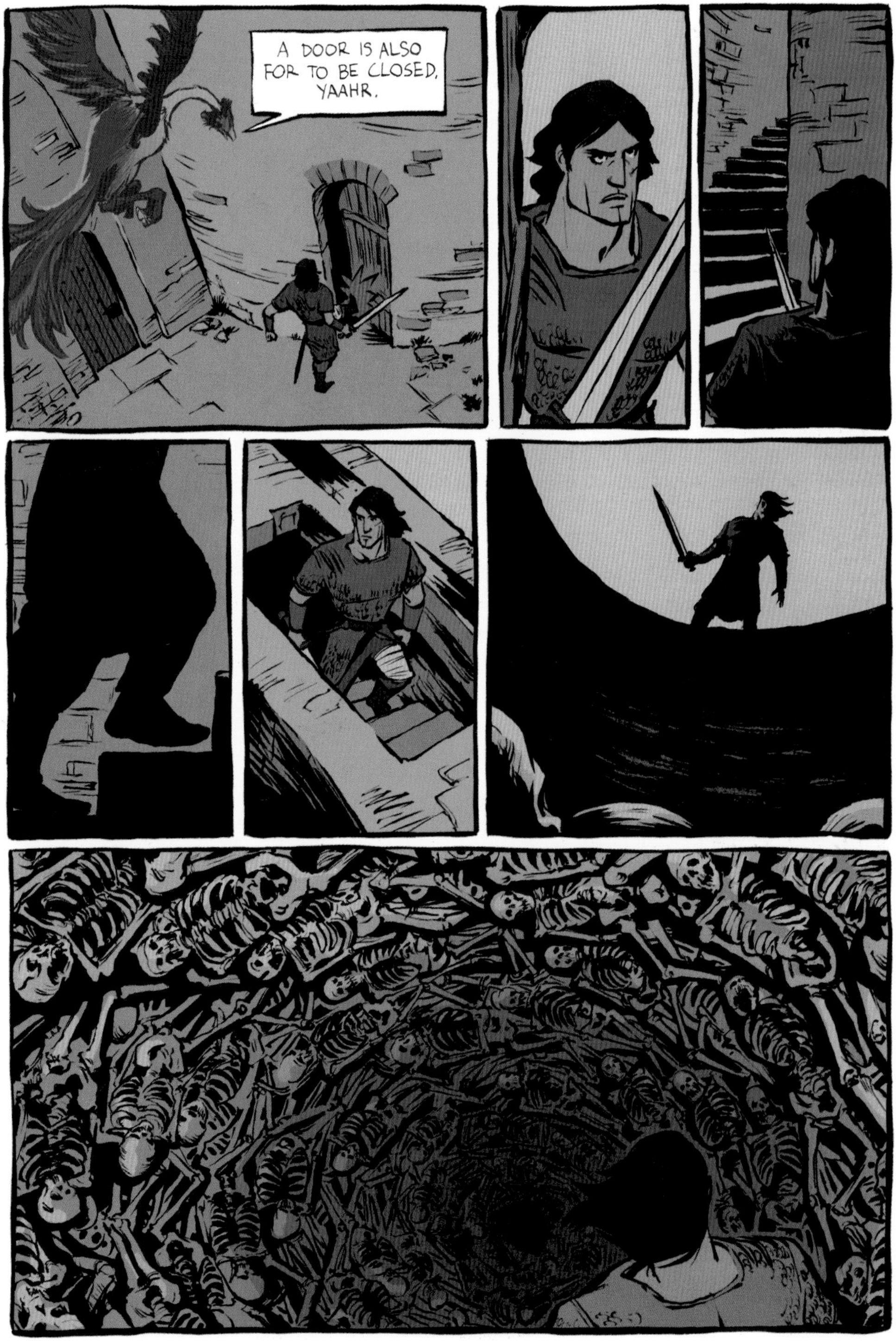
A DOOR IS ALSO FOR TO BE CLOSED, YAAHR.

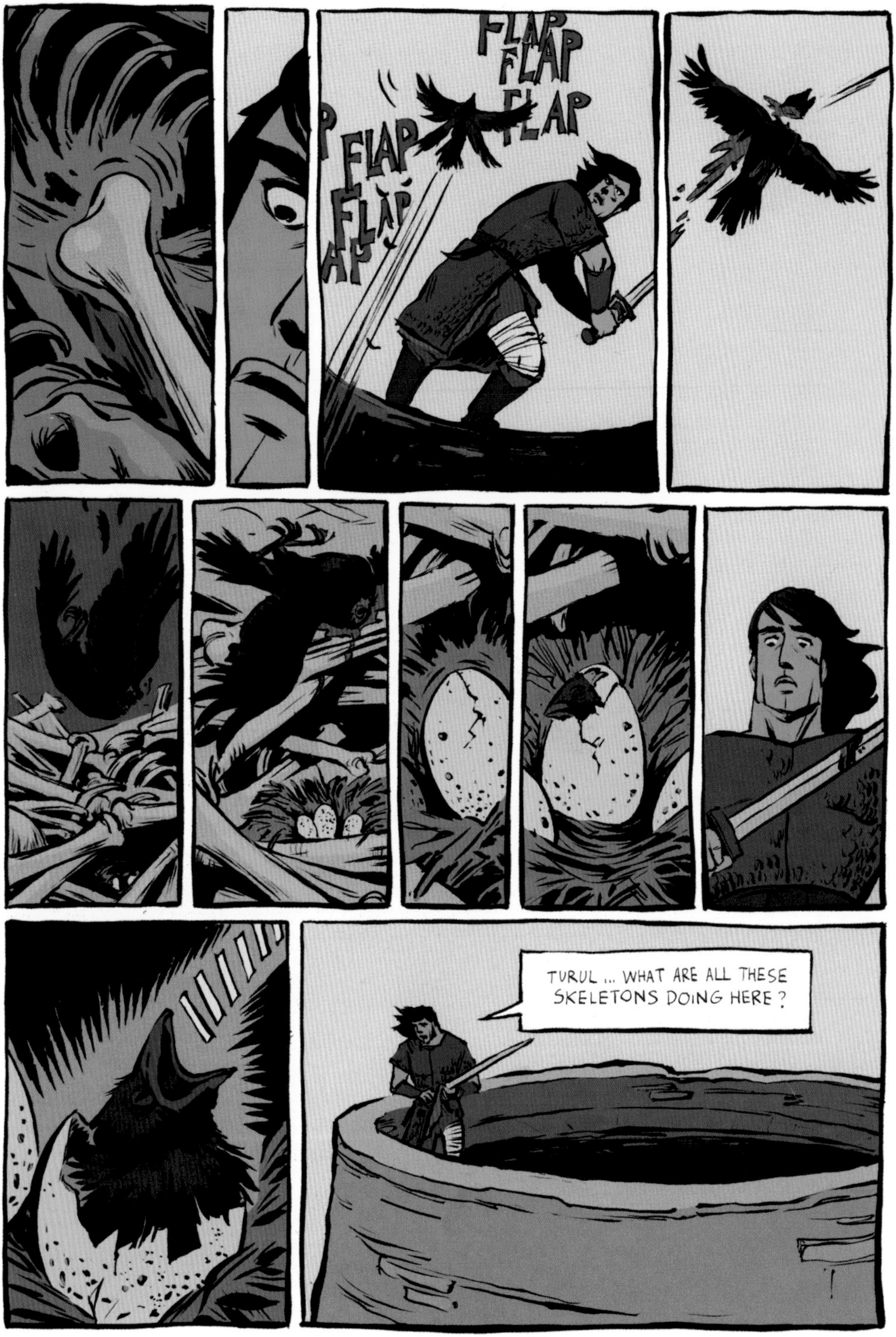
FLAP FLAP FLAP
FLAP FLAP
FLAP FLAP
AP
TURUL ... WHAT ARE ALL THESE SKELETONS DOING HERE?

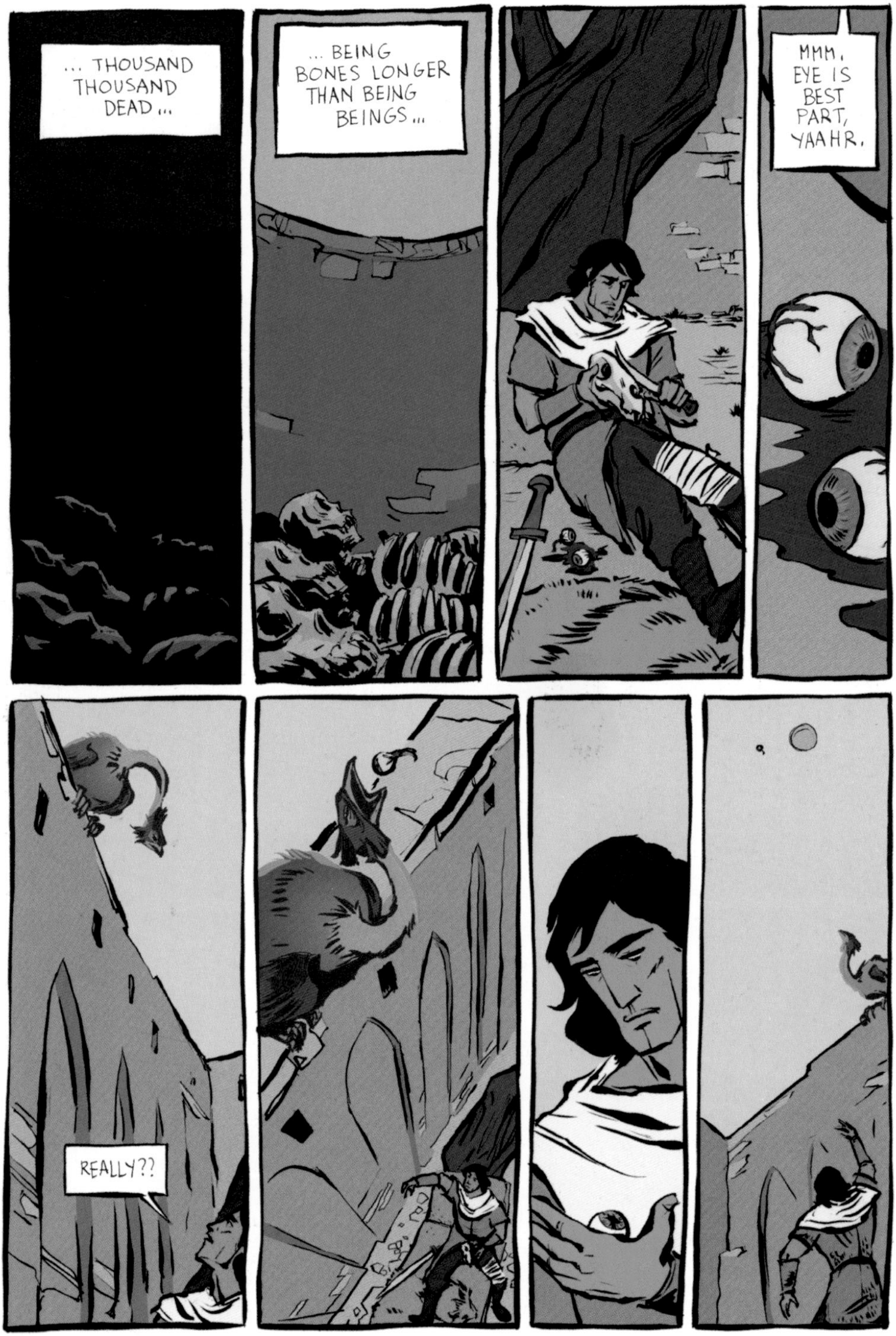
... THOUSAND THOUSAND DEAD ...
... BEING BONES LONGER THAN BEING BEINGS ...
MMM, EYE IS BEST PART, YAAHR.
REALLY??

57

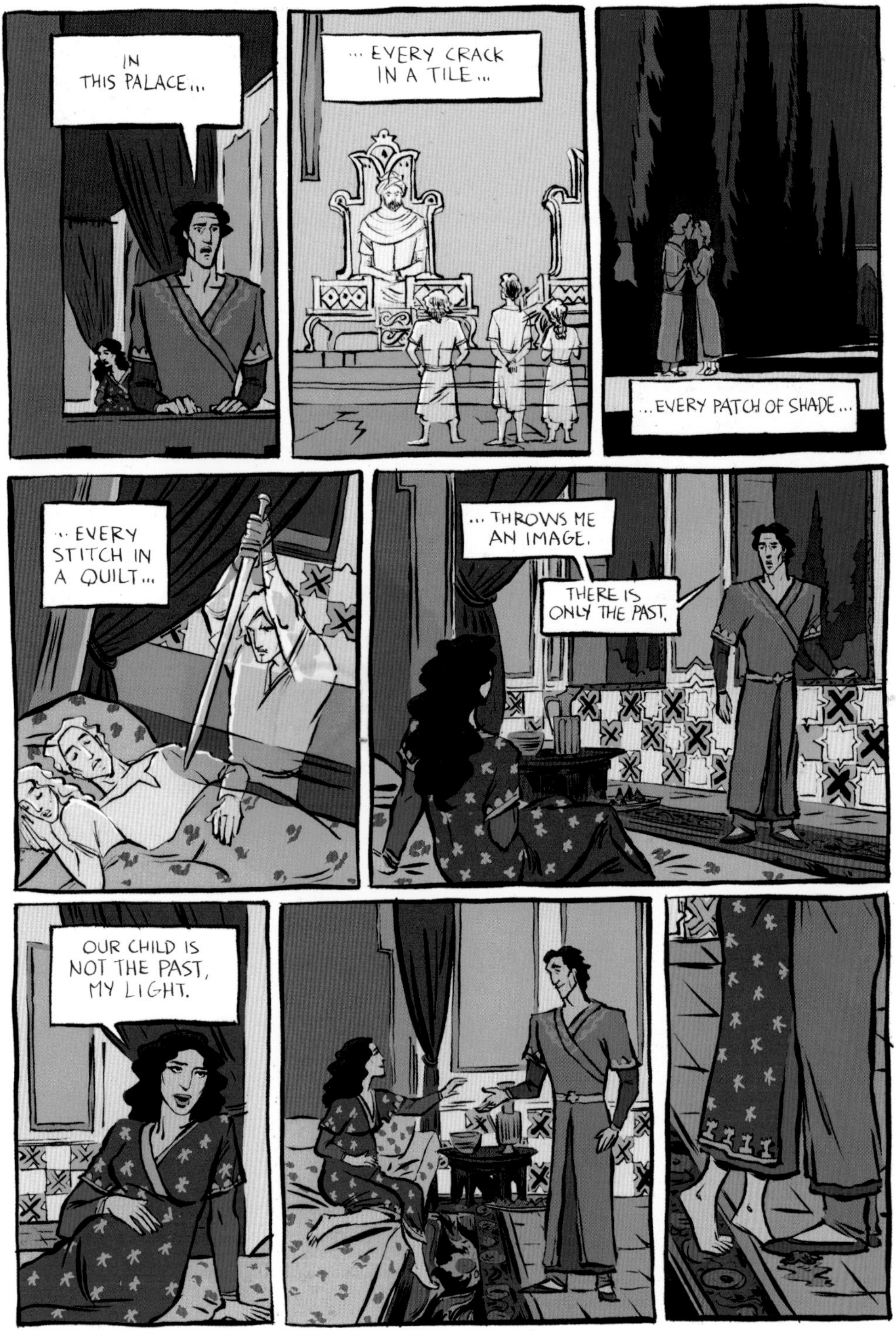
IN THIS PALACE...
...EVERY CRACK IN A TILE...
...EVERY PATCH OF SHADE...
...EVERY STITCH IN A QUILT...
...THROWS ME AN IMAGE.
THERE IS ONLY THE PAST.
OUR CHILD IS NOT THE PAST, MY LIGHT.

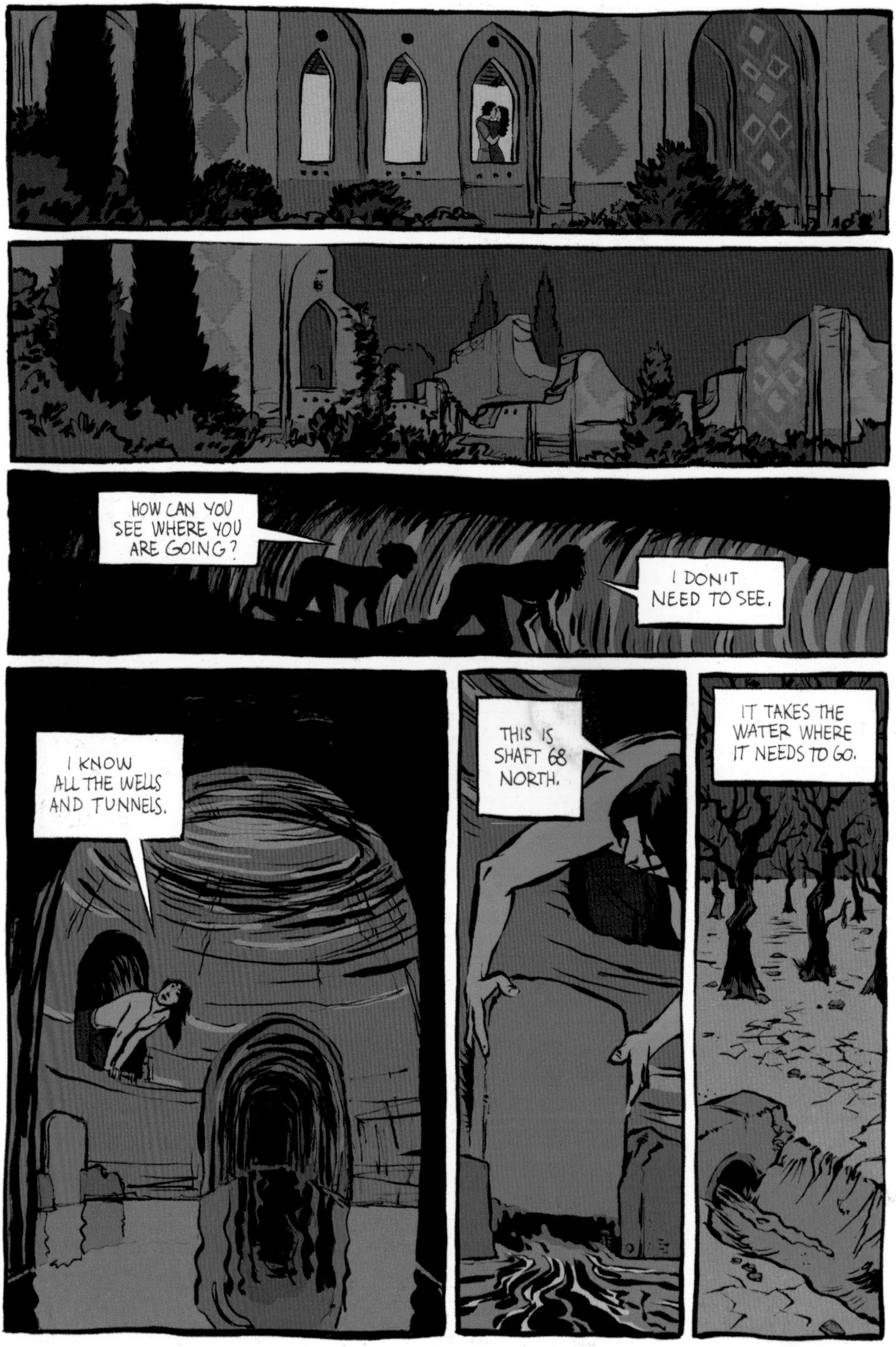
HOW CAN YOU SEE WHERE YOU ARE GOING?
I DON'T NEED TO SEE.
I KNOW ALL THE WELLS AND TUNNELS.
THIS IS SHAFT 68 NORTH.
IT TAKES THE WATER WHERE IT NEEDS TO GO.

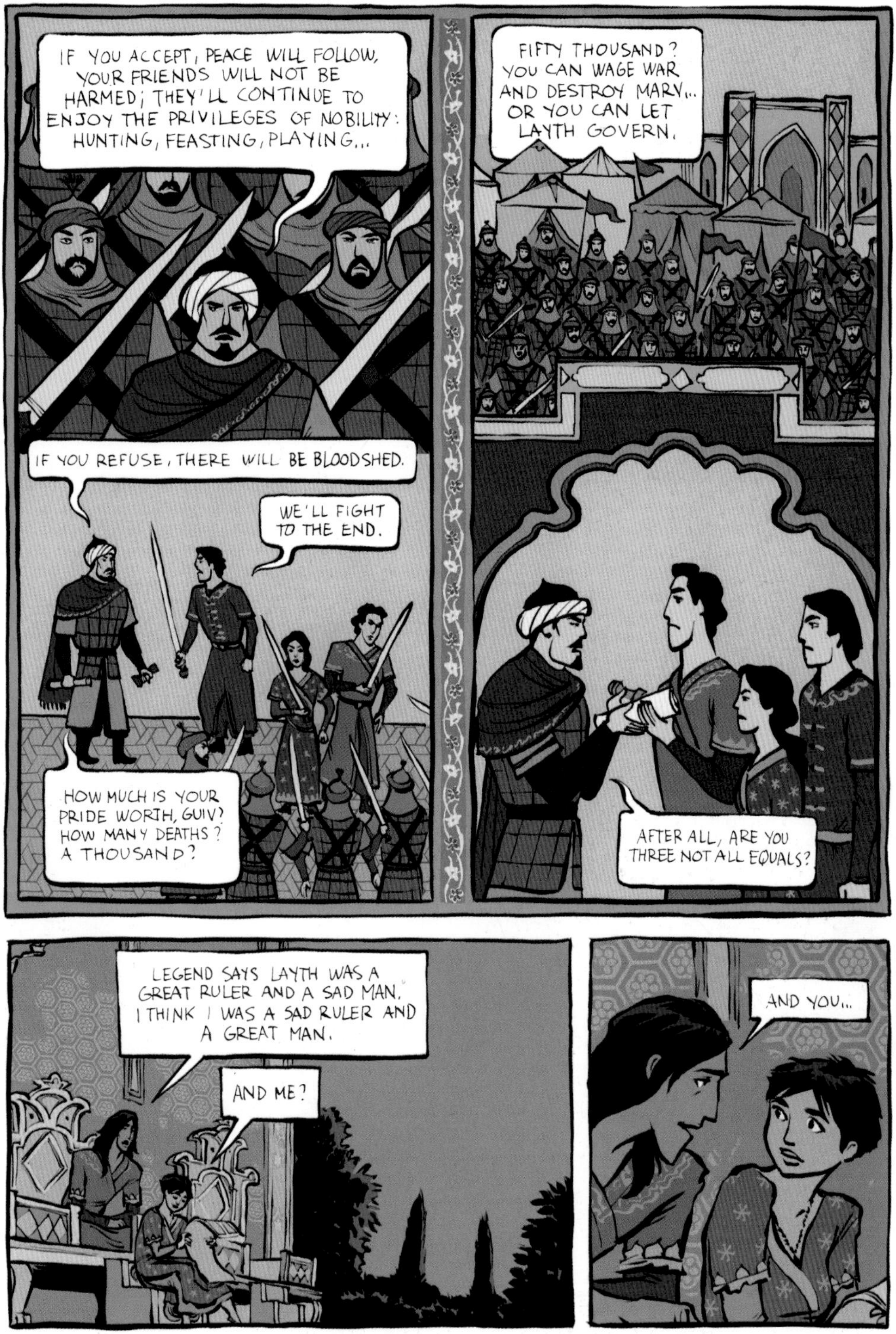
IF YOU ACCEPT, PEACE WILL FOLLOW, YOUR FRIENDS WILL NOT BE HARMED; THEY'LL CONTINUE TO ENJOY THE PRIVILEGES OF NOBILITY: HUNTING, FEASTING, PLAYING...
IF YOU REFUSE, THERE WILL BE BLOODSHED.
WE'LL FIGHT TO THE END.
HOW MUCH IS YOUR PRIDE WORTH, GUIV? HOW MANY DEATHS? A THOUSAND?
FIFTY THOUSAND? YOU CAN WAGE WAR AND DESTROY MARV... OR YOU CAN LET LAYTH GOVERN.
AFTER ALL, ARE YOU THREE NOT ALL EQUALS?
LEGEND SAYS LAYTH WAS A GREAT RULER AND A SAD MAN. I THINK I WAS A SAD RULER AND A GREAT MAN.
AND ME?
AND YOU...

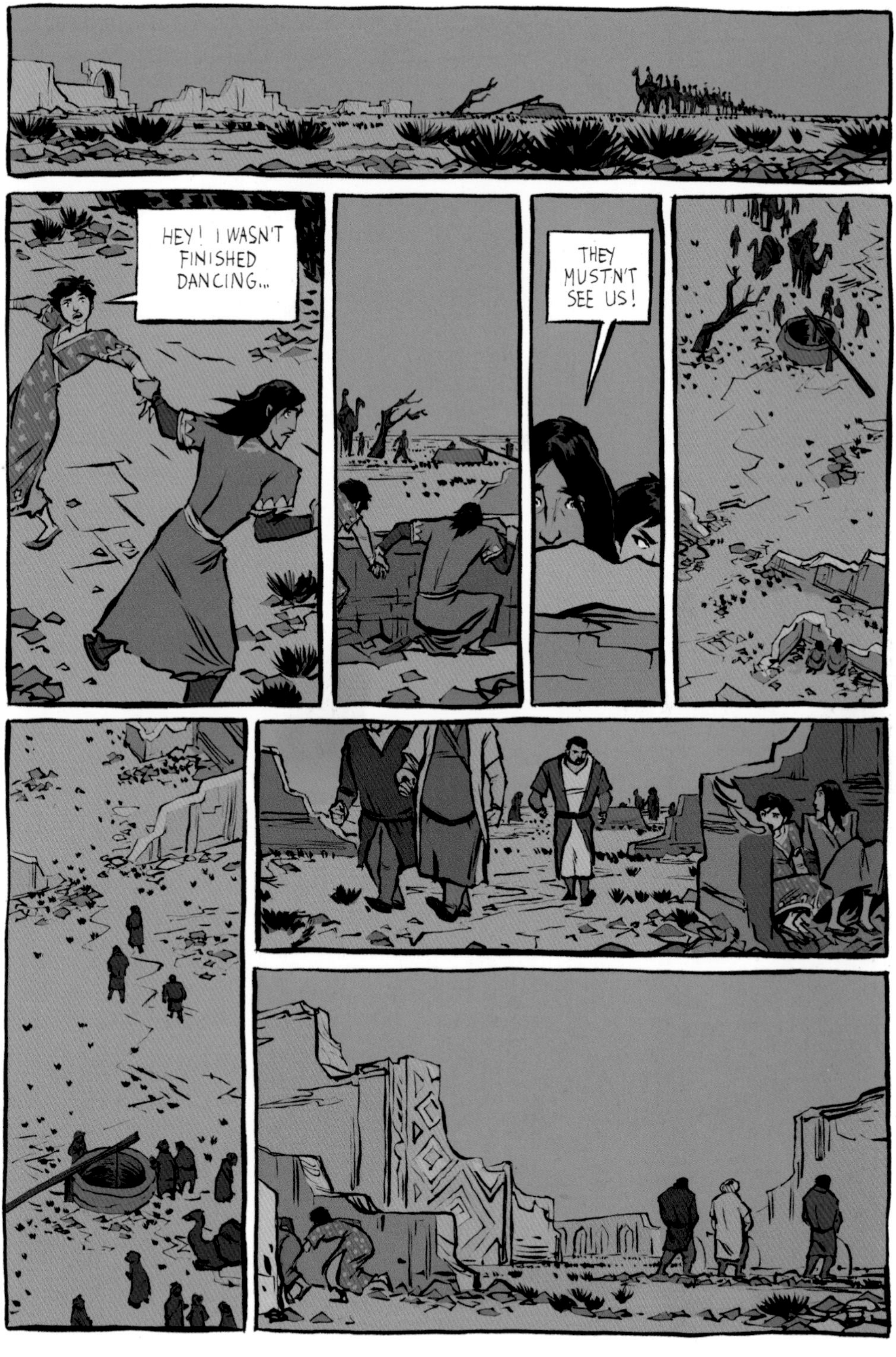
HEY! I WASN'T FINISHED DANCING...
THEY MUSTN'T SEE US!

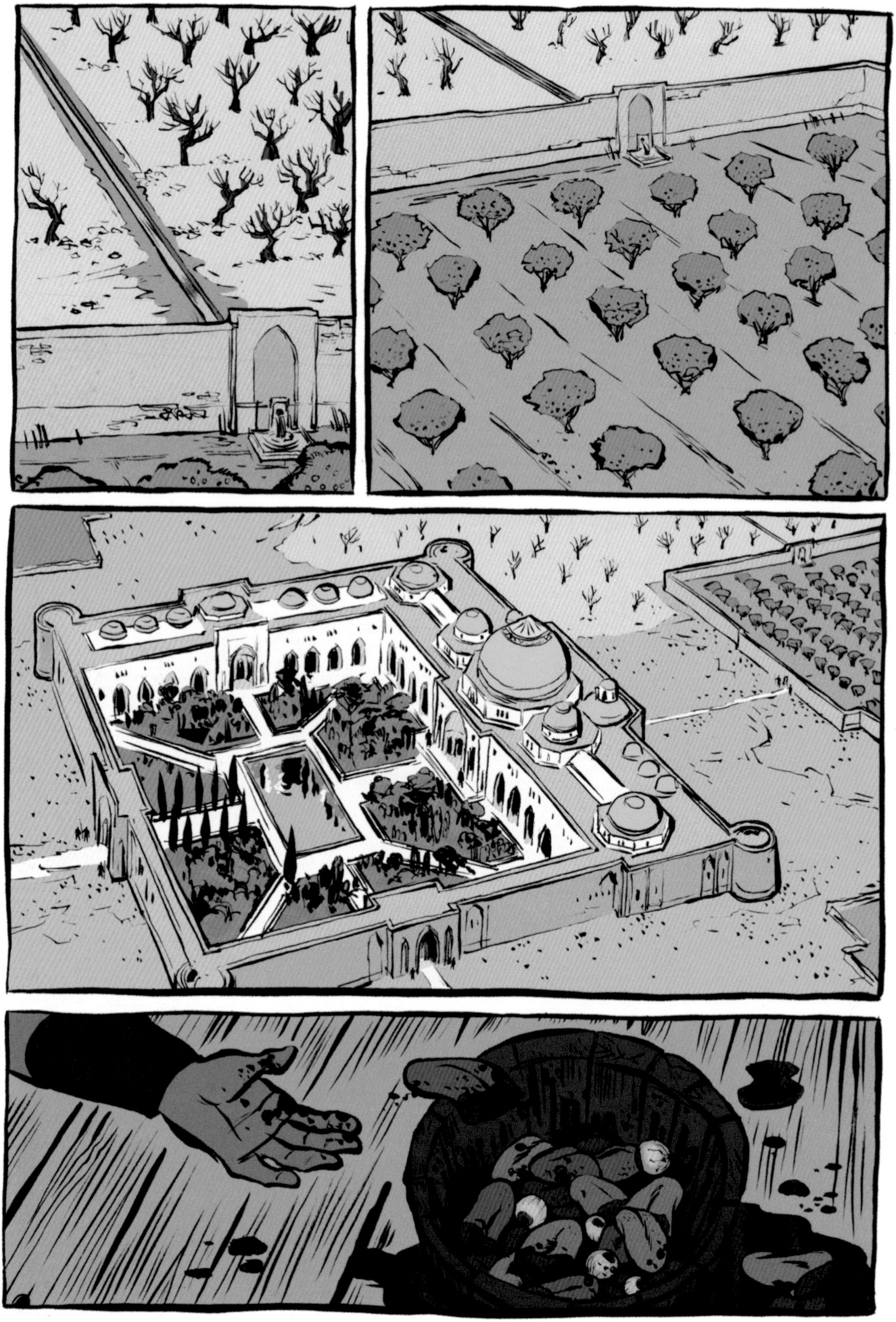

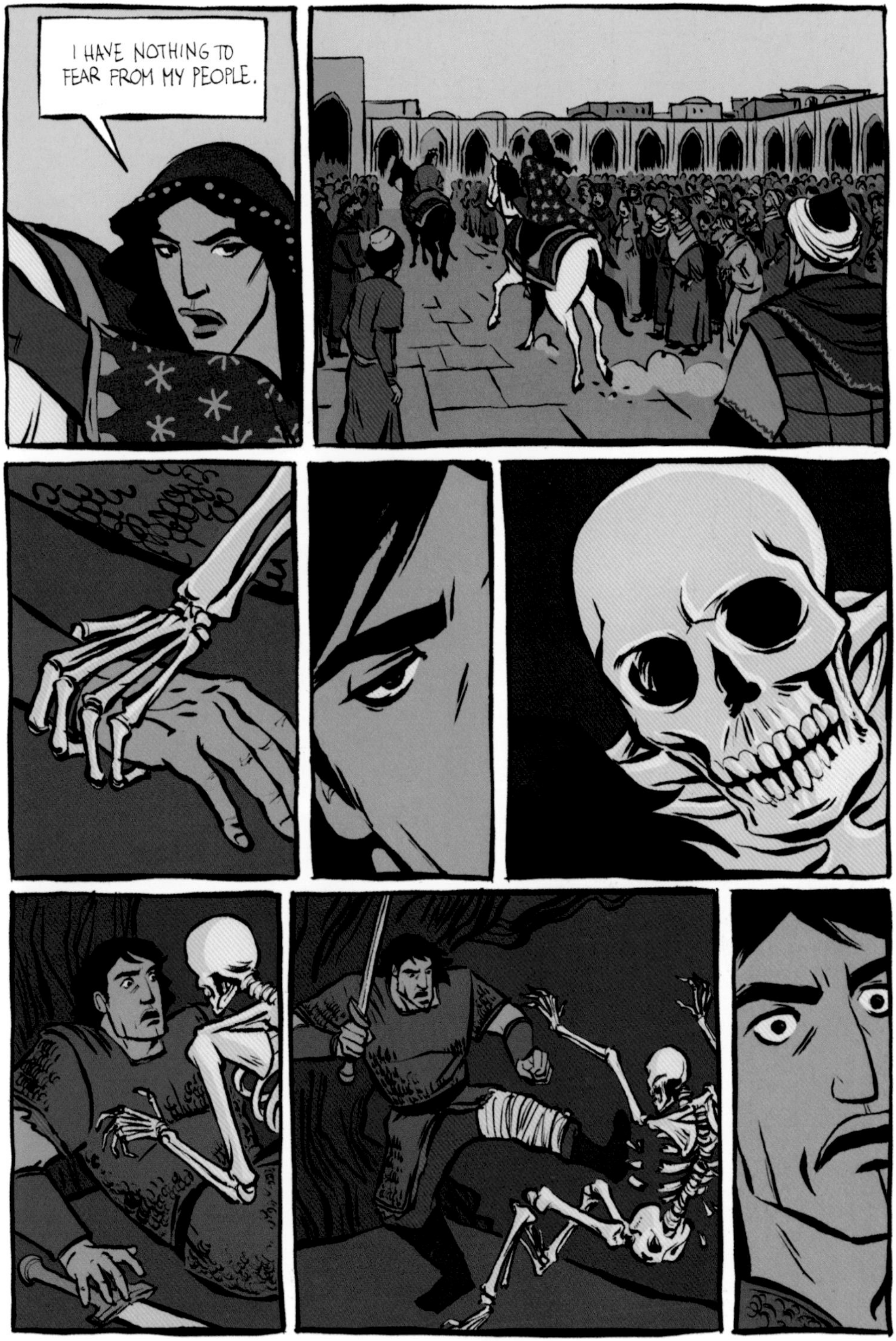
I HAVE NOTHING TO FEAR FROM MY PEOPLE.

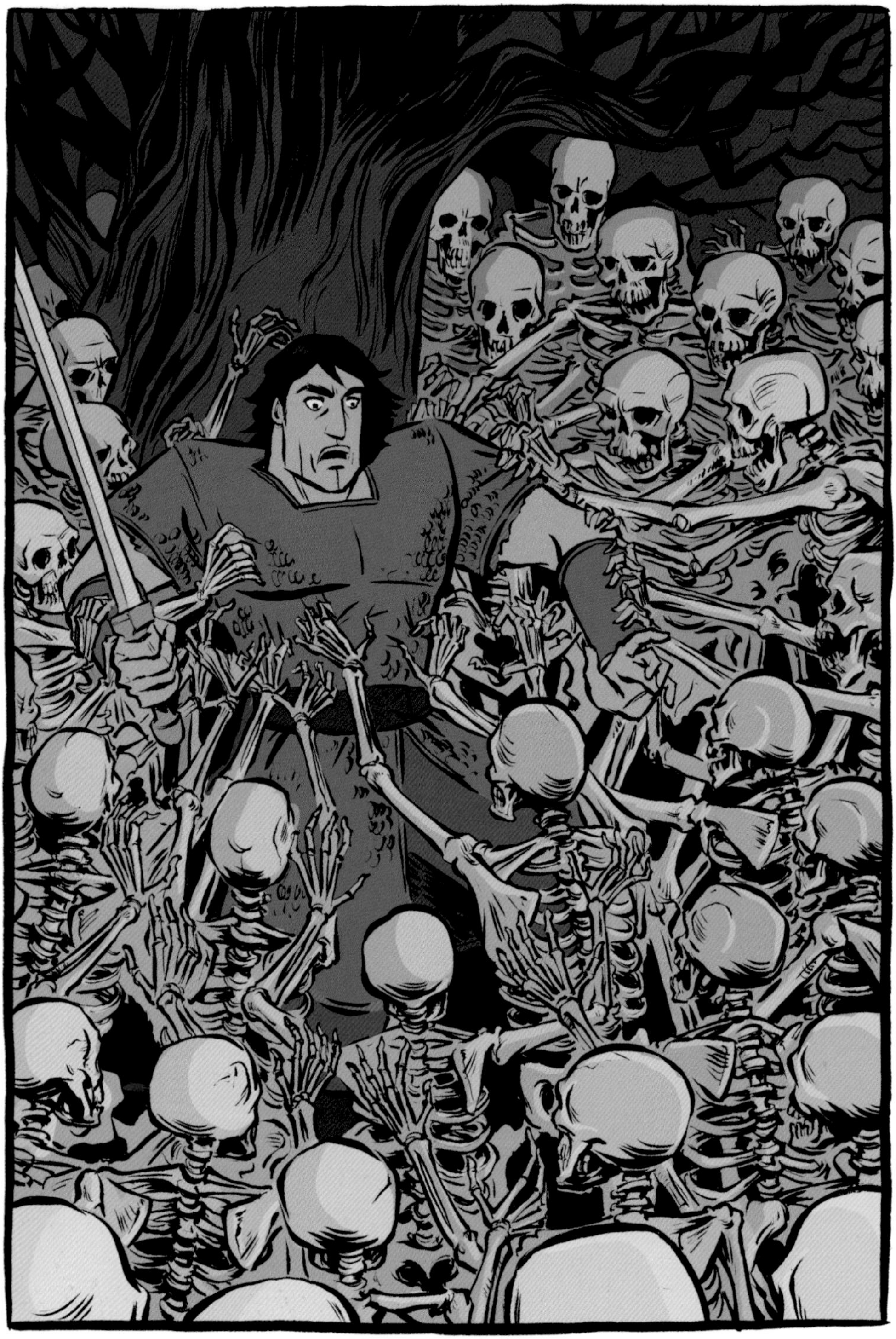

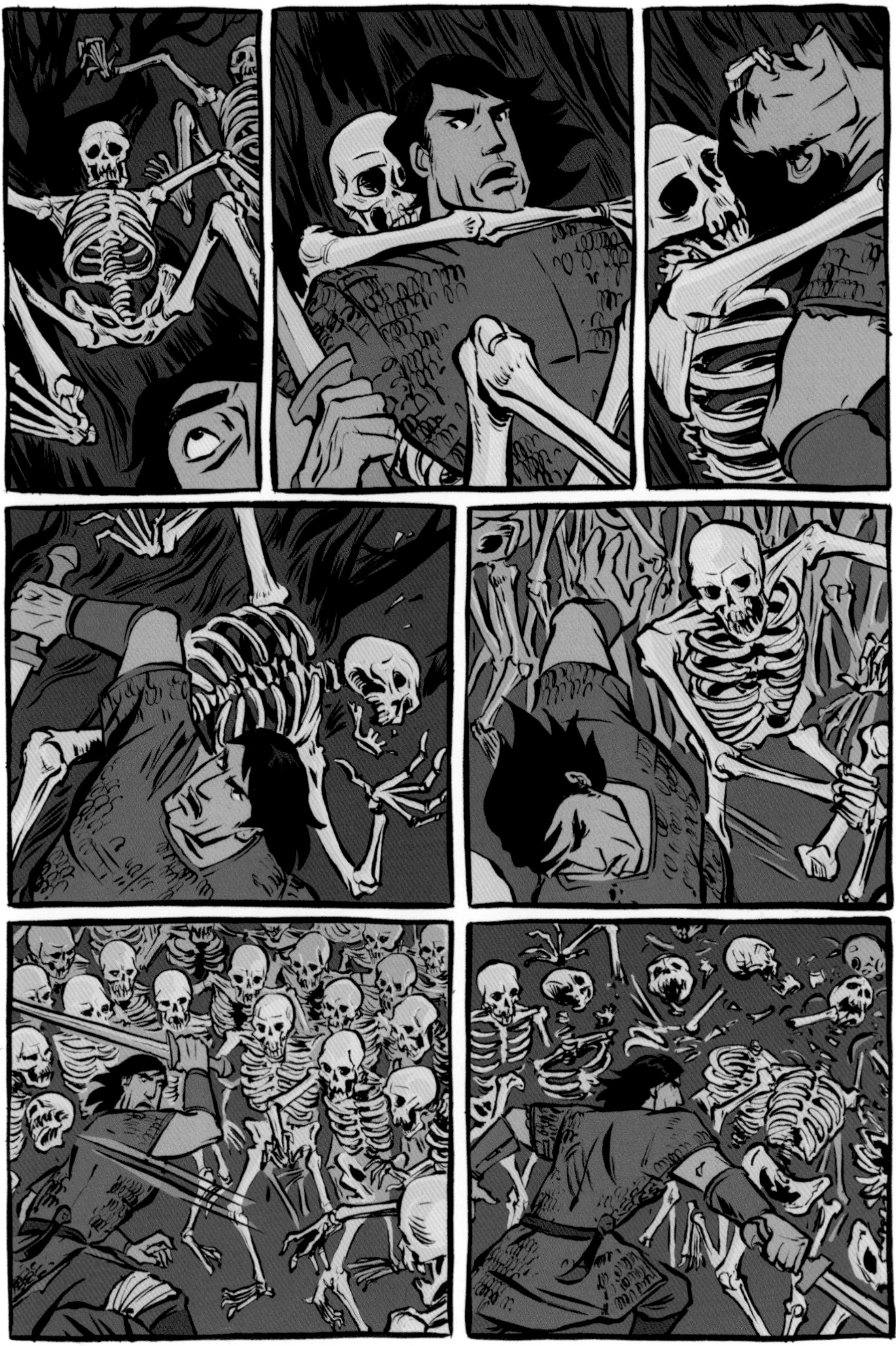

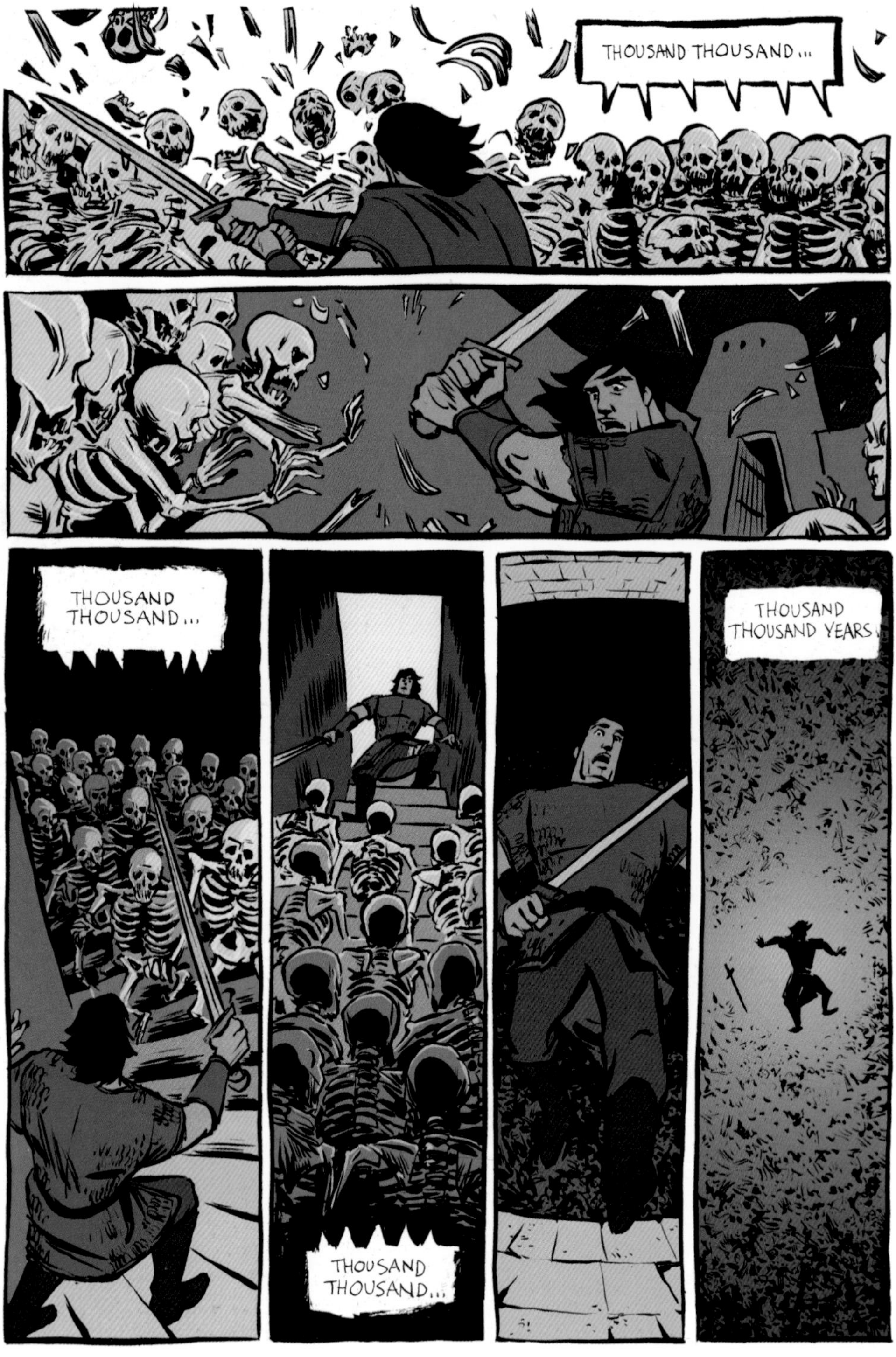
THOUSAND THOUSAND...
THOUSAND THOUSAND...
THOUSAND THOUSAND...
THOUSAND THOUSAND YEARS

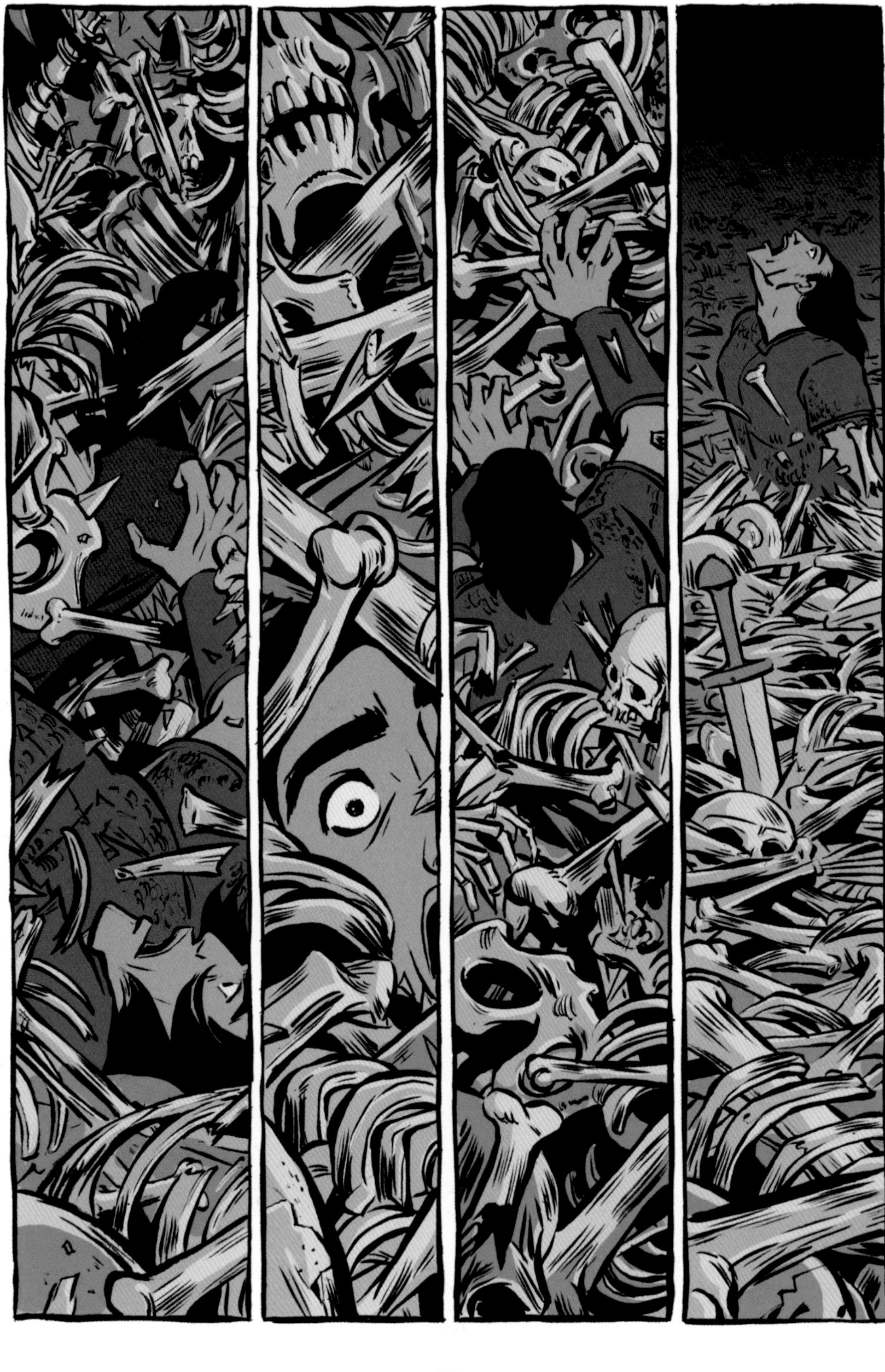

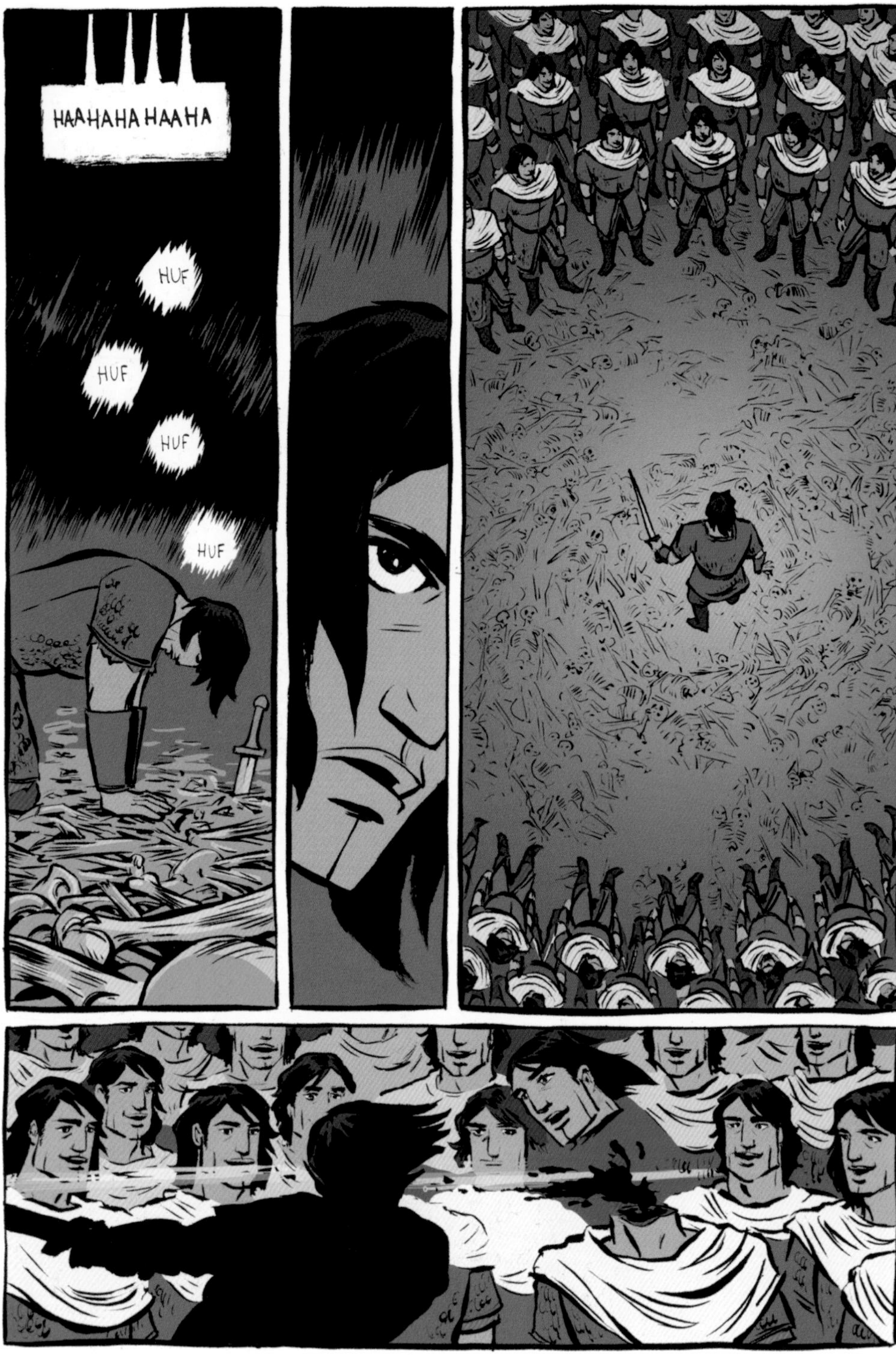
HAAHAHA HAAHA
HUF
HUF
HUF
HUF

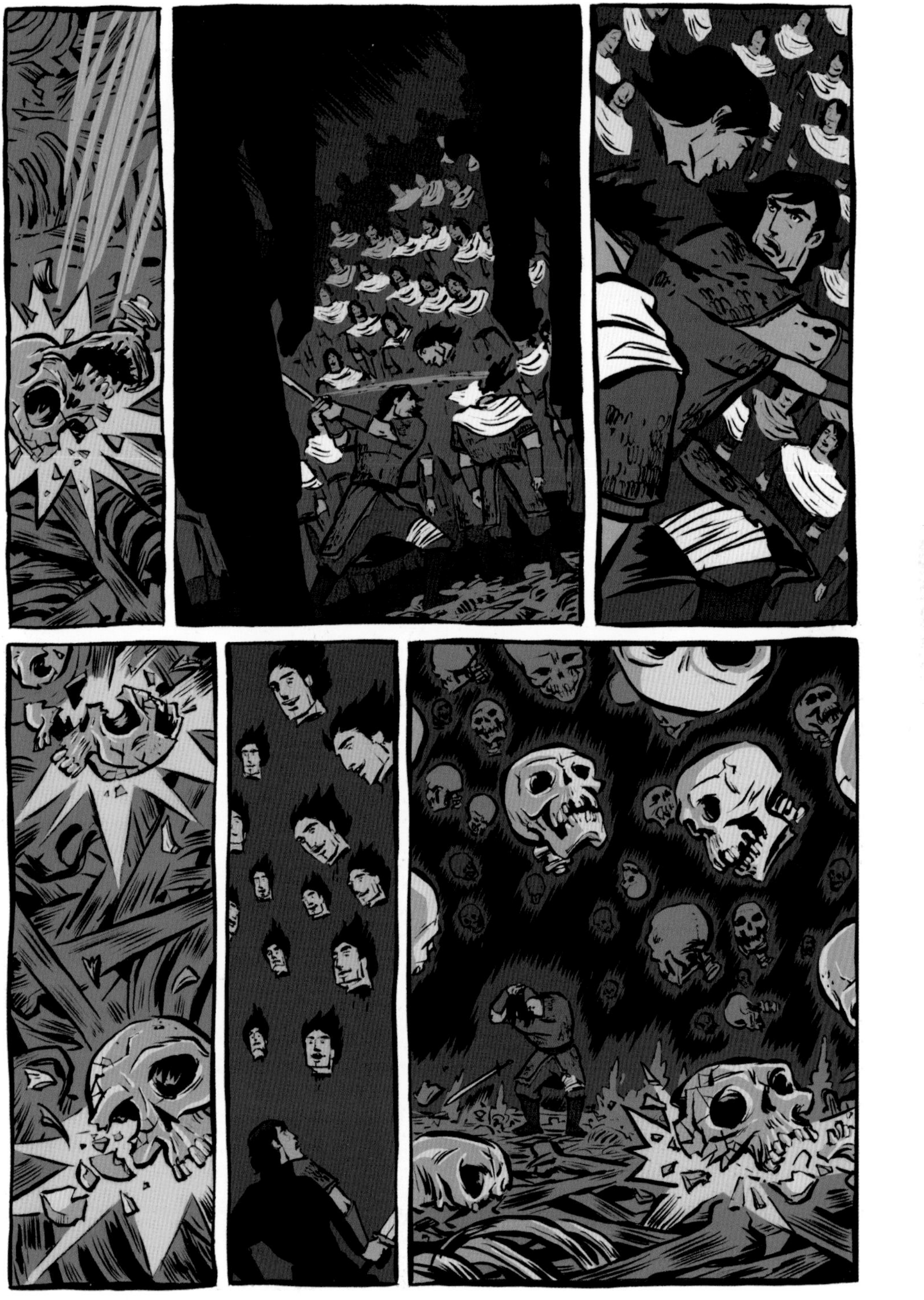

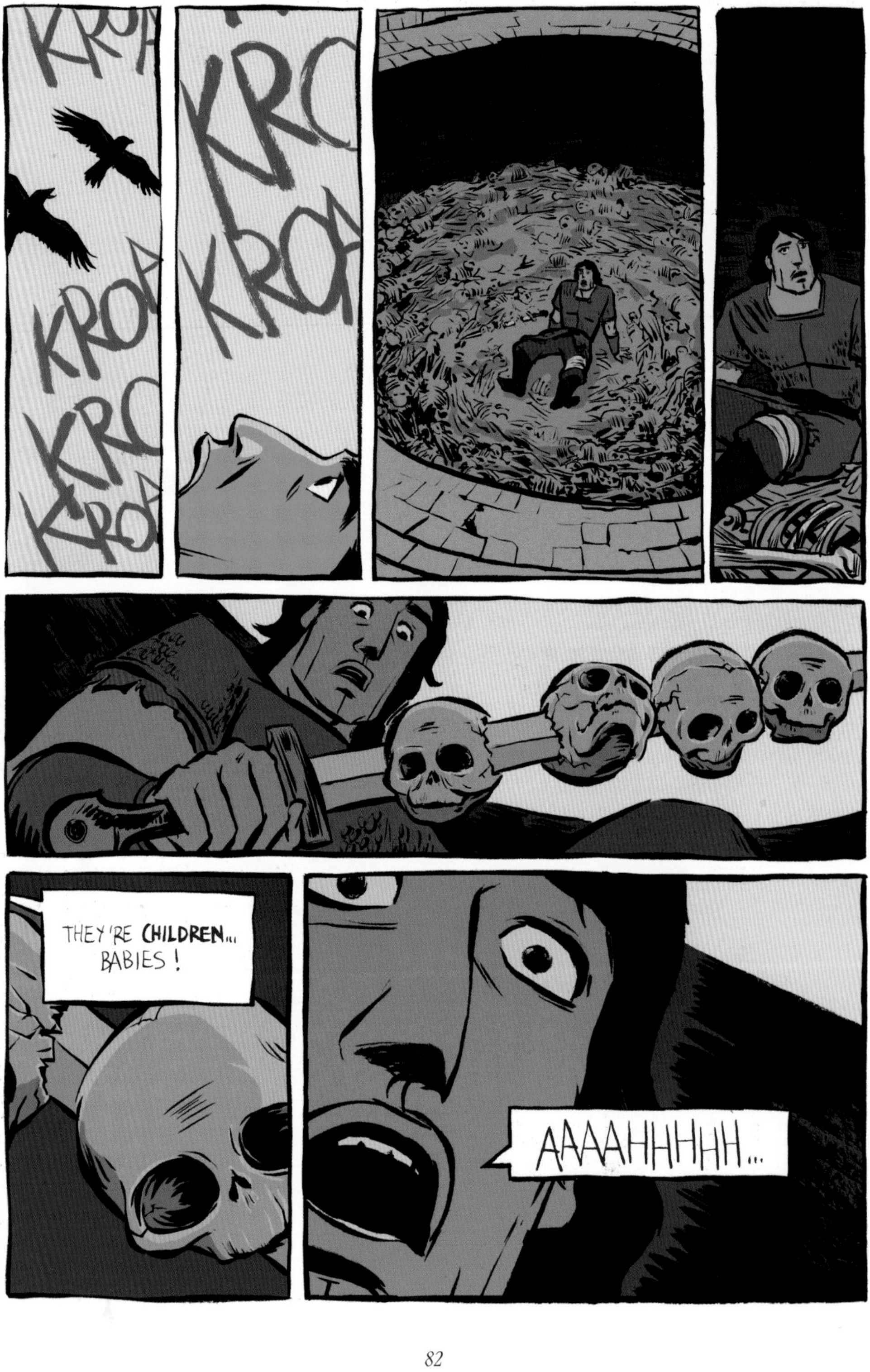
KROA
KROA
KRO
KROA
KRO
KROA
THEY'RE CHILDREN...
BABIES!
AAAAHHHHH...

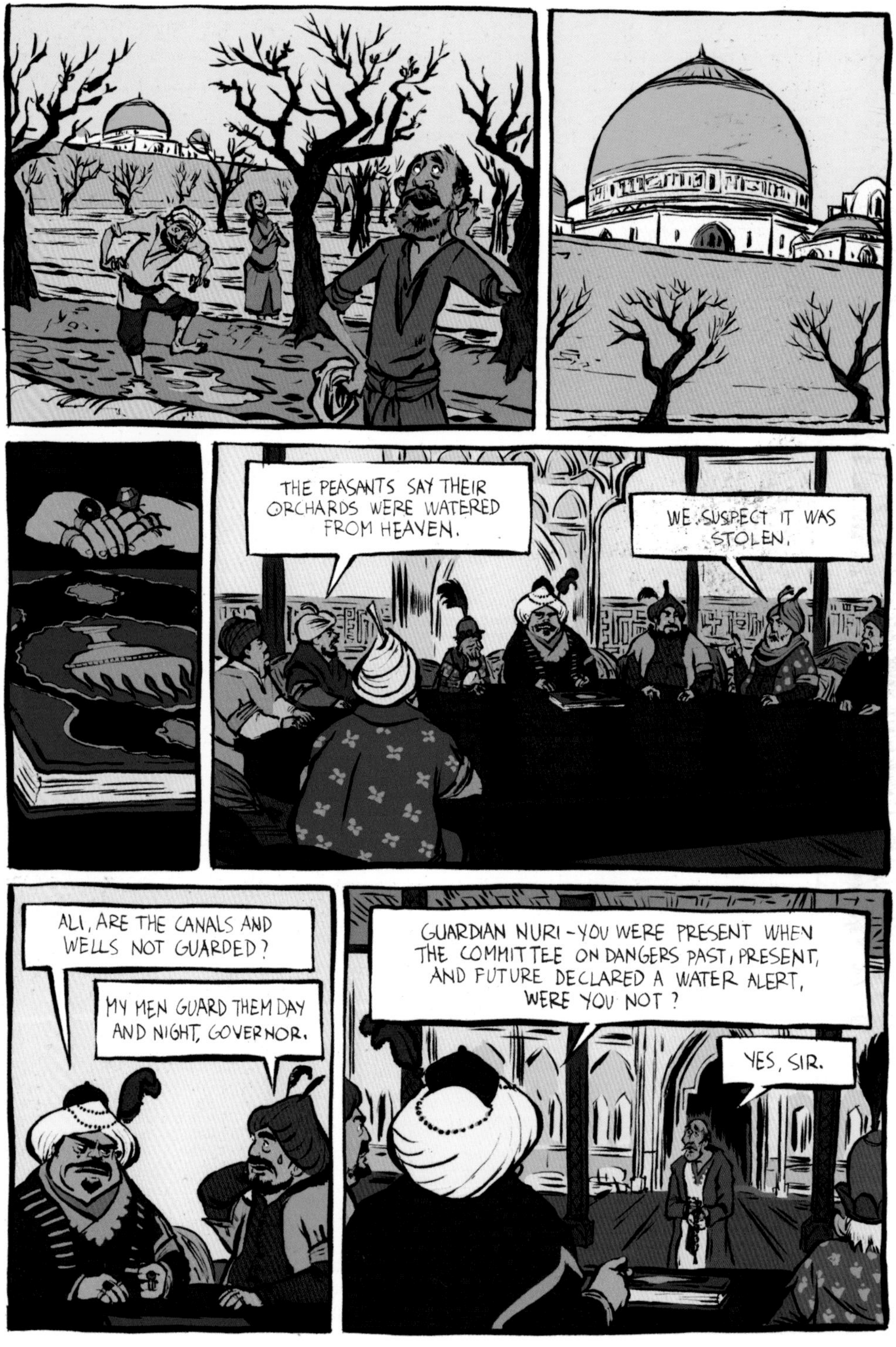
THE PEASANTS SAY THEIR ORCHARDS WERE WATERED FROM HEAVEN.
WE SUSPECT IT WAS STOLEN.
ALI, ARE THE CANALS AND WELLS NOT GUARDED?
MY MEN GUARD THEM DAY AND NIGHT, GOVERNOR.
GUARDIAN NURI - YOU WERE PRESENT WHEN THE COMMITTEE ON DANGERS PAST, PRESENT, AND FUTURE DECLARED A WATER ALERT, WERE YOU NOT?
YES, SIR.

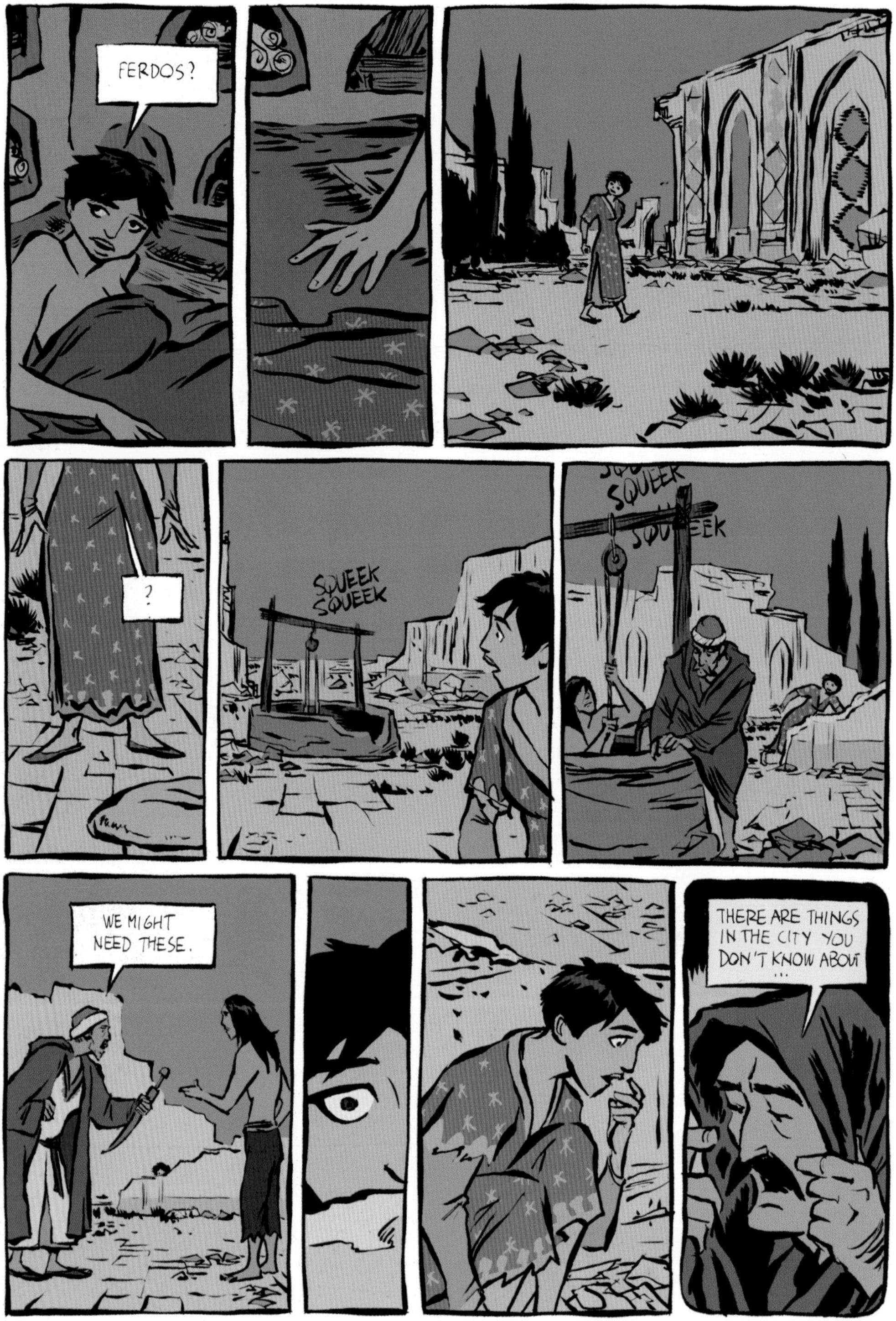
FERDOS?
?
SQUEEK
SQUEEK
SQUEEK
SQUEEK
WE MIGHT NEED THESE.
THERE ARE THINGS IN THE CITY YOU DON'T KNOW ABOUT ...

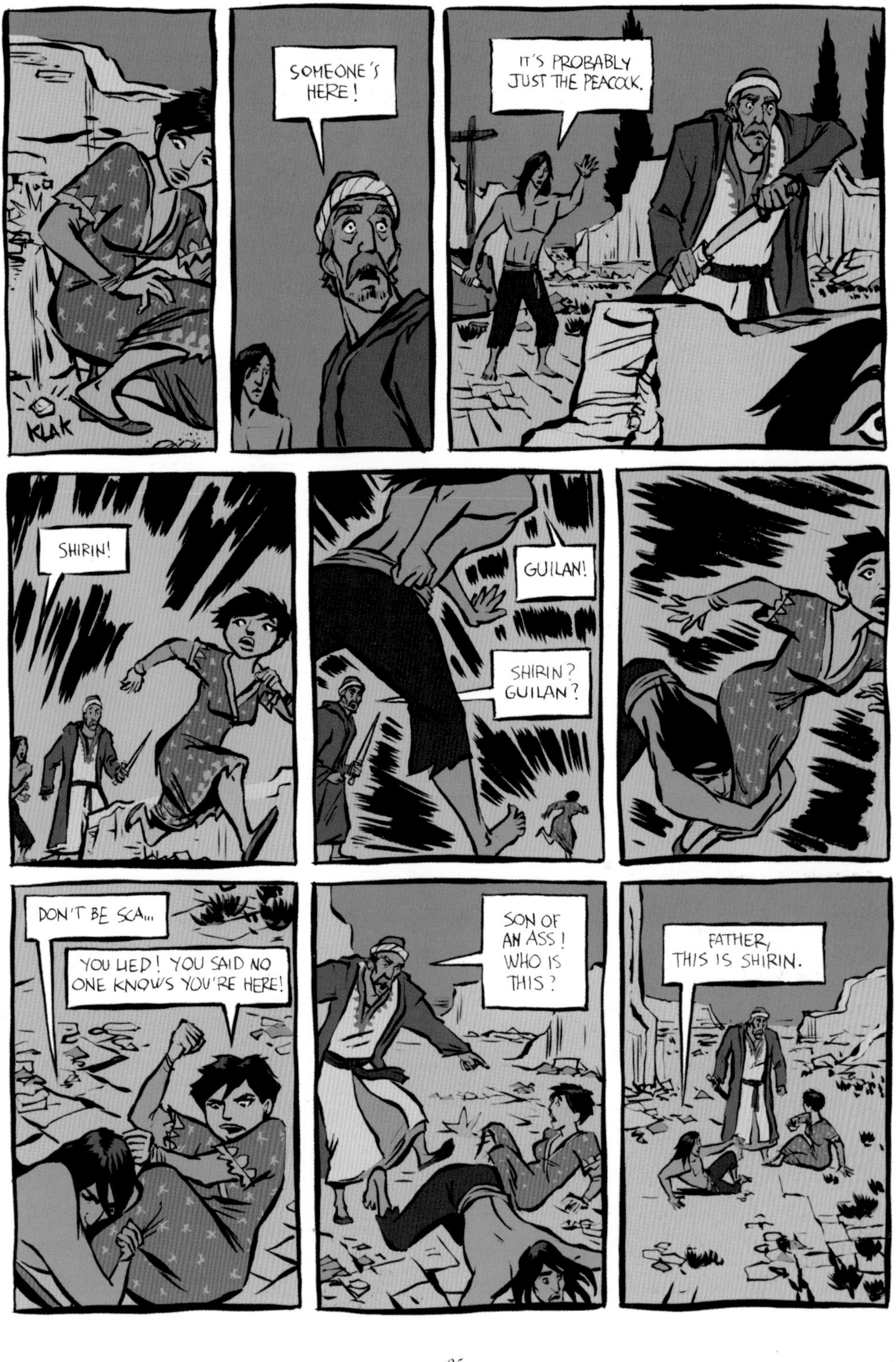
KLAK
SOMEONE'S HERE!
IT'S PROBABLY JUST THE PEACOCK.
SHIRIN!
GUILAN!
SHIRIN? GUILAN?
DON'T BE SCA...
YOU LIED! YOU SAID NO ONE KNOWS YOU'RE HERE!
SON OF AN ASS! WHO IS THIS?
FATHER, THIS IS SHIRIN.

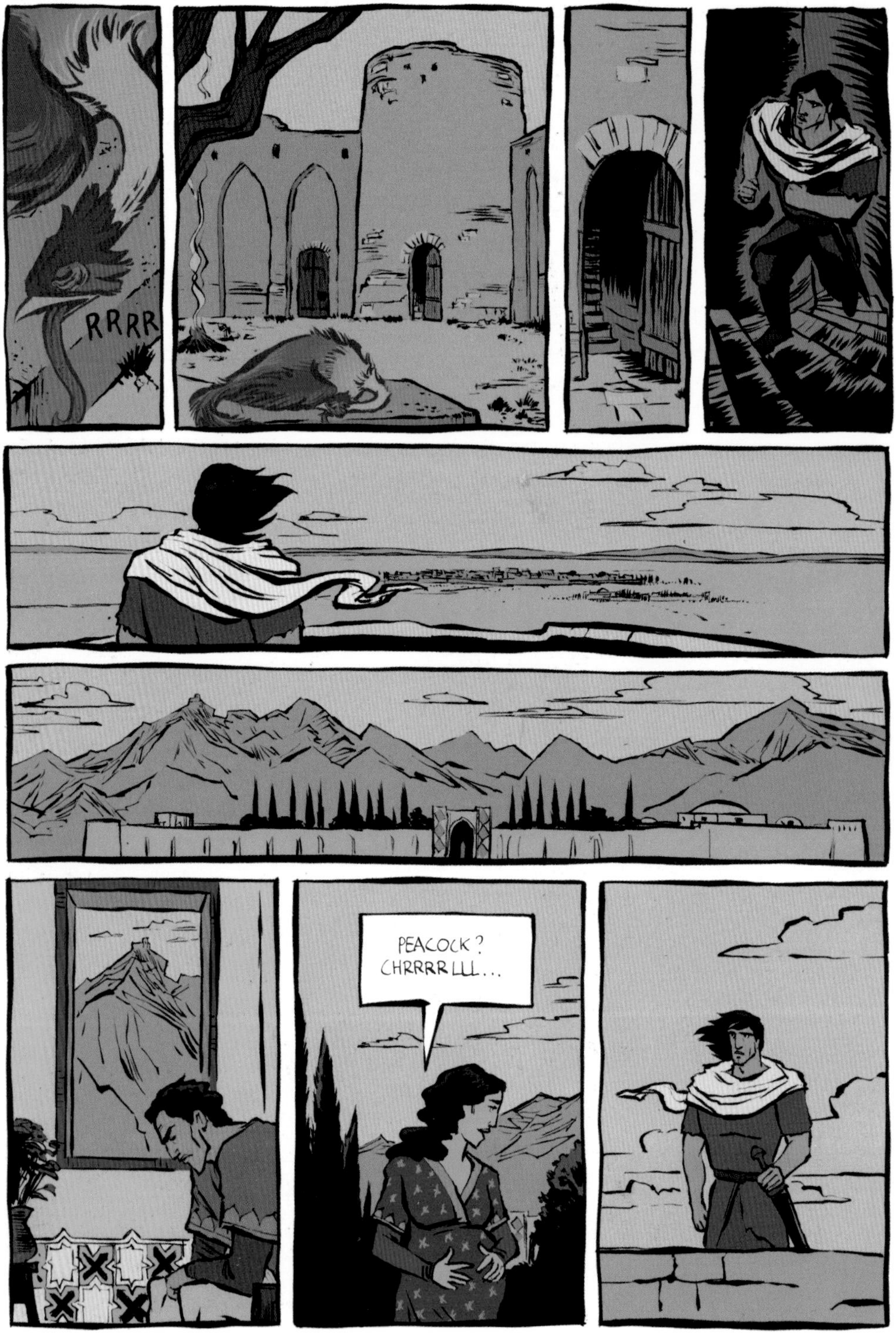
RRRR
PEACOCK?
CHRRRRLLL...

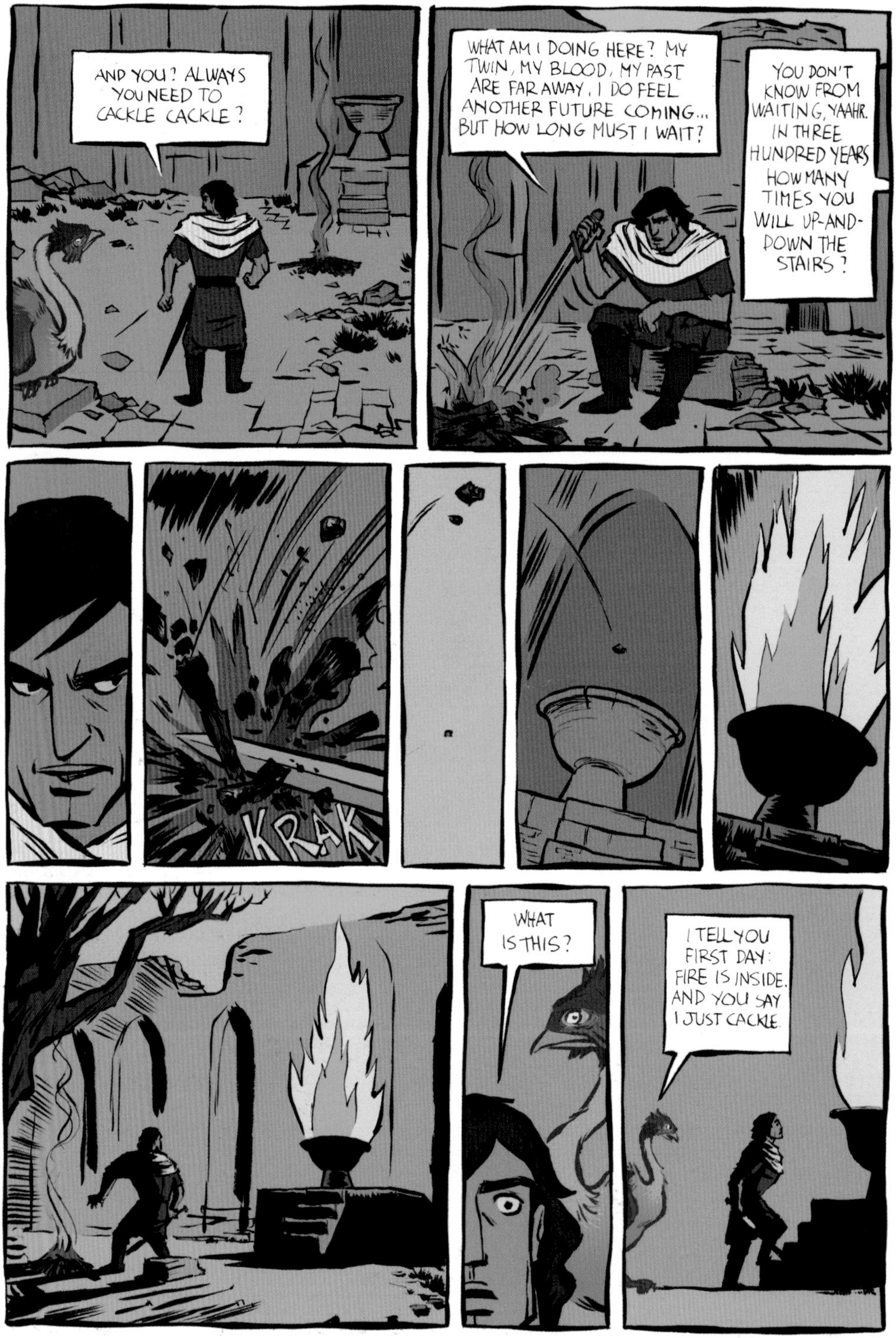
AND YOU? ALWAYS YOU NEED TO CACKLE CACKLE?
WHAT AM I DOING HERE? MY TWIN, MY BLOOD, MY PAST ARE FAR AWAY. I DO FEEL ANOTHER FUTURE COMING... BUT HOW LONG MUST I WAIT?
YOU DON'T KNOW FROM WAITING, YAAHR. IN THREE HUNDRED YEARS HOW MANY TIMES YOU WILL UP-AND-DOWN THE STAIRS?
KRAK
WHAT IS THIS?
I TELL YOU FIRST DAY: FIRE IS INSIDE. AND YOU SAY I JUST CACKLE.

100

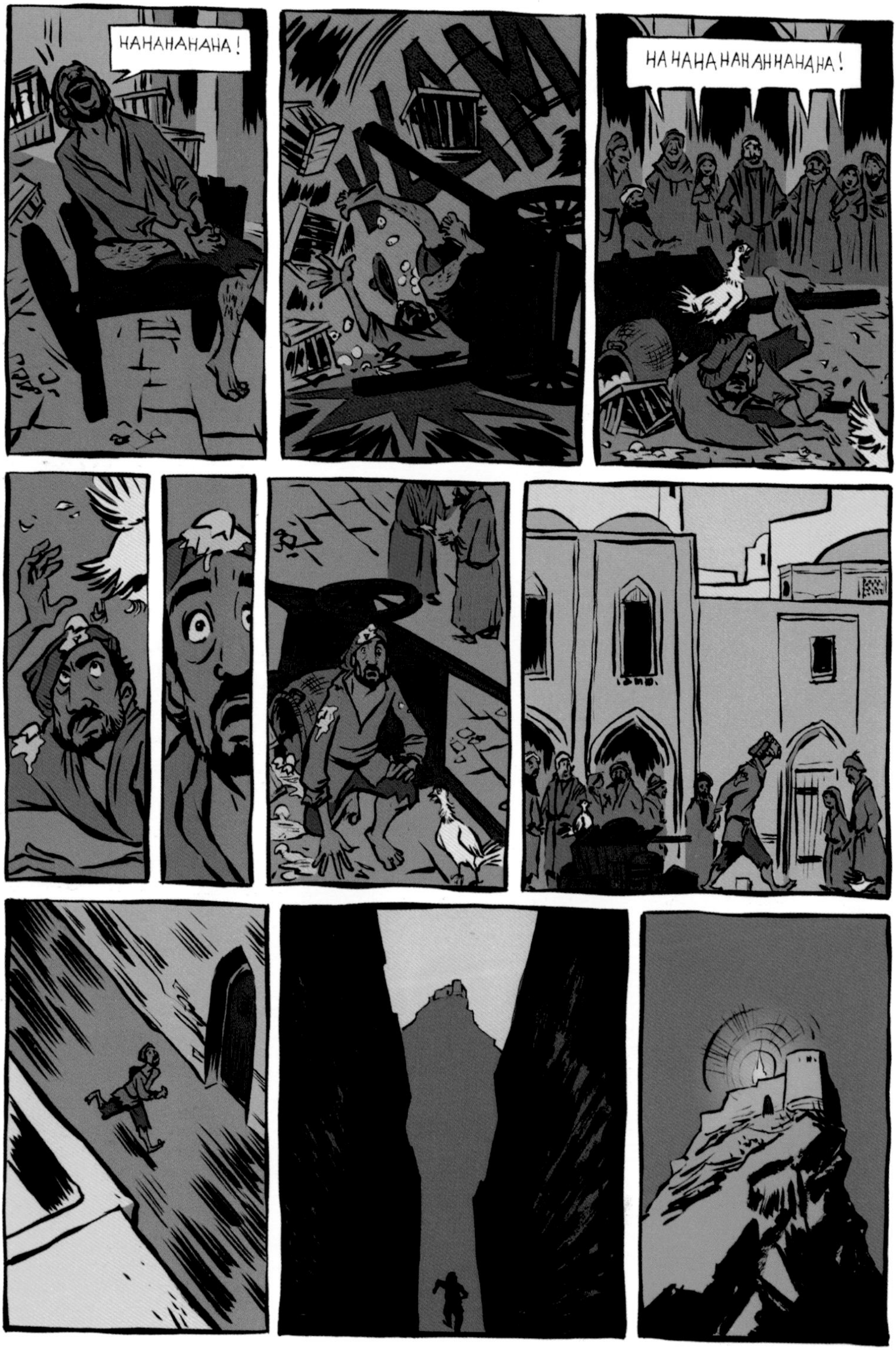
HAHAHAHAHA!
HAHAHAHAHAHHAHAHA!

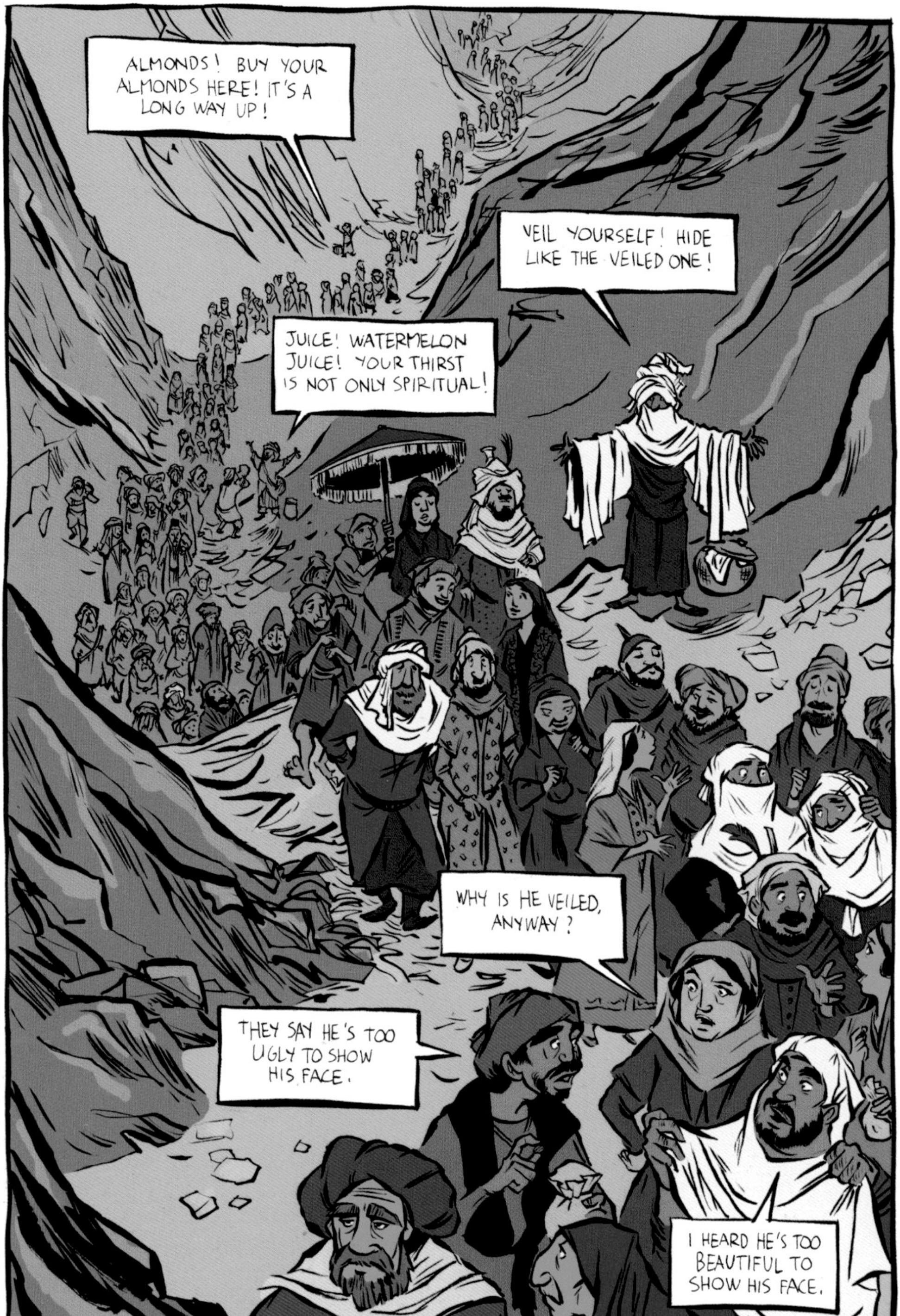
ALMONDS! BUY YOUR ALMONDS HERE! IT'S A LONG WAY UP!
VEIL YOURSELF! HIDE LIKE THE VEILED ONE!
JUICE! WATERMELON JUICE! YOUR THIRST IS NOT ONLY SPIRITUAL!
WHY IS HE VEILED, ANYWAY?
THEY SAY HE'S TOO UGLY TO SHOW HIS FACE.
I HEARD HE'S TOO BEAUTIFUL TO SHOW HIS FACE.

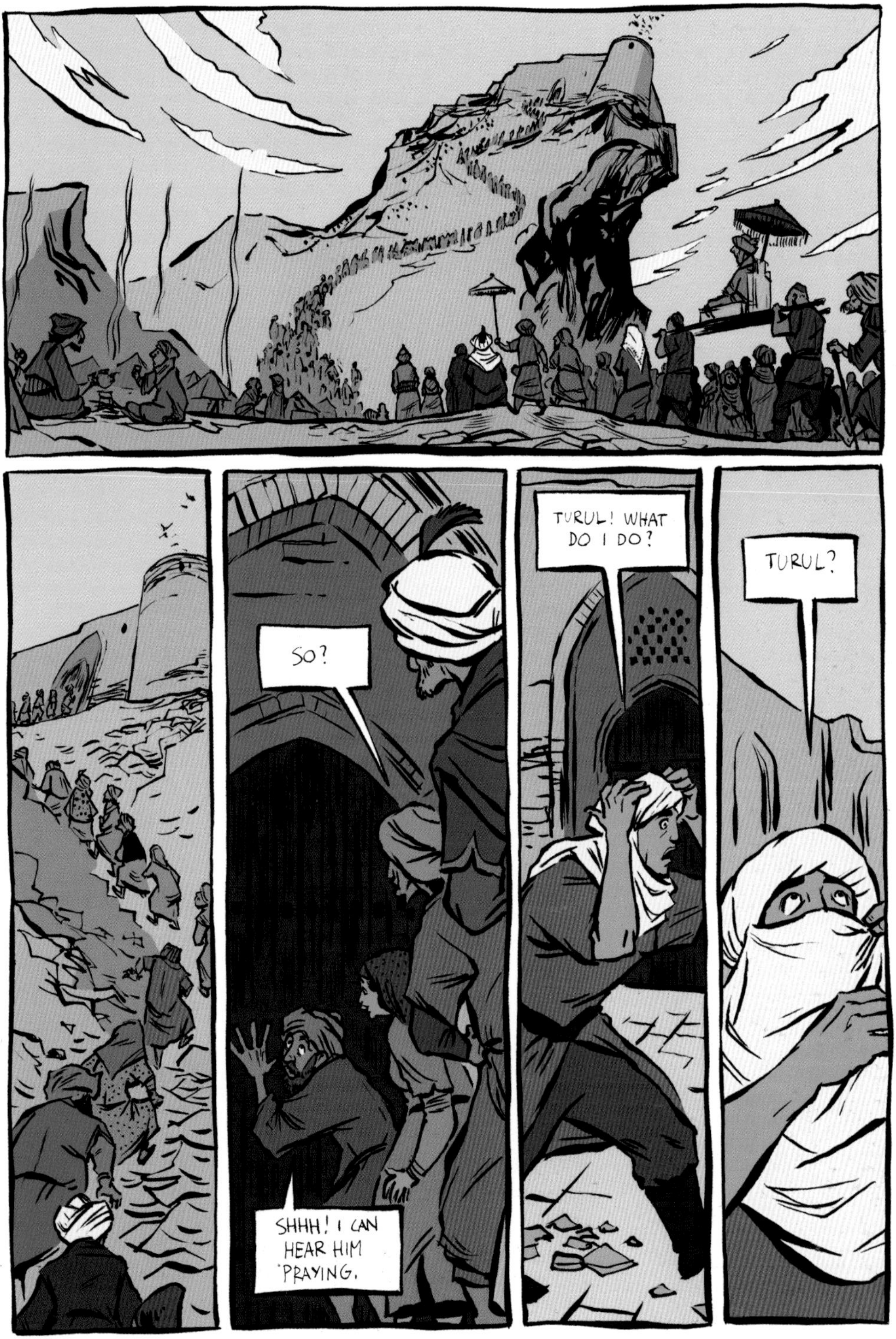
SO?
SHHH! I CAN HEAR HIM PRAYING.
TURUL! WHAT DO I DO?
TURUL?

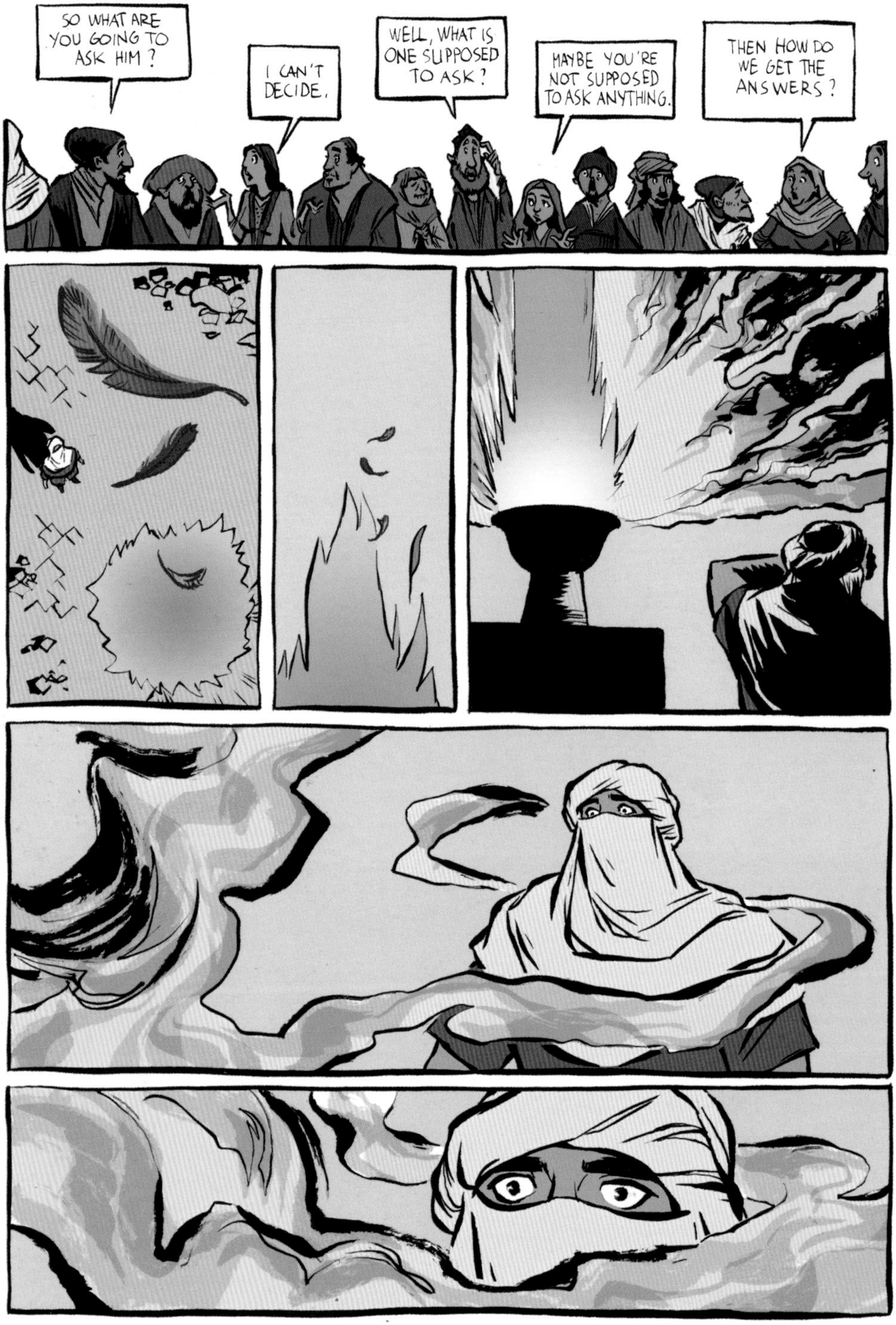
SO WHAT ARE YOU GOING TO ASK HIM?
I CAN'T DECIDE.
WELL, WHAT IS ONE SUPPOSED TO ASK?
MAYBE YOU'RE NOT SUPPOSED TO ASK ANYTHING.
THEN HOW DO WE GET THE ANSWERS?

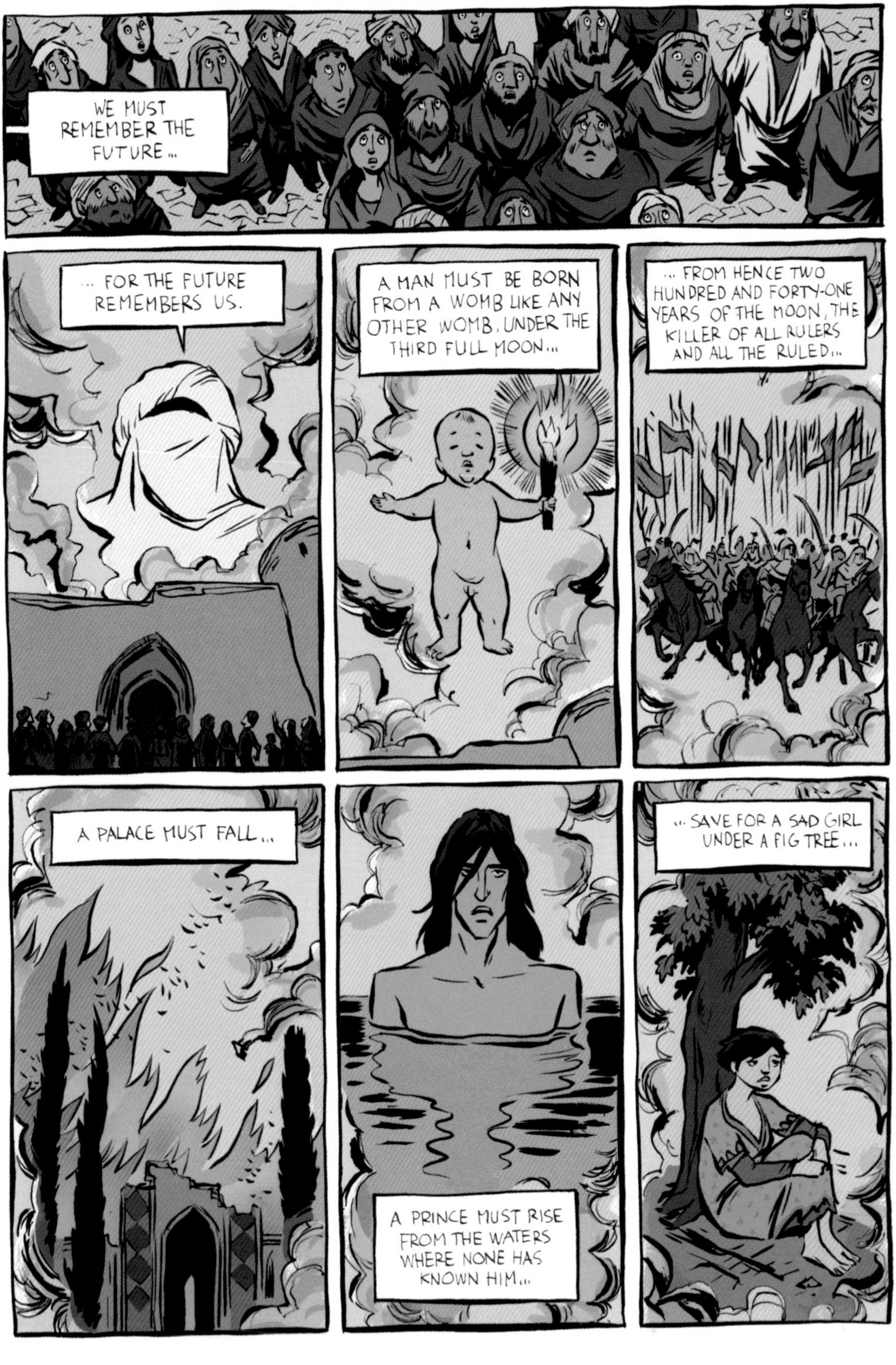
WE MUST REMEMBER THE FUTURE...
... FOR THE FUTURE REMEMBERS US.
A MAN MUST BE BORN FROM A WOMB LIKE ANY OTHER WOMB, UNDER THE THIRD FULL MOON...
... FROM HENCE TWO HUNDRED AND FORTY-ONE YEARS OF THE MOON, THE KILLER OF ALL RULERS AND ALL THE RULED...
A PALACE MUST FALL...
A PRINCE MUST RISE FROM THE WATERS WHERE NONE HAS KNOWN HIM...
... SAVE FOR A SAD GIRL UNDER A FIG TREE...

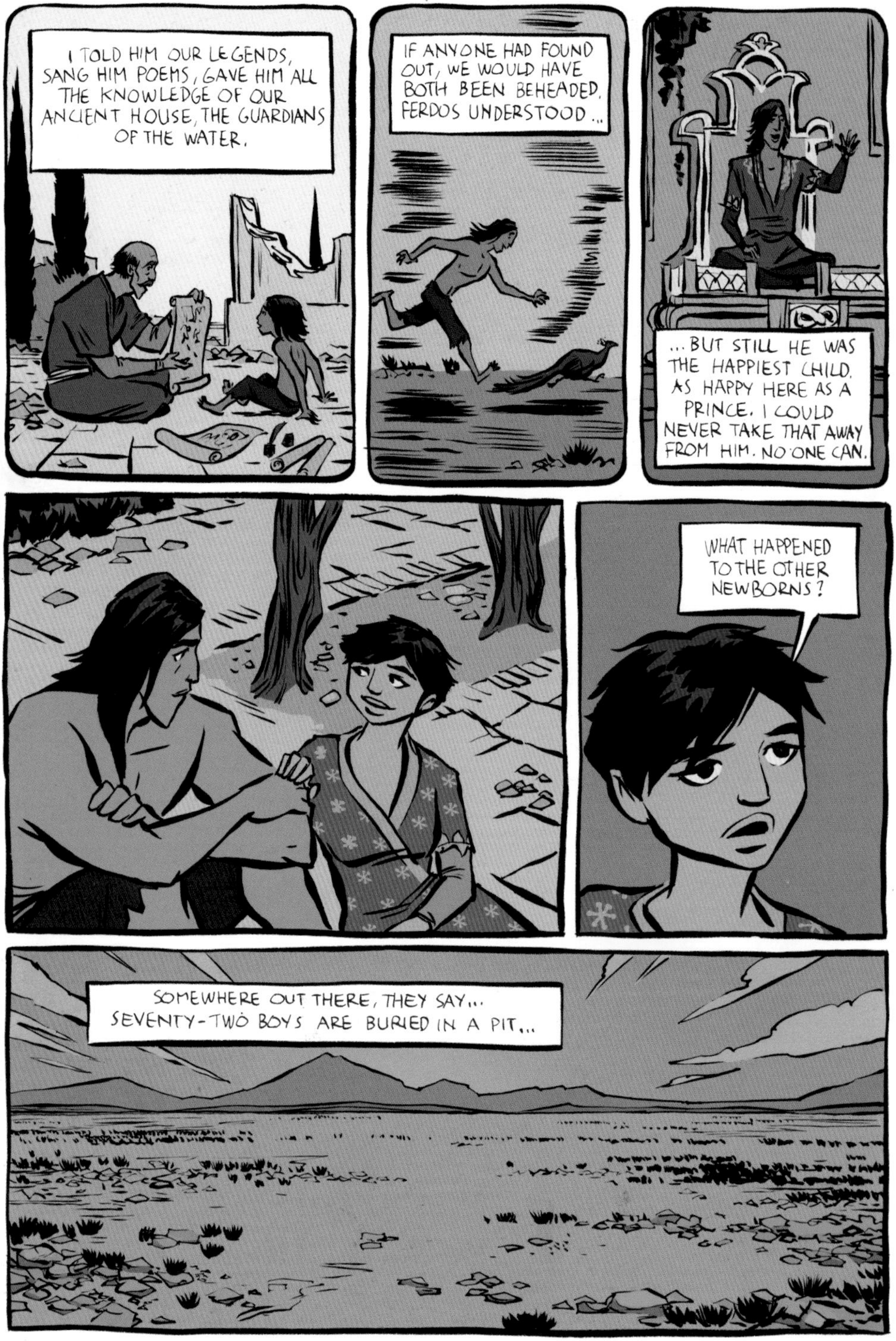
I TOLD HIM OUR LEGENDS, SANG HIM POEMS, GAVE HIM ALL THE KNOWLEDGE OF OUR ANCIENT HOUSE, THE GUARDIANS OF THE WATER.
IF ANYONE HAD FOUND OUT, WE WOULD HAVE BOTH BEEN BEHEADED. FERDOS UNDERSTOOD...
...BUT STILL HE WAS THE HAPPIEST CHILD. AS HAPPY HERE AS A PRINCE. I COULD NEVER TAKE THAT AWAY FROM HIM. NO ONE CAN.
WHAT HAPPENED TO THE OTHER NEWBORNS?
SOMEWHERE OUT THERE, THEY SAY... SEVENTY-TWO BOYS ARE BURIED IN A PIT...

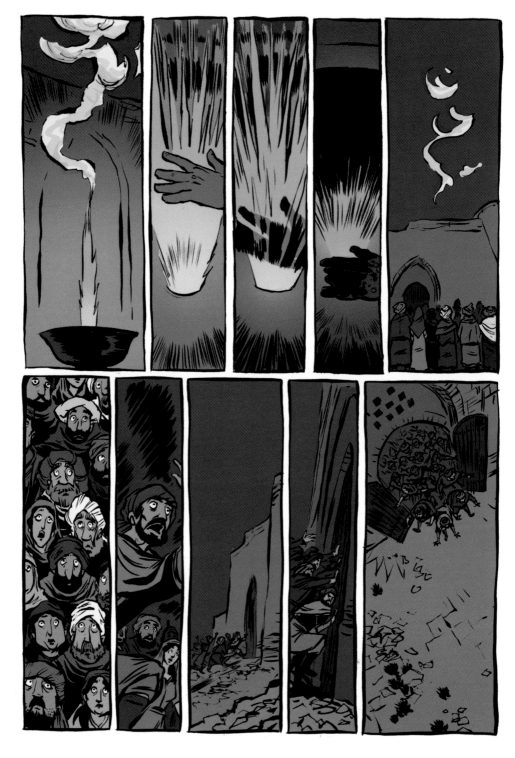

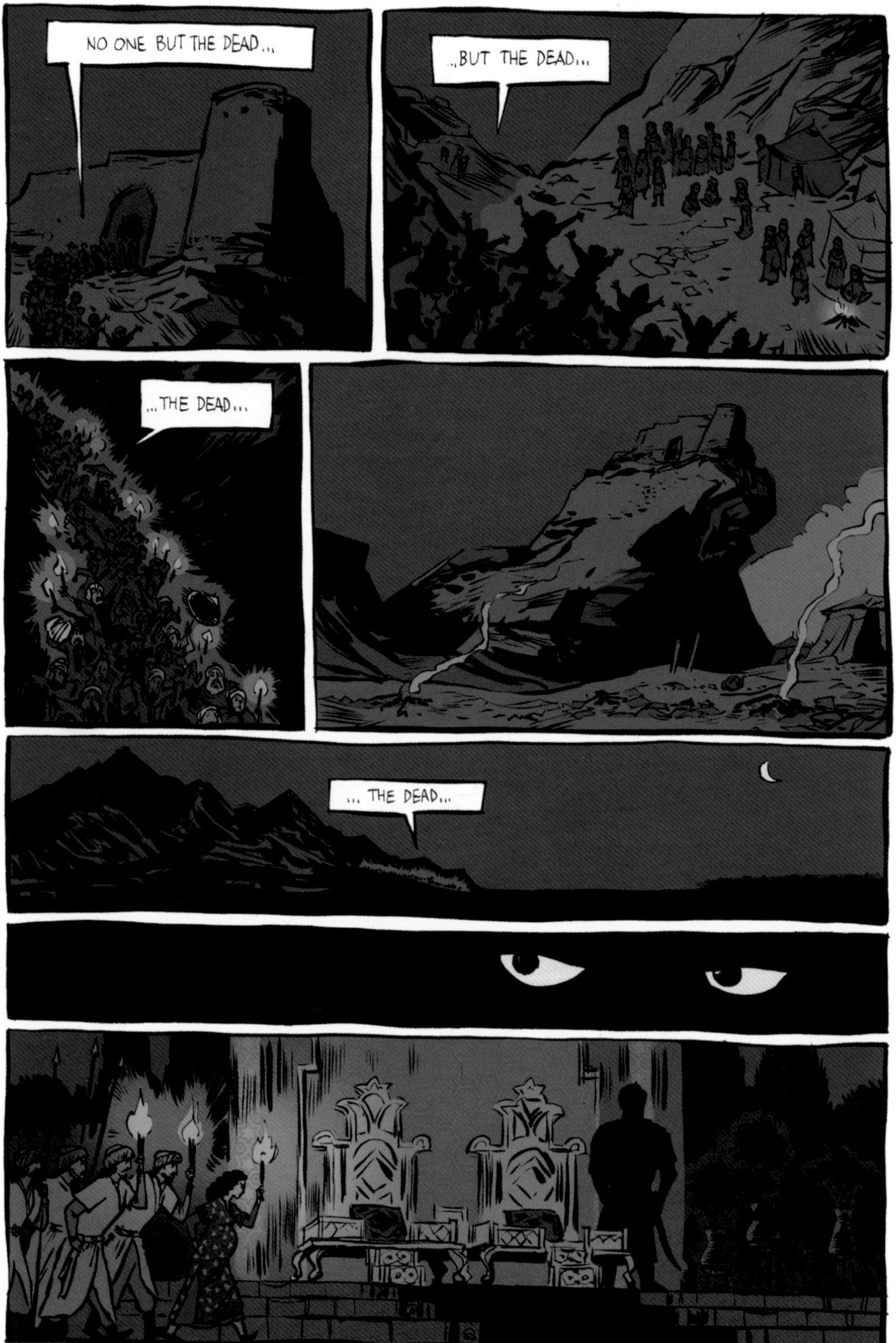
NO ONE BUT THE DEAD...
...BUT THE DEAD...
...THE DEAD...
... THE DEAD...

PRINCESS, YOUR FACE IS AS THE MOON TONIGHT: AN ORB OF LIGHT IN OUR DARKNESS.

GENERAL AMIR, WHY ARE YOUR SOLDIERS ALL AROUND THE CITY AND THE PALACE?

THE PEOPLE ARE RESTLESS, FEARFUL. THE VEILED ONE OF MARV PROPHESIED THAT THE PALACE WILL BE BURNED DOWN, PERHAPS BY GUIV.

GENERAL, SUCH DECISIONS ARE TO BE MADE BY MY HUSBAND, LAYTH.

SO, PRINCESS, I THOUGHT PROTECTION MIGHT BE NECESSARY.

A PITY, THEN, THAT HE DOES NOT MAKE THEM.

TO QUELL RUMORS, I'M HAVING THE WORDS OF THAT VEILED FOOL TRANSCRIBED. WE MUST KNOW EXACTLY WHAT HE SAID.

HE SAID, "FROM HENCE TWO HUNDRED AND FORTY-ONE YEARS." THAT PUTS US IN THE 481ST YEAR OF THE MOON.

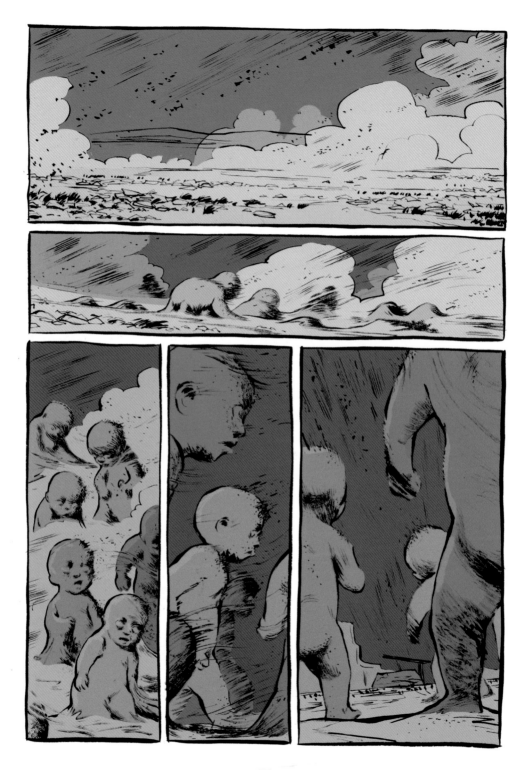

121

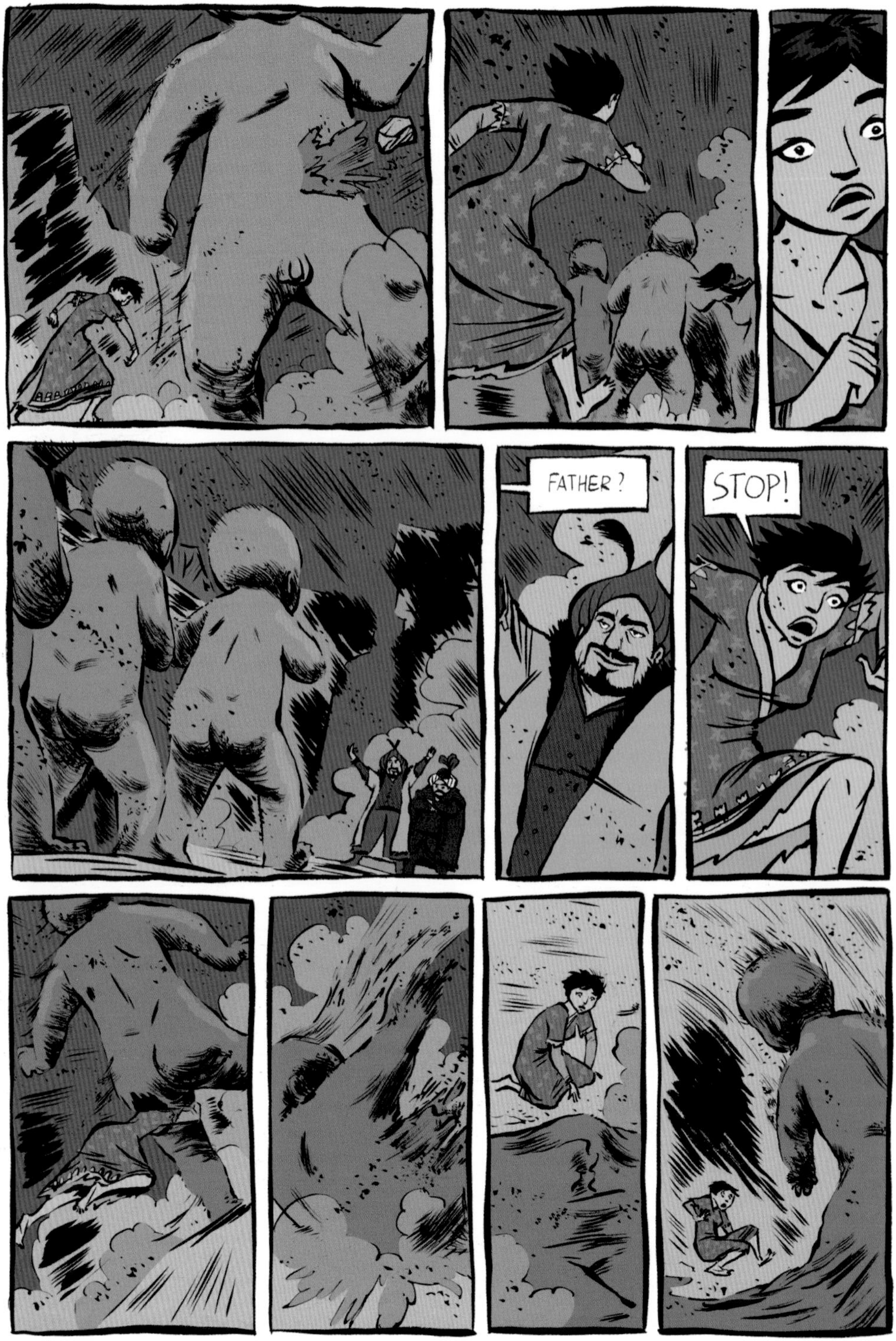
FATHER?
STOP!

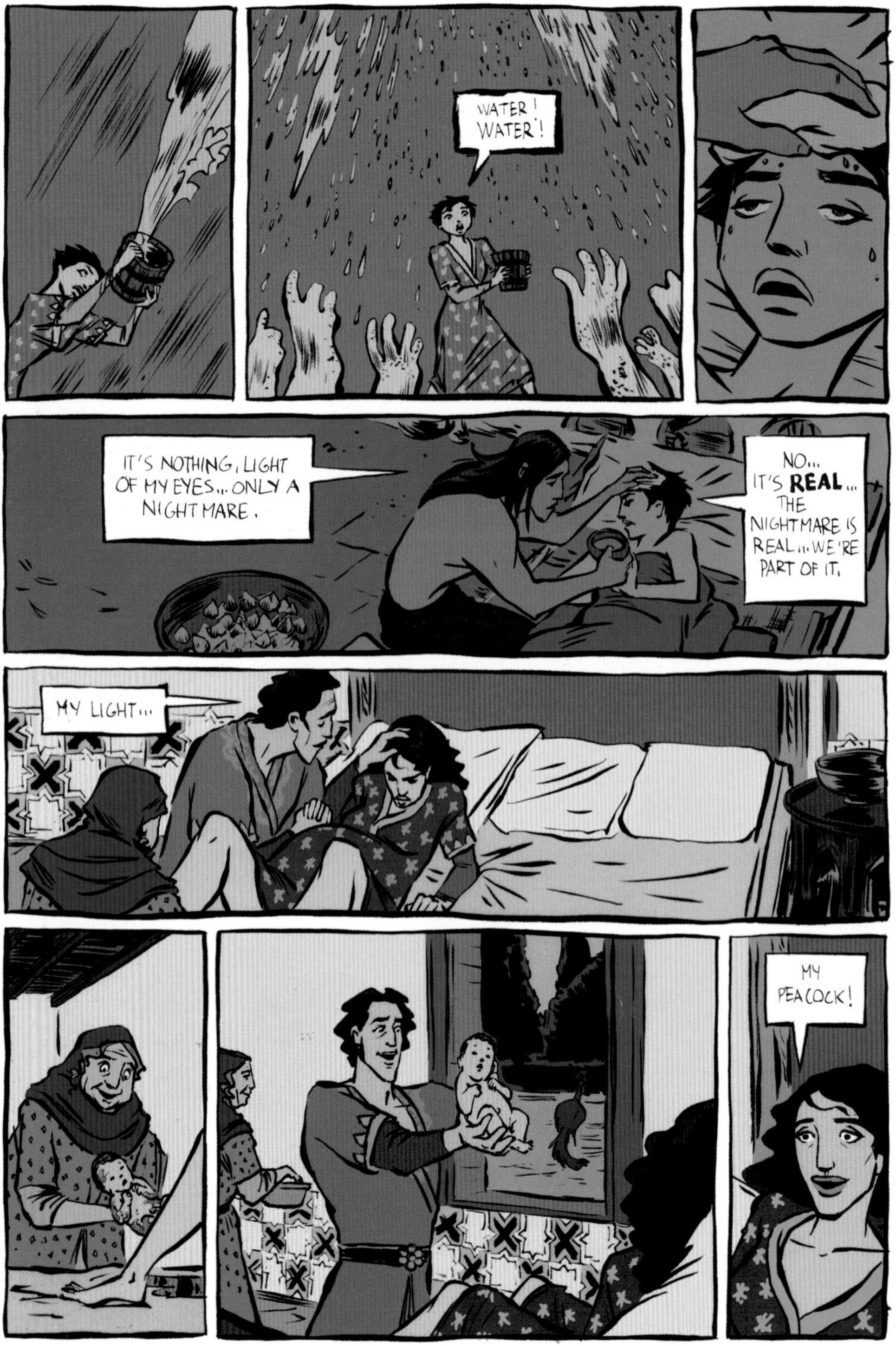
WATER! WATER!
IT'S NOTHING, LIGHT OF MY EYES... ONLY A NIGHTMARE.
NO... IT'S **REAL**... THE NIGHTMARE IS REAL... WE'RE PART OF IT.
MY LIGHT...
MY PEACOCK!

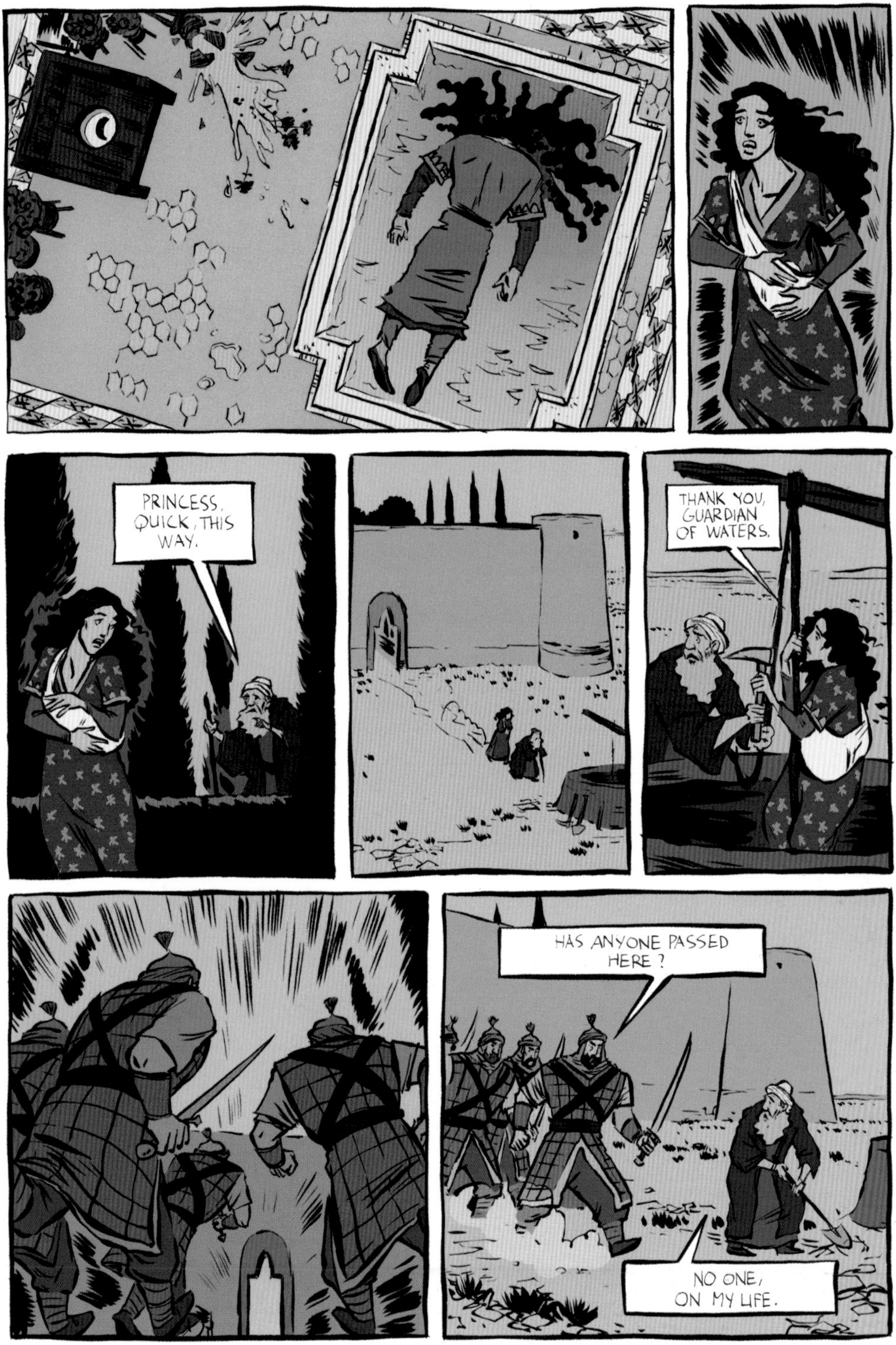
PRINCESS, QUICK, THIS WAY.
THANK YOU, GUARDIAN OF WATERS.
HAS ANYONE PASSED HERE ?
NO ONE, ON MY LIFE.

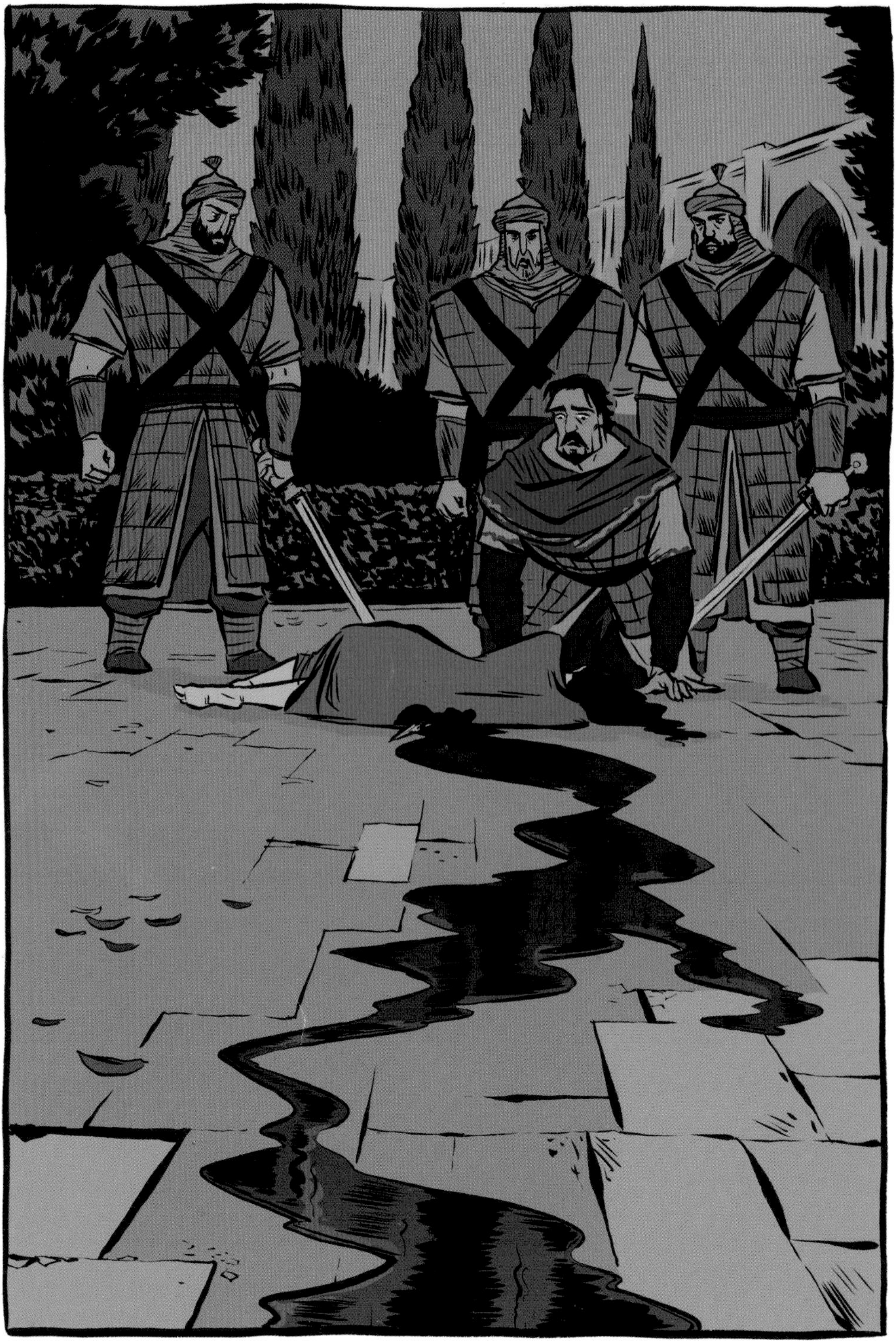

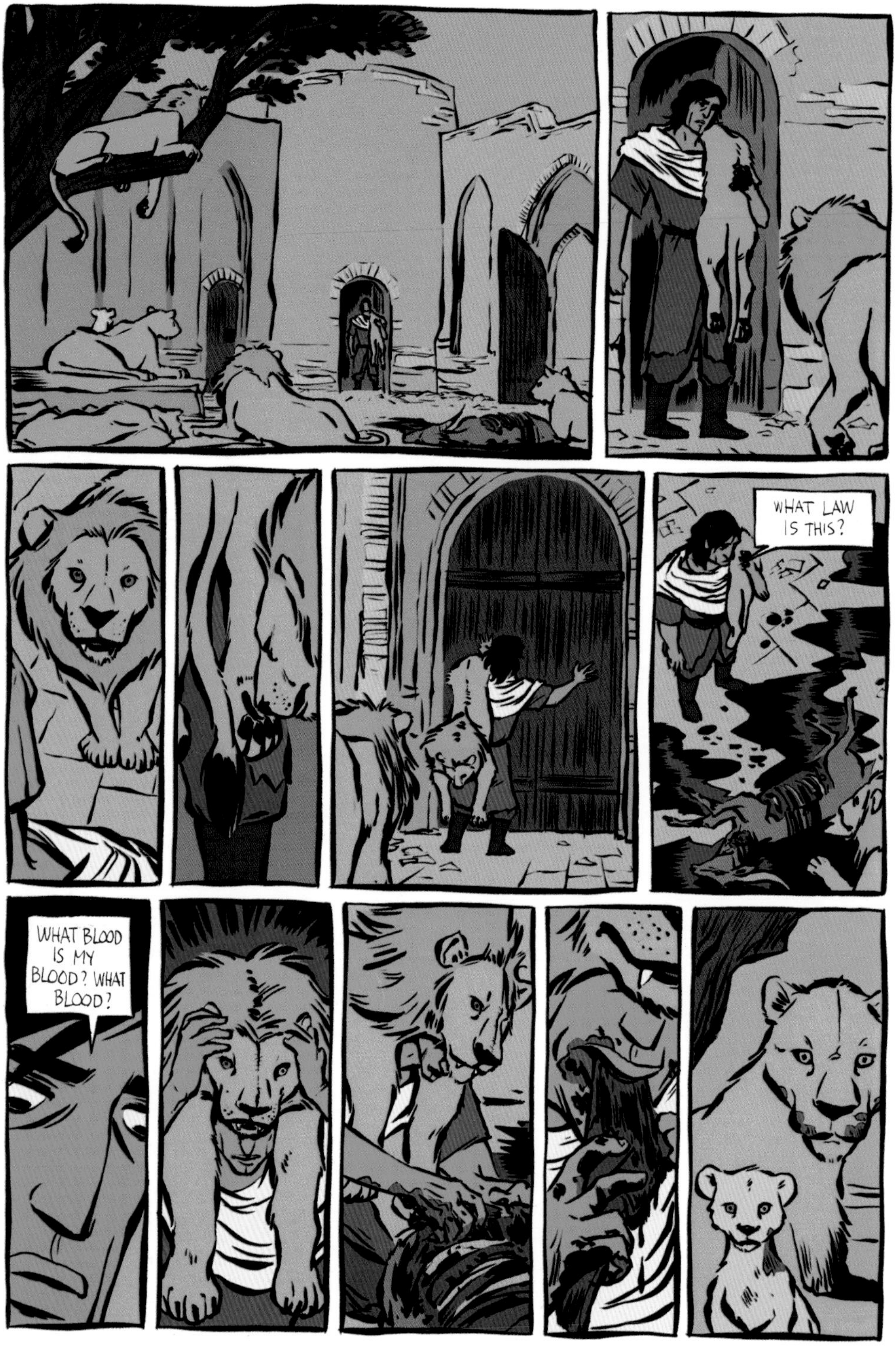
WHAT LAW IS THIS?
WHAT BLOOD IS MY BLOOD? WHAT BLOOD?

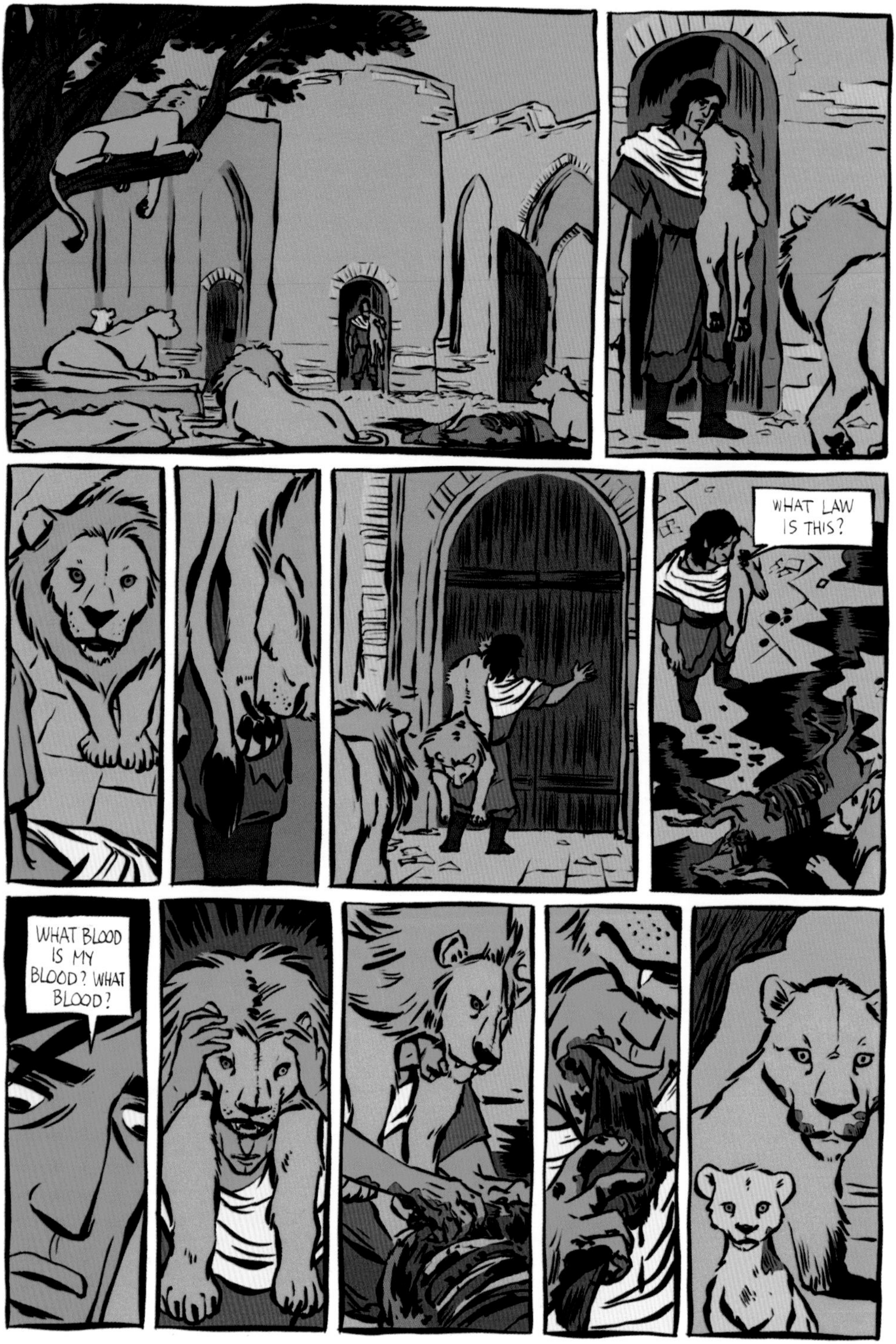
WHAT LAW IS THIS?
WHAT BLOOD IS MY BLOOD? WHAT BLOOD?

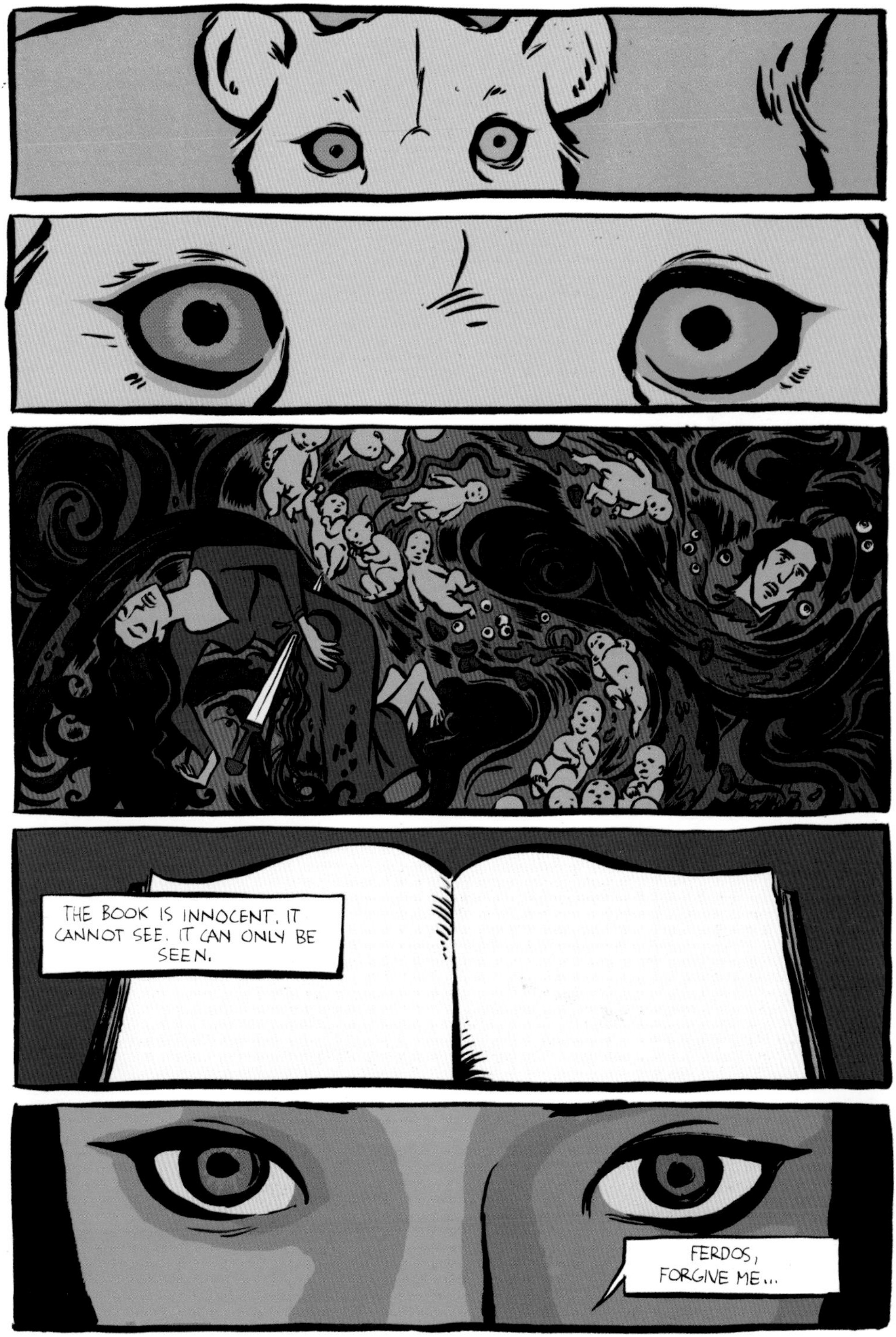
THE BOOK IS INNOCENT. IT CANNOT SEE. IT CAN ONLY BE SEEN.
FERDOS, FORGIVE ME...

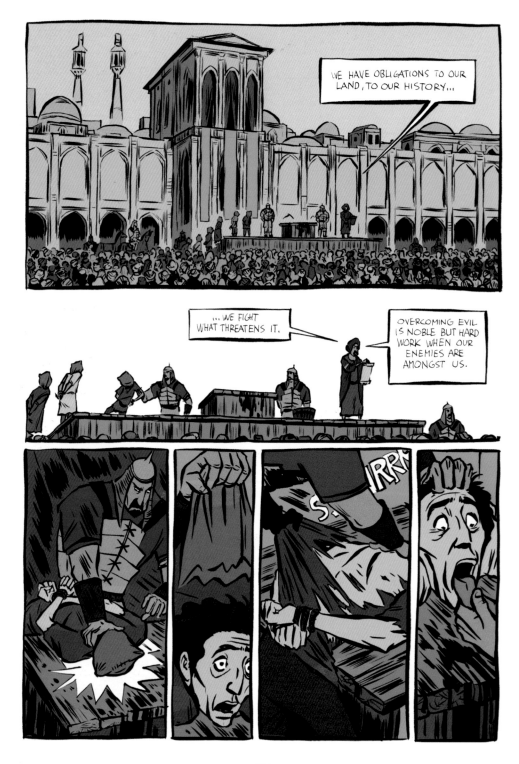

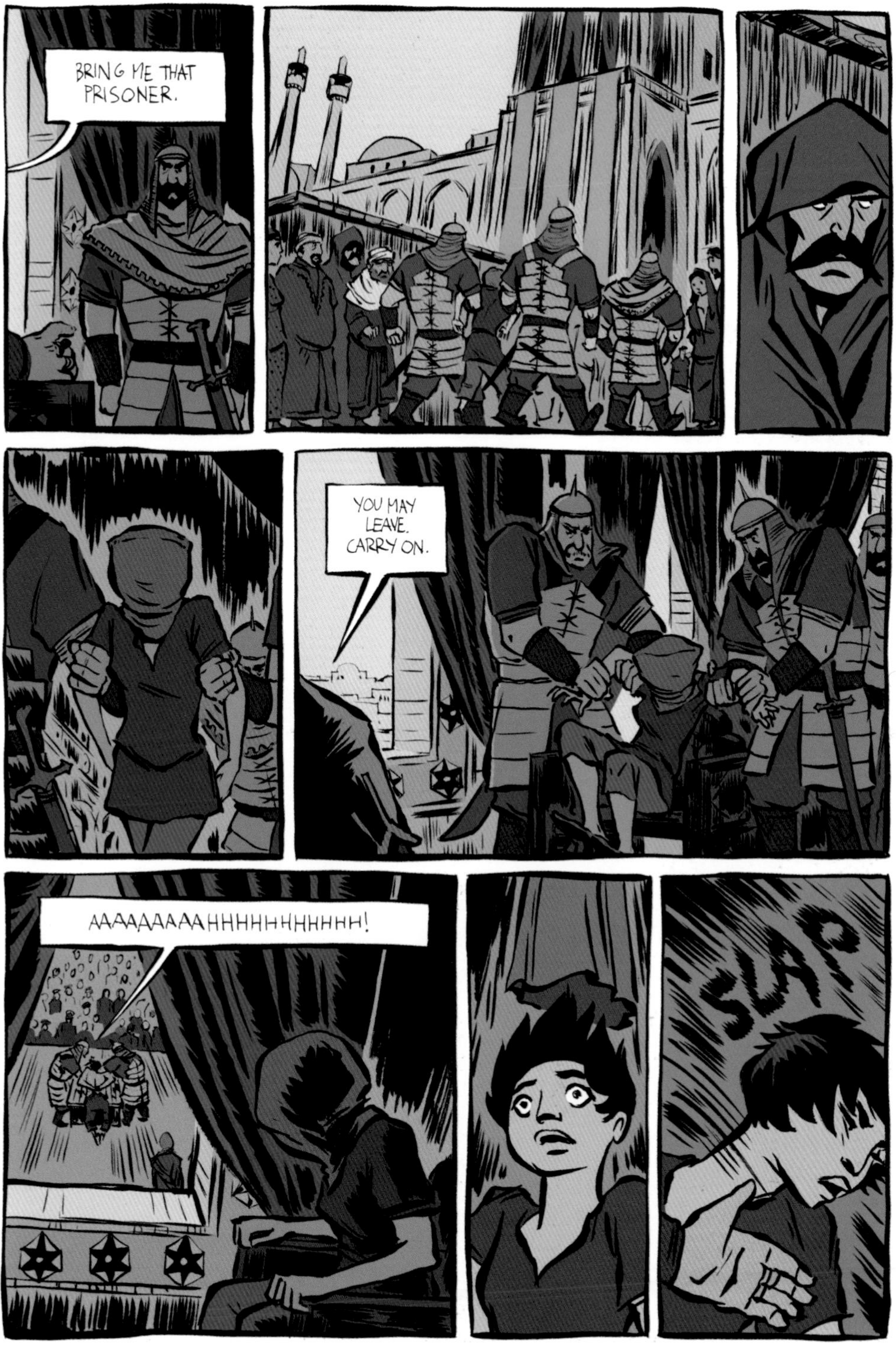
BRING ME THAT PRISONER.
YOU MAY LEAVE. CARRY ON.
AAAAAAAAAHHHHHHHHHHH!
SLAP

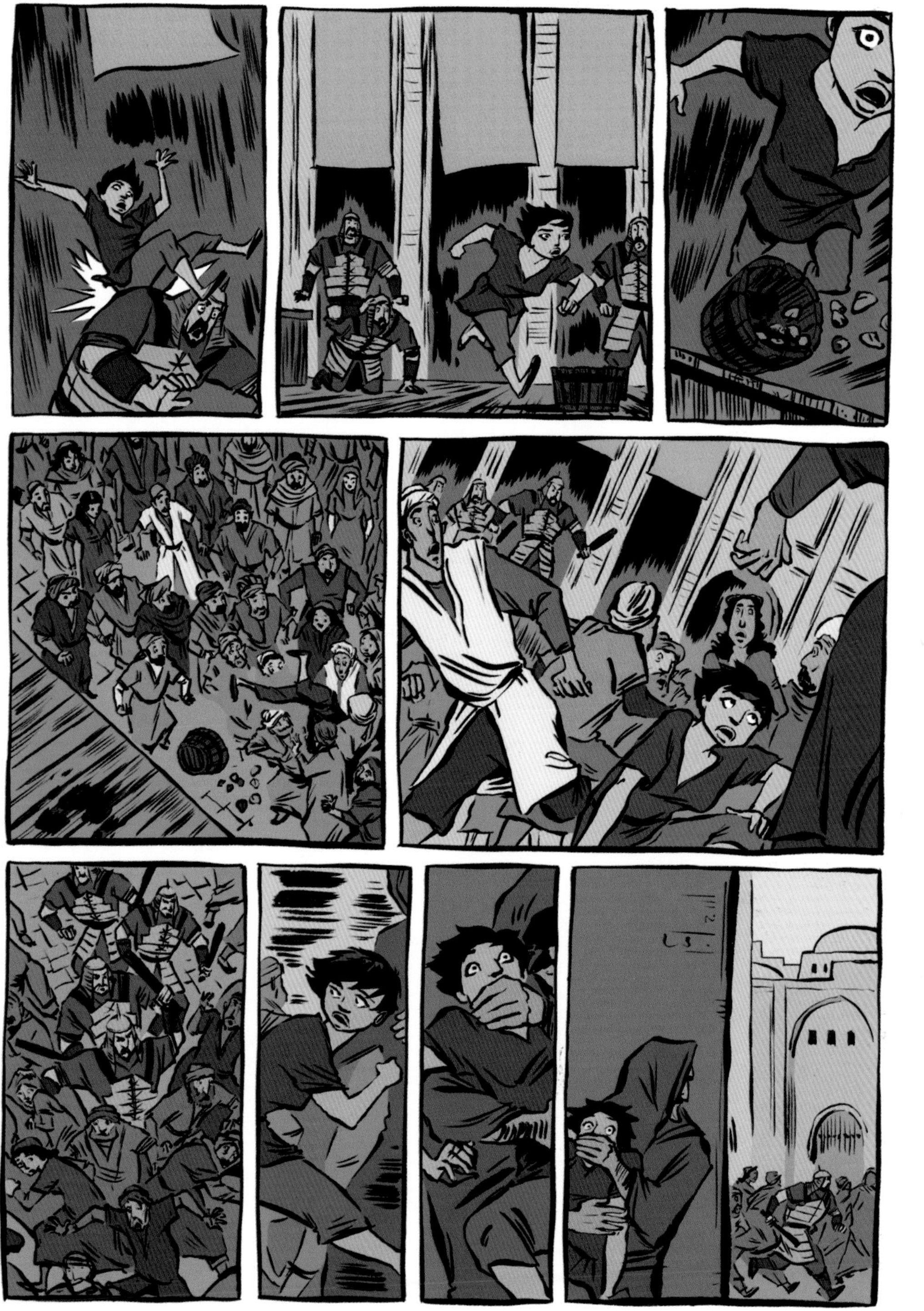

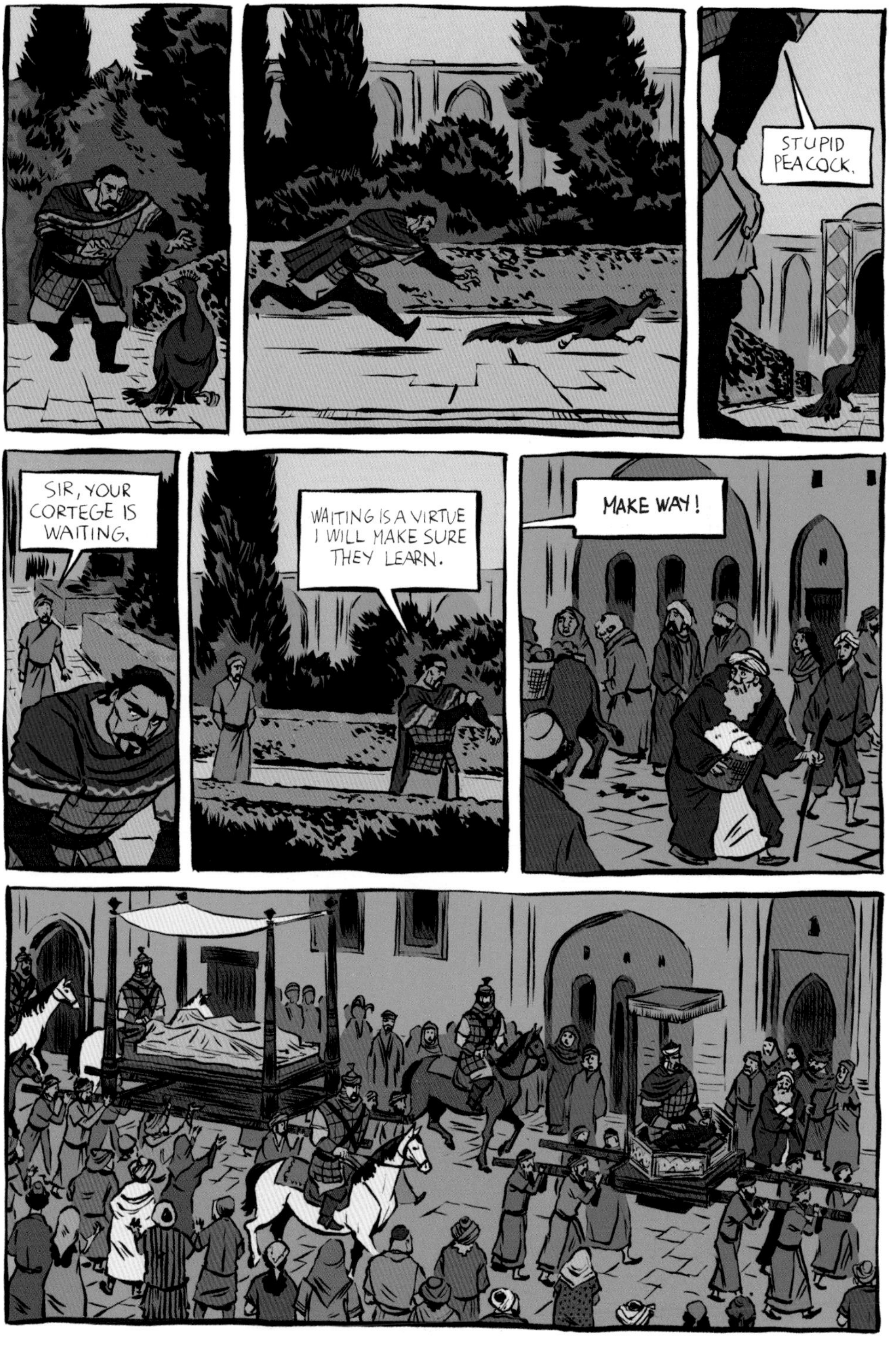
STUPID PEACOCK.
SIR, YOUR CORTEGE IS WAITING.
WAITING IS A VIRTUE I WILL MAKE SURE THEY LEARN.
MAKE WAY!

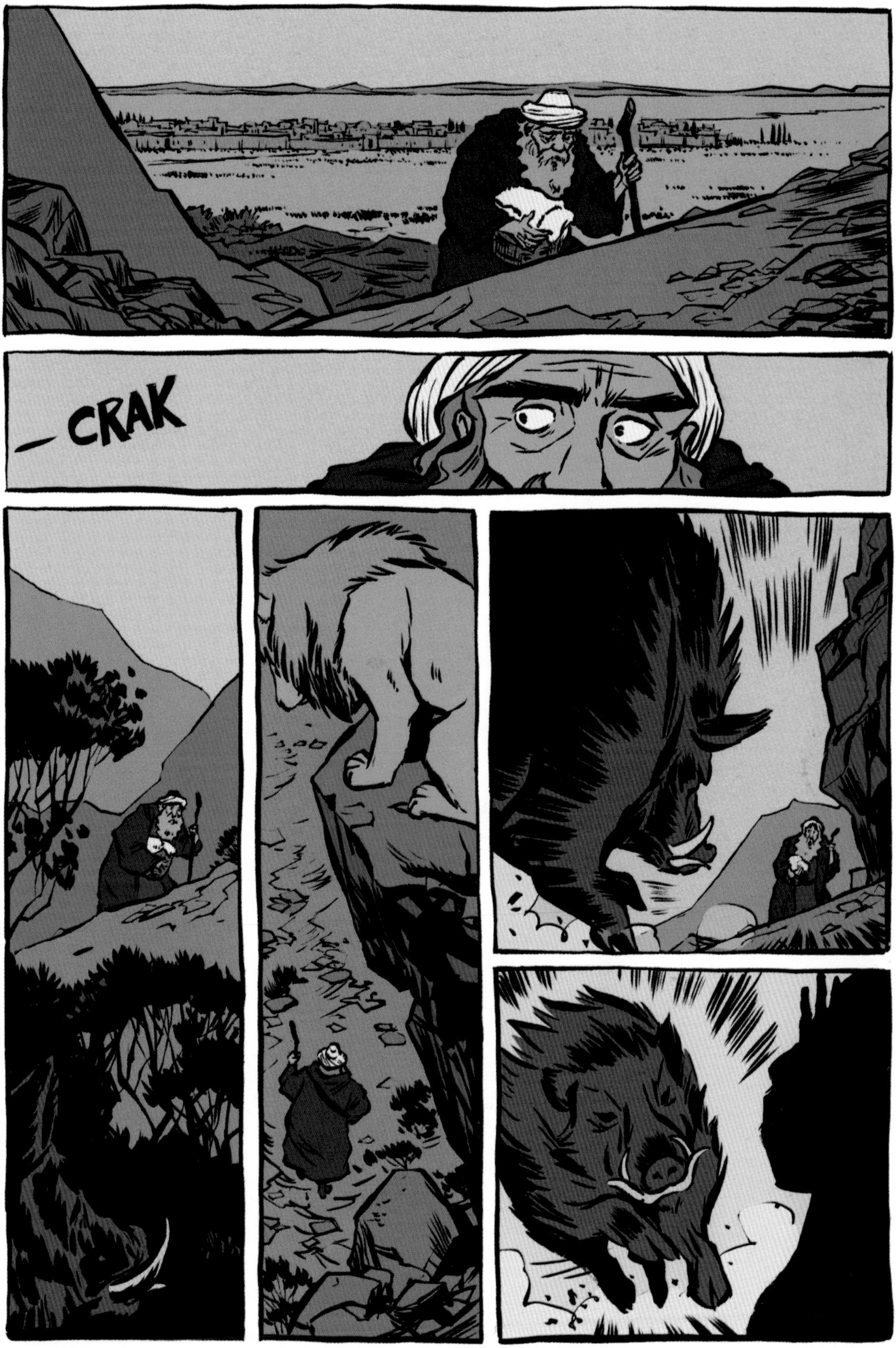
CRAK

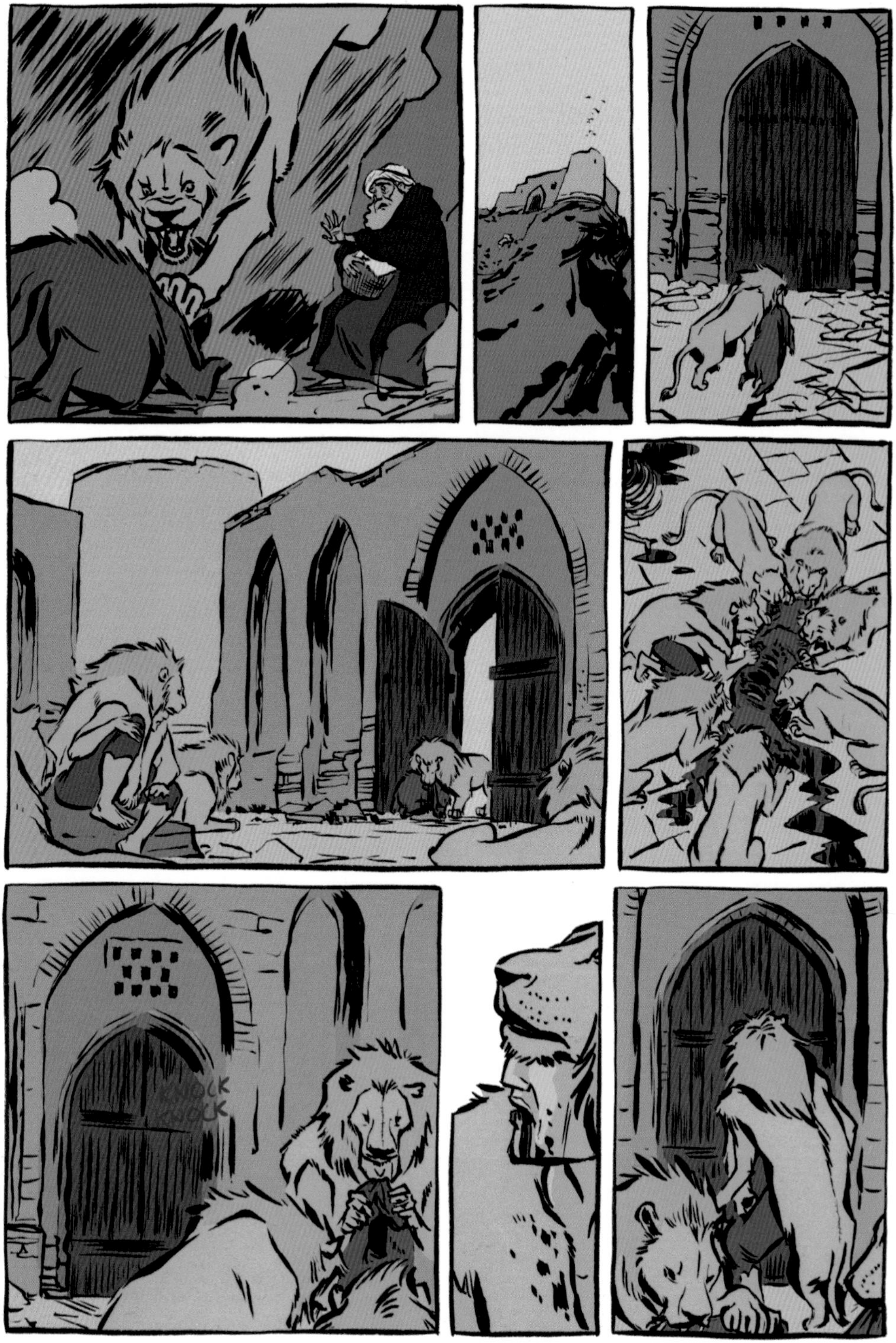
KNOCK
KNOCK

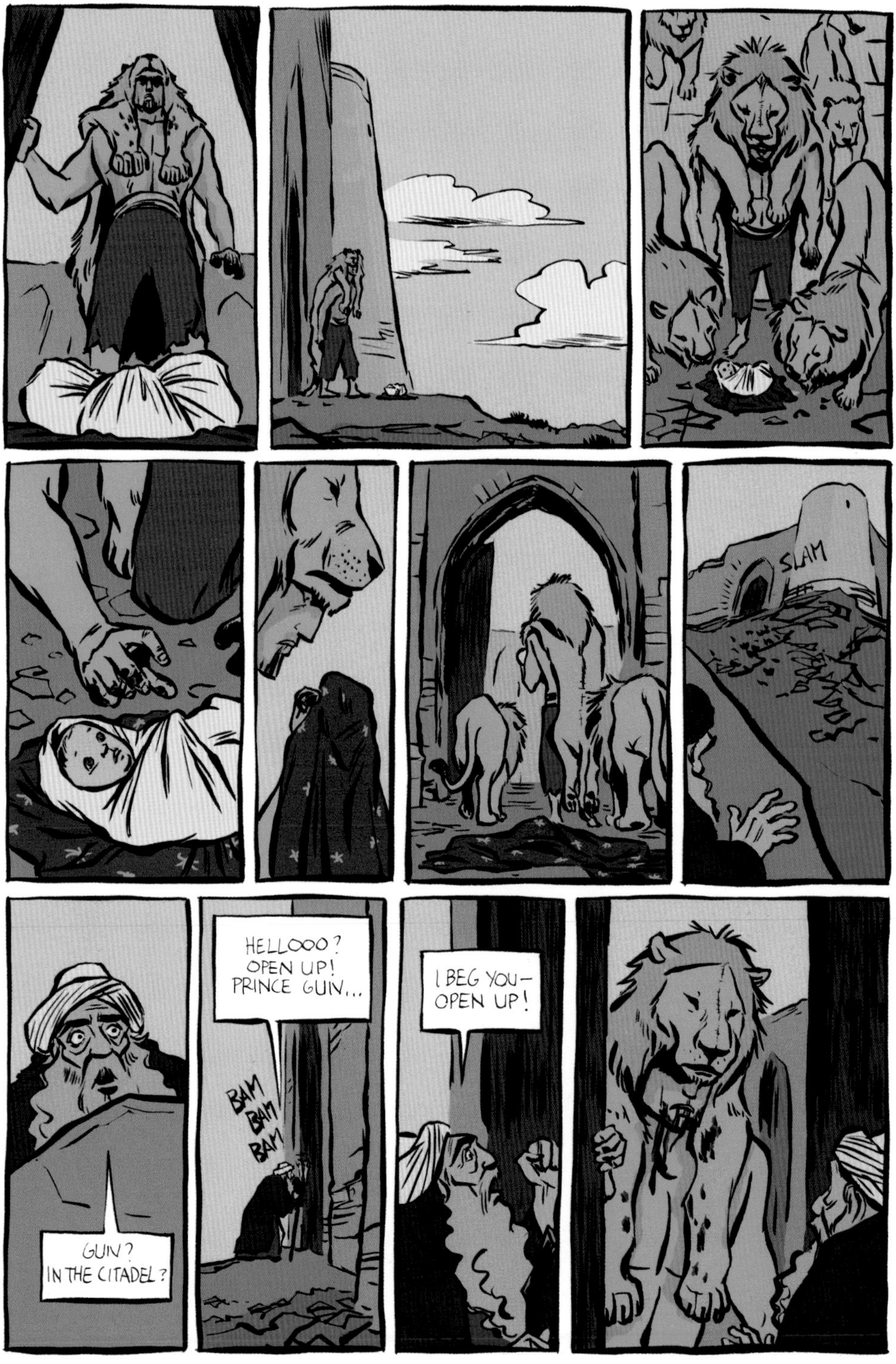
SLAM
GUIN? IN THE CITADEL?
HELLOOO? OPEN UP! PRINCE GUIN...
BAM BAM BAM
I BEG YOU— OPEN UP!

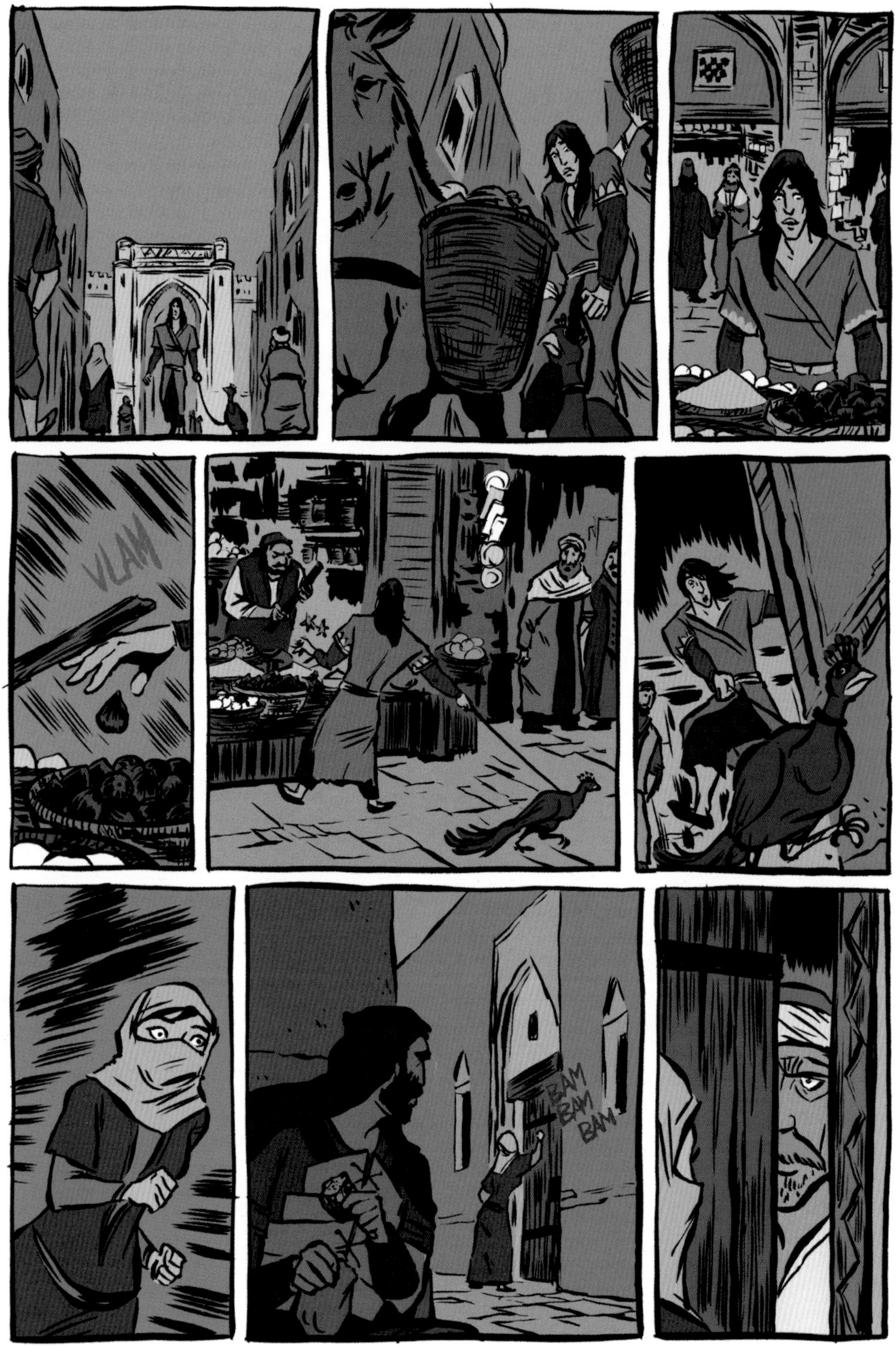
VLAM
BAM
BAM
BAM

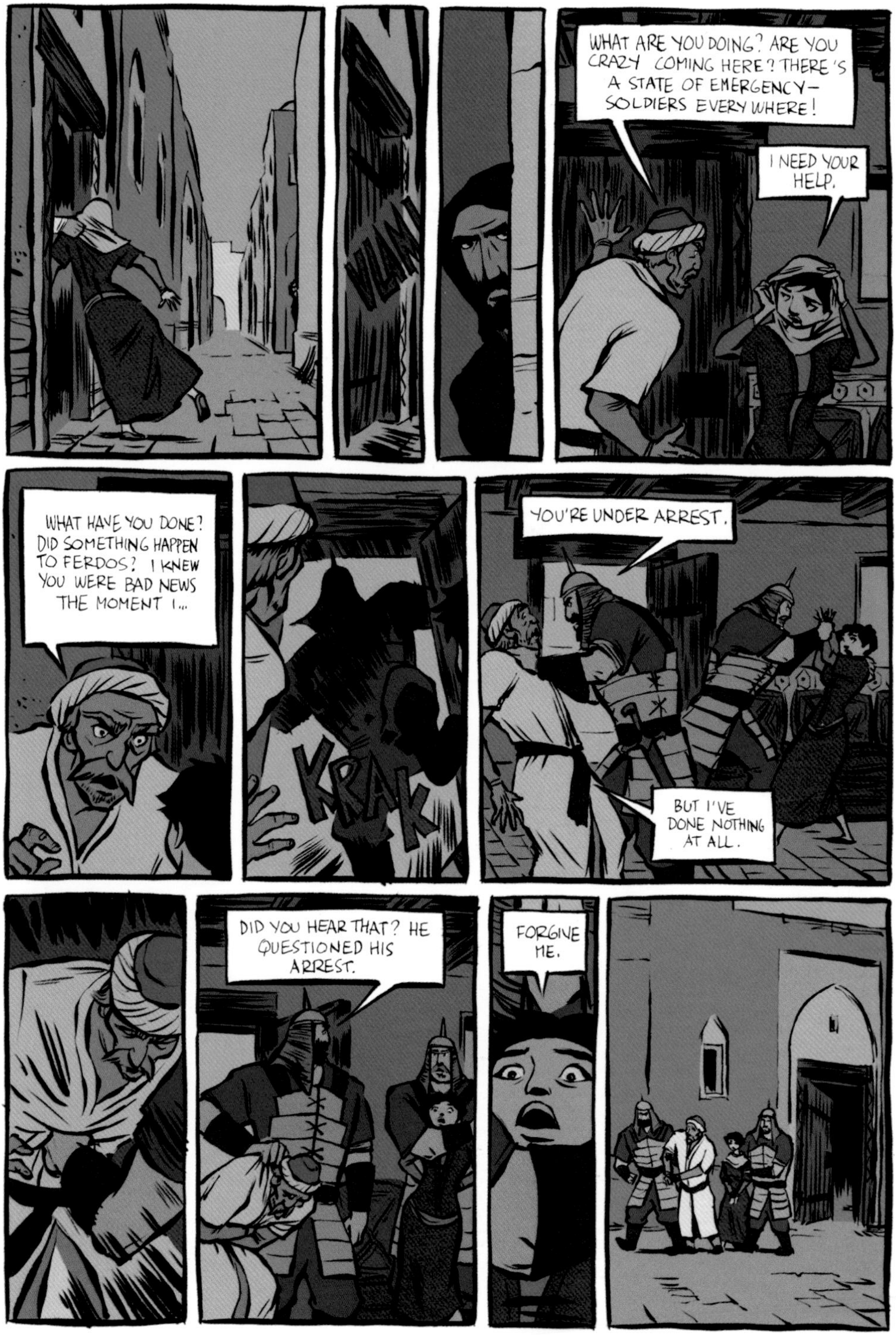
WHAT ARE YOU DOING? ARE YOU CRAZY COMING HERE? THERE'S A STATE OF EMERGENCY– SOLDIERS EVERYWHERE!
I NEED YOUR HELP.
WHAT HAVE YOU DONE? DID SOMETHING HAPPEN TO FERDOS? I KNEW YOU WERE BAD NEWS THE MOMENT I...
KRAK
YOU'RE UNDER ARREST.
BUT I'VE DONE NOTHING AT ALL.
DID YOU HEAR THAT? HE QUESTIONED HIS ARREST.
FORGIVE ME.

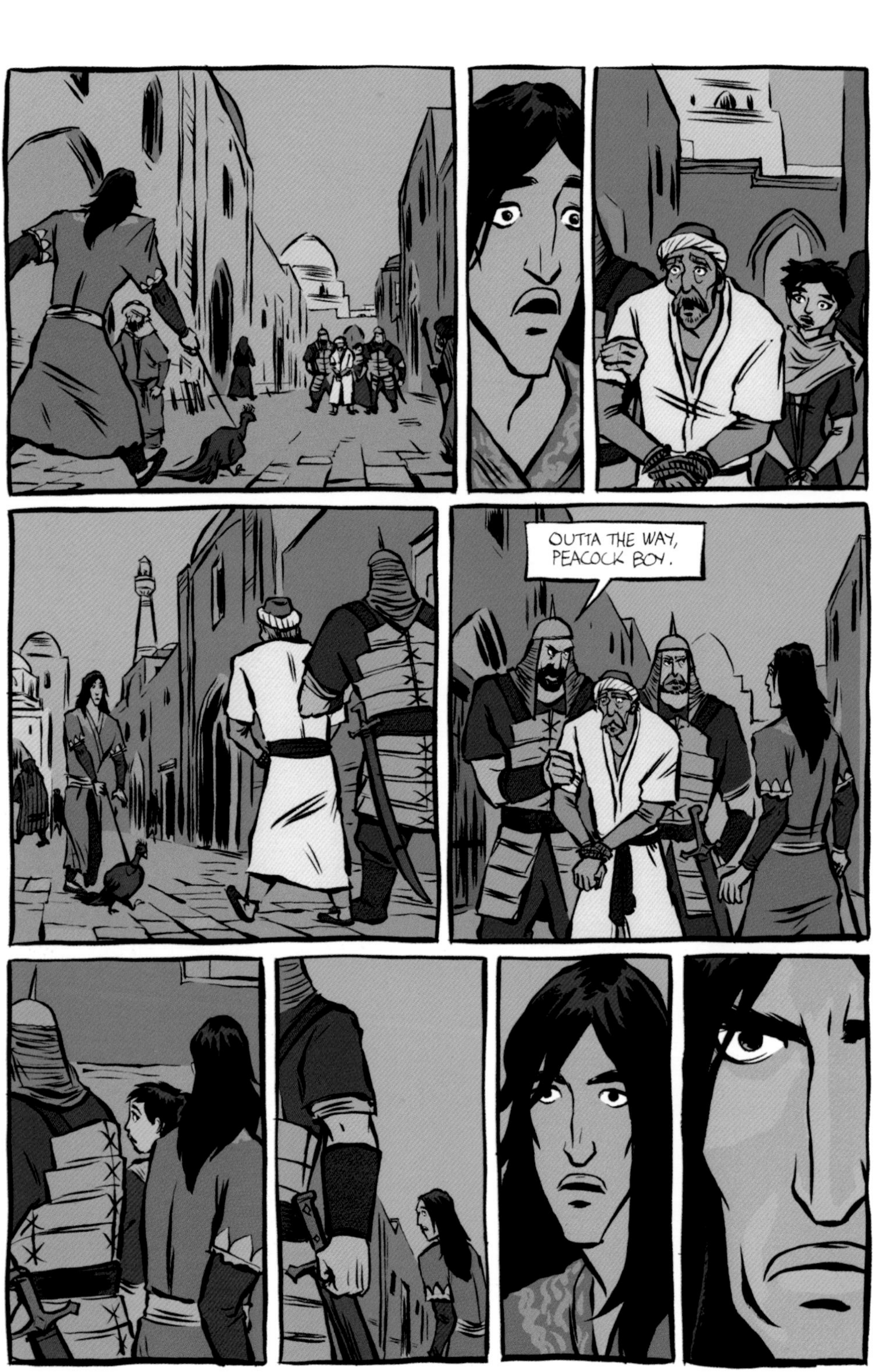
OUTTA THE WAY, PEACOCK BOY.

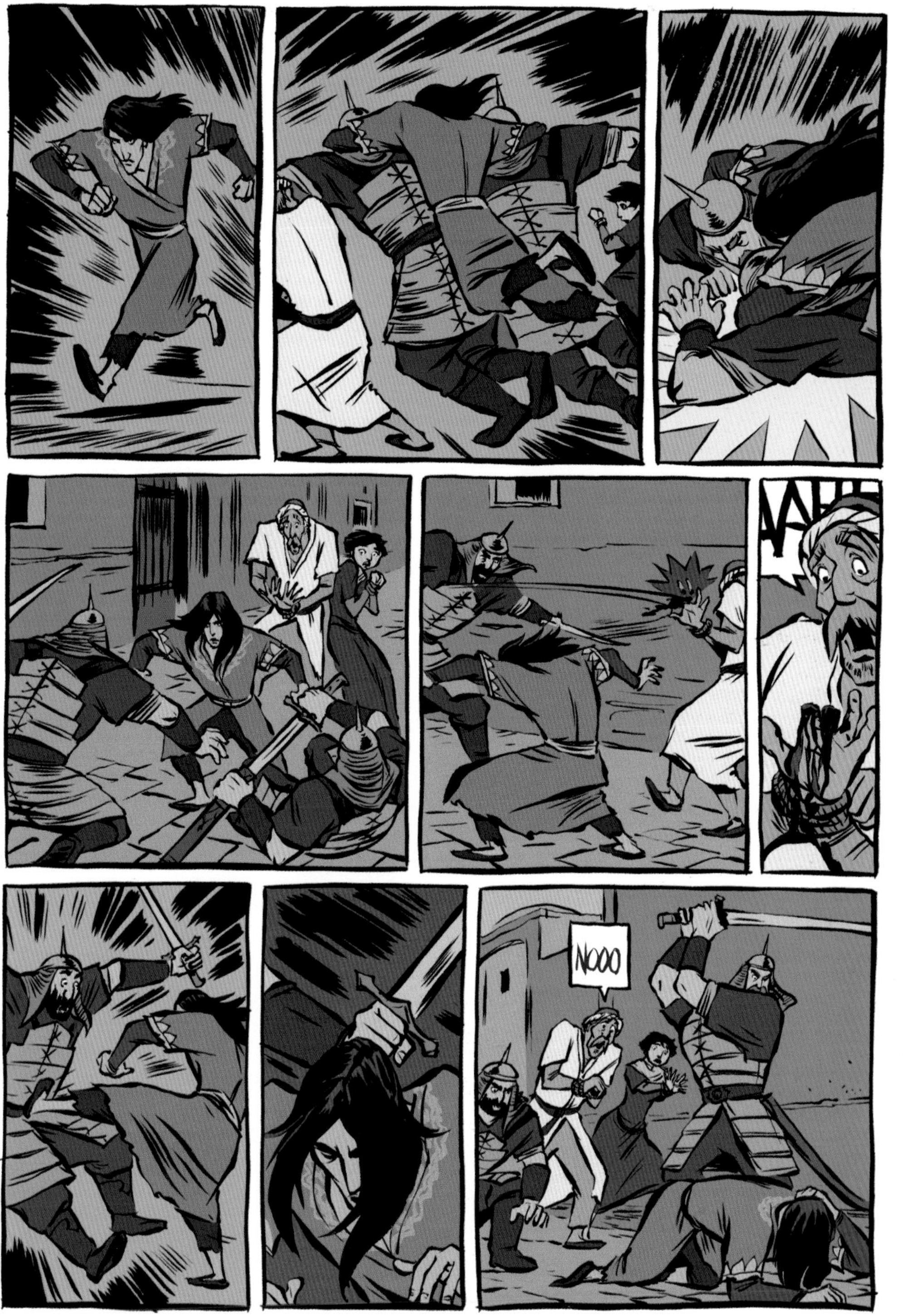
NOOO

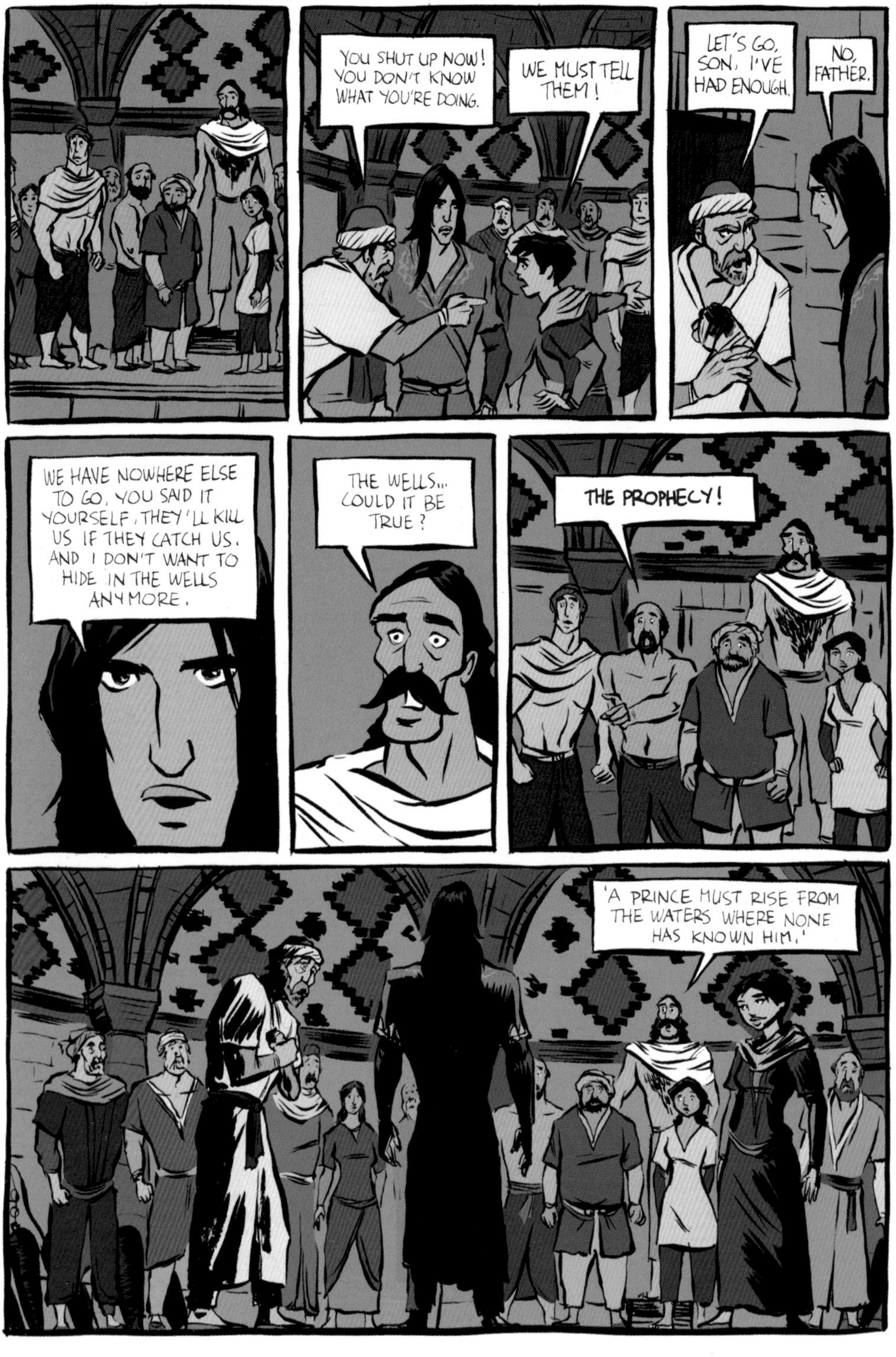
YOU SHUT UP NOW! YOU DON'T KNOW WHAT YOU'RE DOING.
WE MUST TELL THEM!
LET'S GO, SON, I'VE HAD ENOUGH.
NO, FATHER.
WE HAVE NOWHERE ELSE TO GO. YOU SAID IT YOURSELF, THEY'LL KILL US IF THEY CATCH US. AND I DON'T WANT TO HIDE IN THE WELLS ANYMORE.
THE WELLS... COULD IT BE TRUE?
THE PROPHECY!
'A PRINCE MUST RISE FROM THE WATERS WHERE NONE HAS KNOWN HIM.'

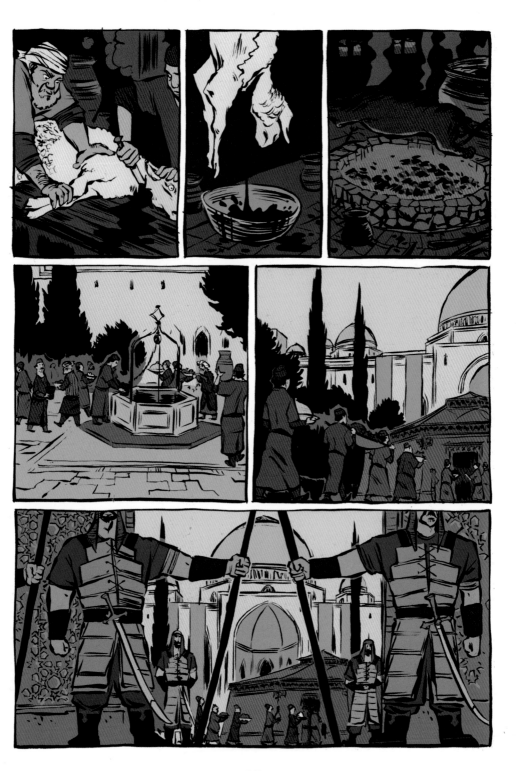

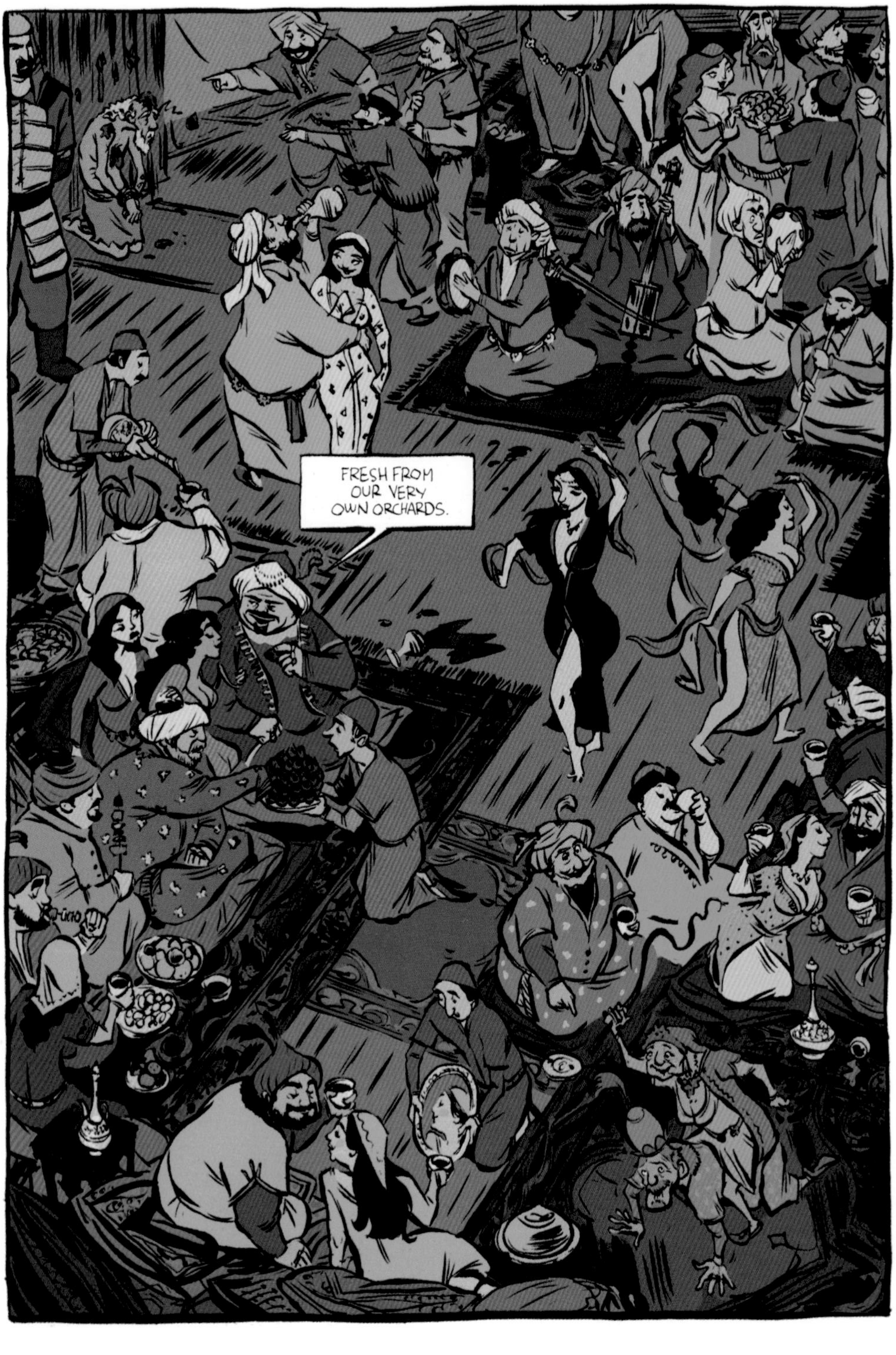
FRESH FROM OUR VERY OWN ORCHARDS.

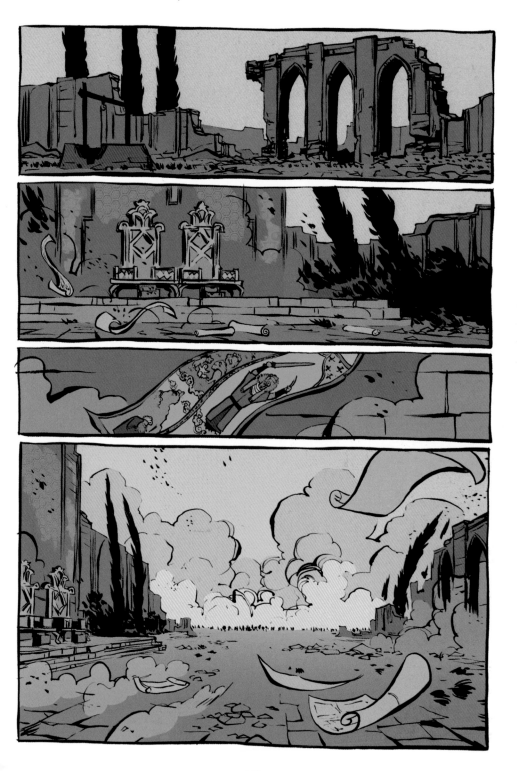

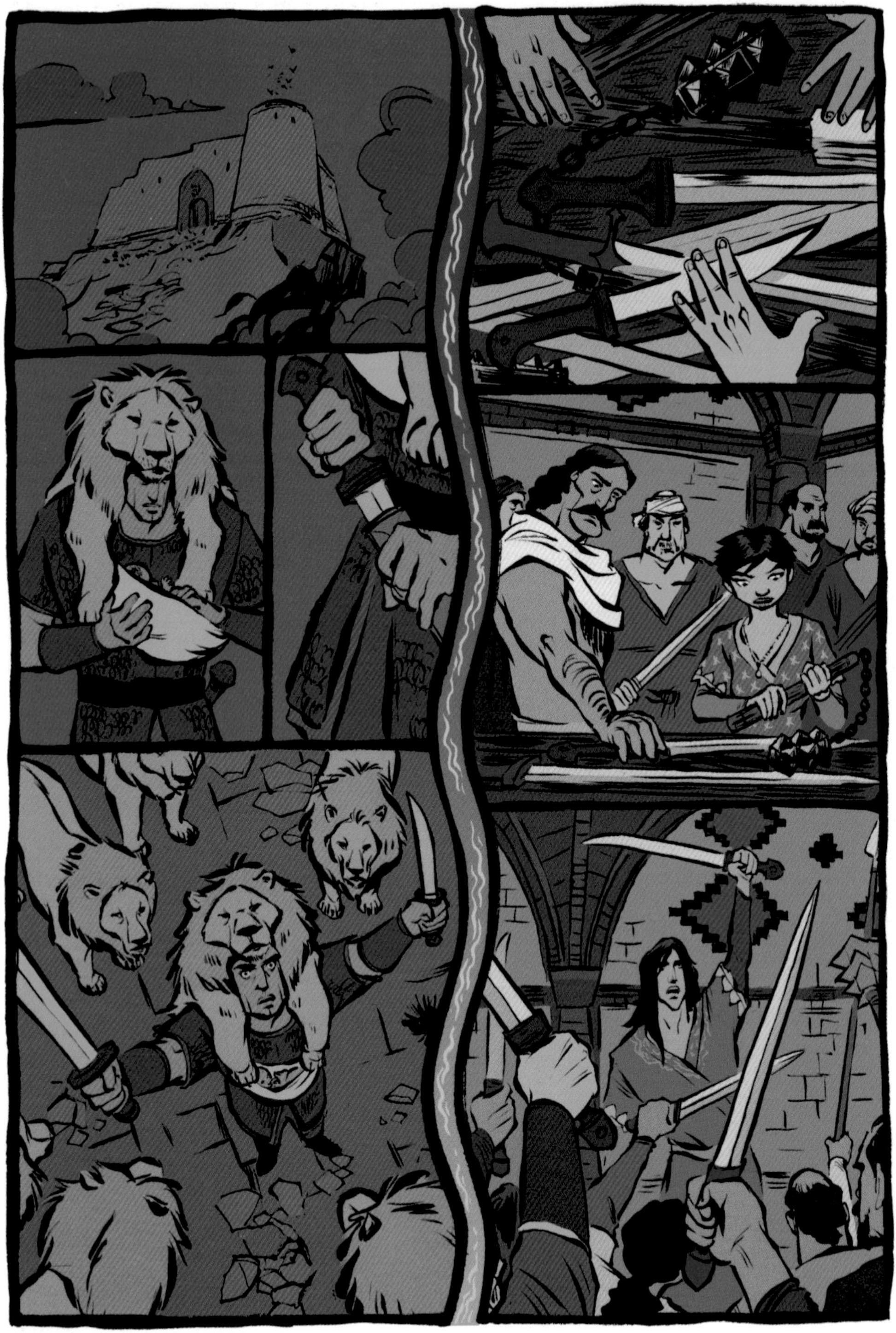

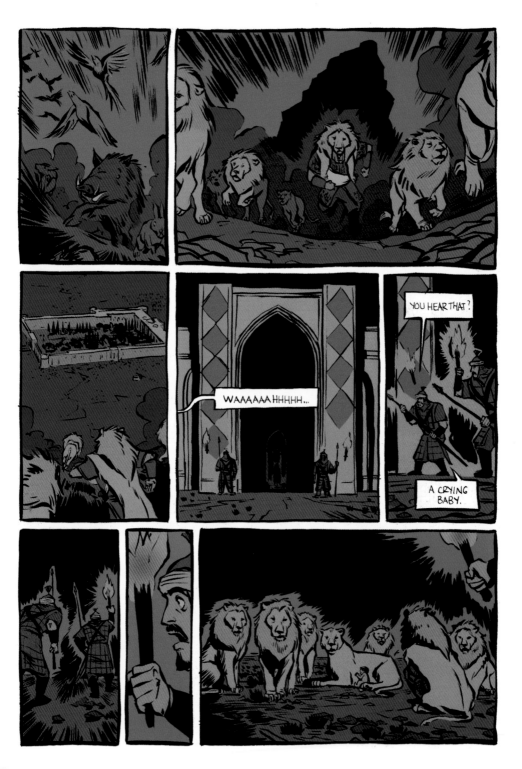

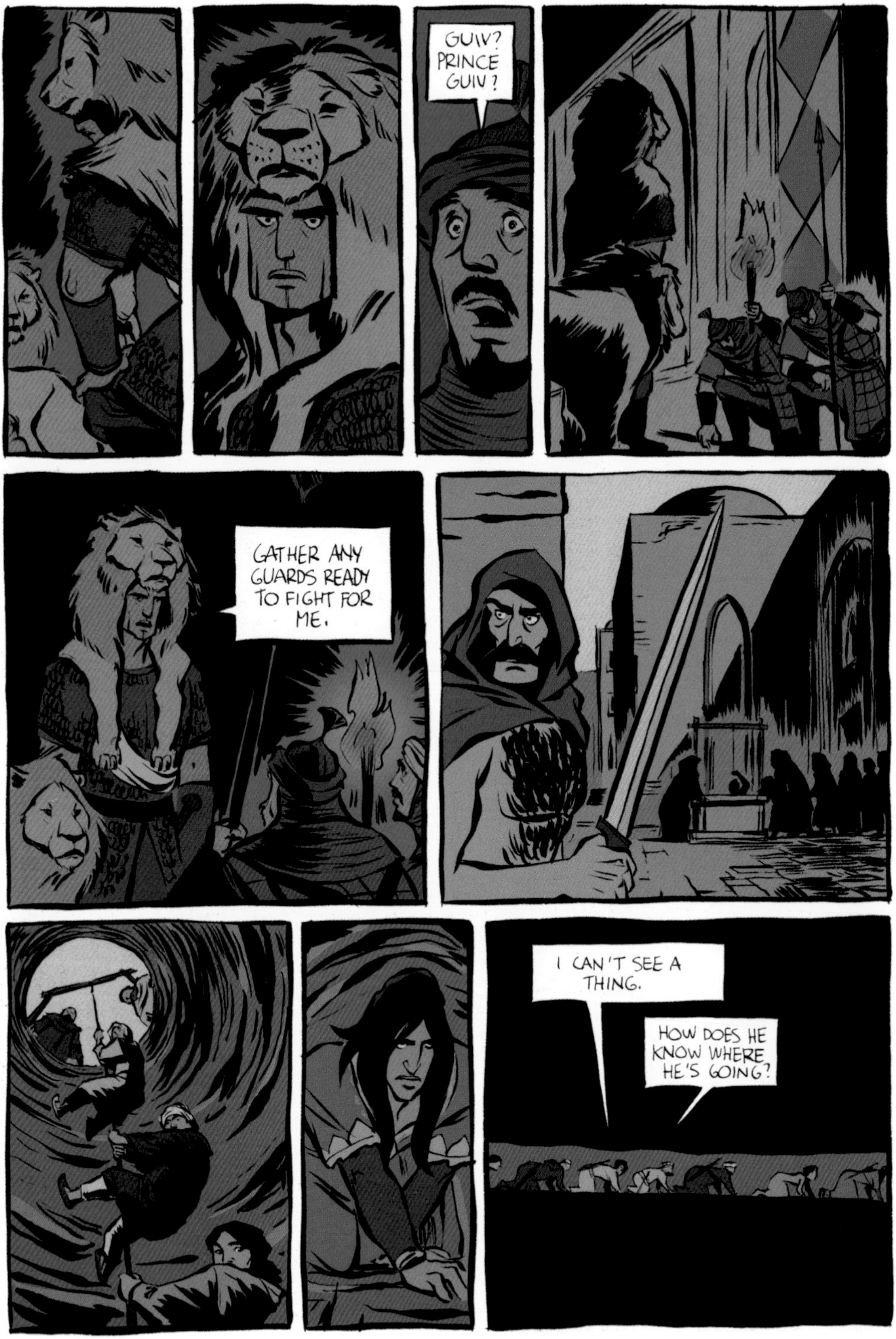
GUIV? PRINCE GUIV?
GATHER ANY GUARDS READY TO FIGHT FOR ME.
I CAN'T SEE A THING.
HOW DOES HE KNOW WHERE HE'S GOING?

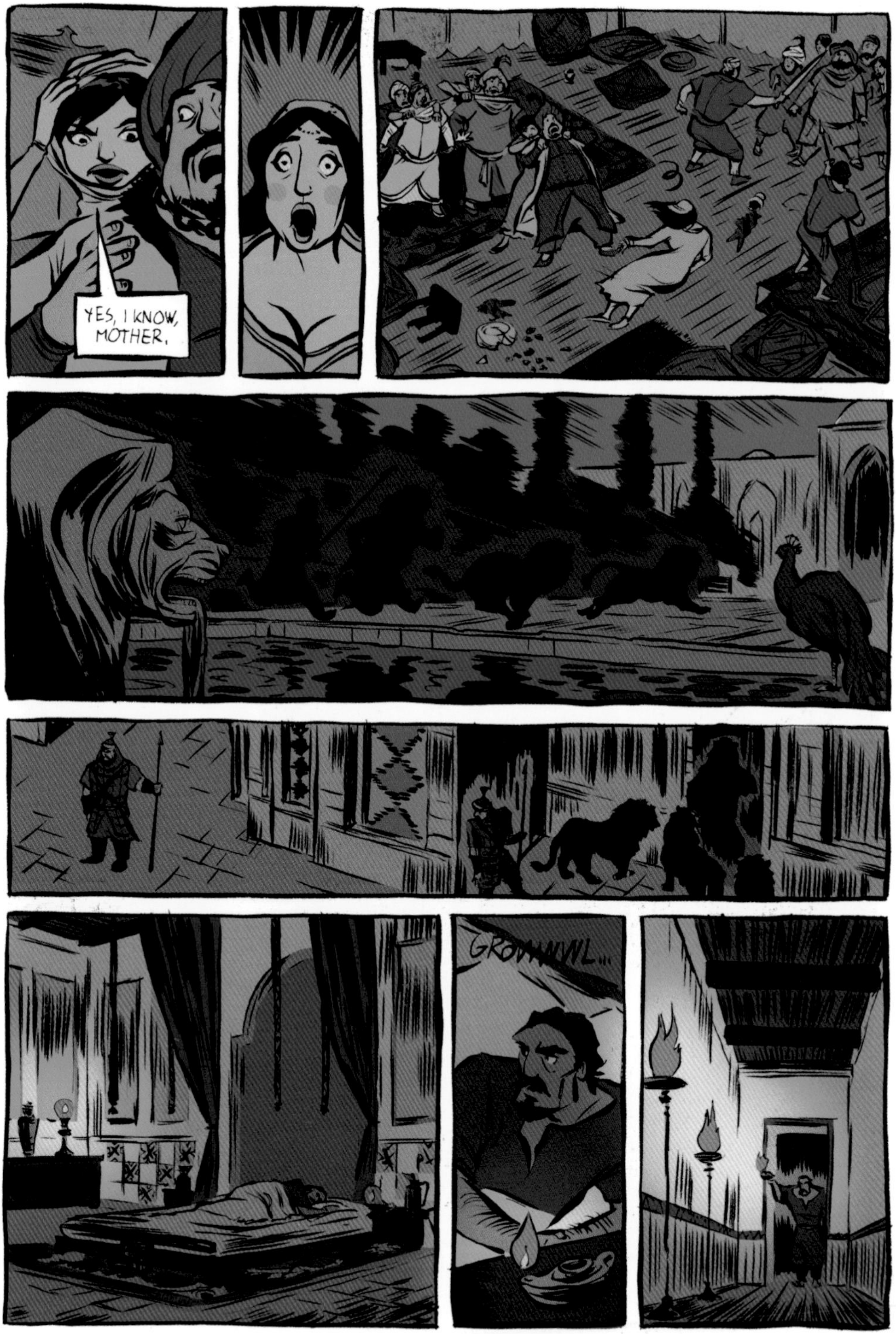
YES, I KNOW, MOTHER.
GROWWWL...

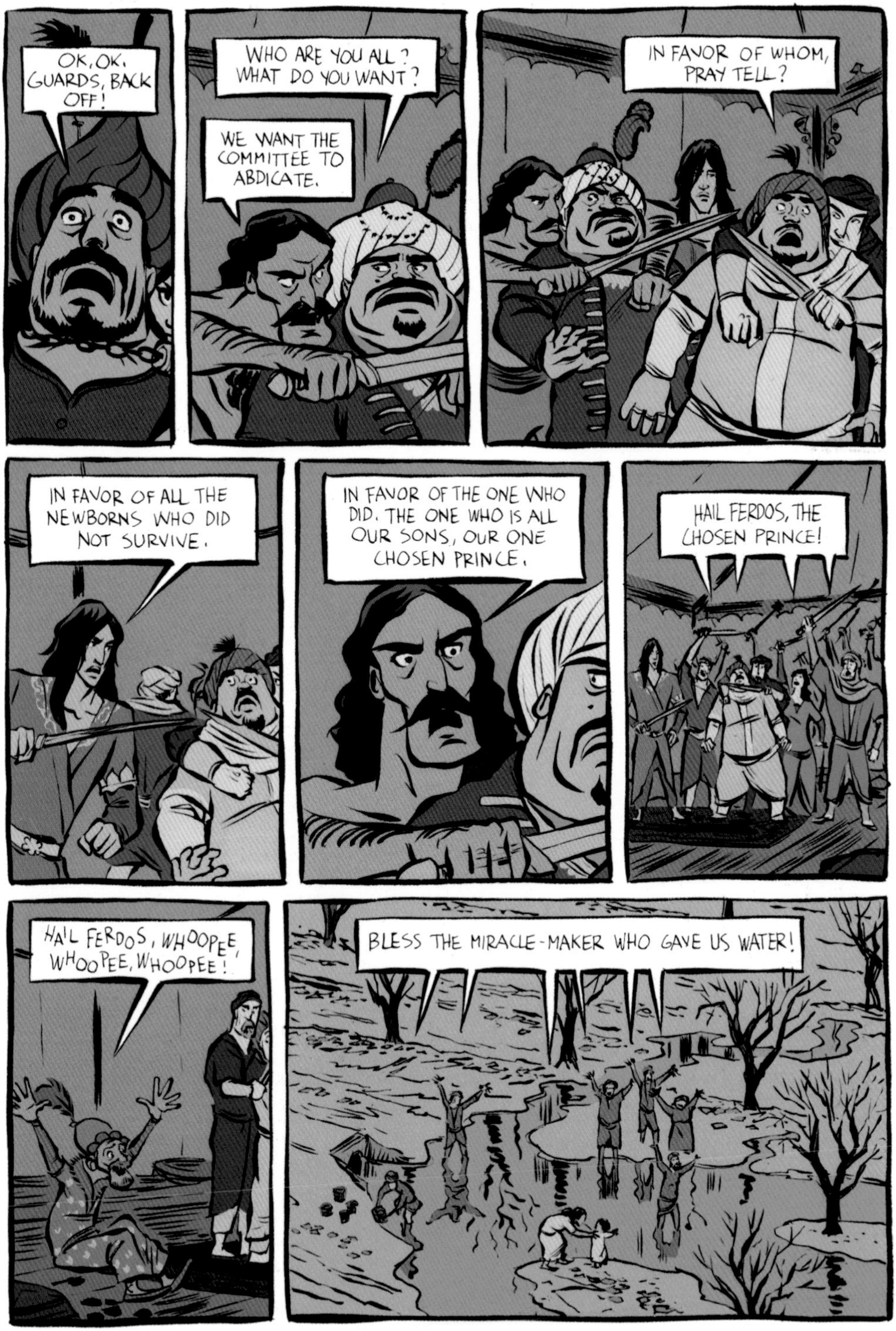
OK, OK. GUARDS, BACK OFF!
WHO ARE YOU ALL? WHAT DO YOU WANT?
WE WANT THE COMMITTEE TO ABDICATE.
IN FAVOR OF WHOM, PRAY TELL?
IN FAVOR OF ALL THE NEWBORNS WHO DID NOT SURVIVE.
IN FAVOR OF THE ONE WHO DID. THE ONE WHO IS ALL OUR SONS, OUR ONE CHOSEN PRINCE.
HAIL FERDOS, THE CHOSEN PRINCE!
HAIL FERDOS, WHOOPEE, WHOOPEE, WHOOPEE!
BLESS THE MIRACLE-MAKER WHO GAVE US WATER!

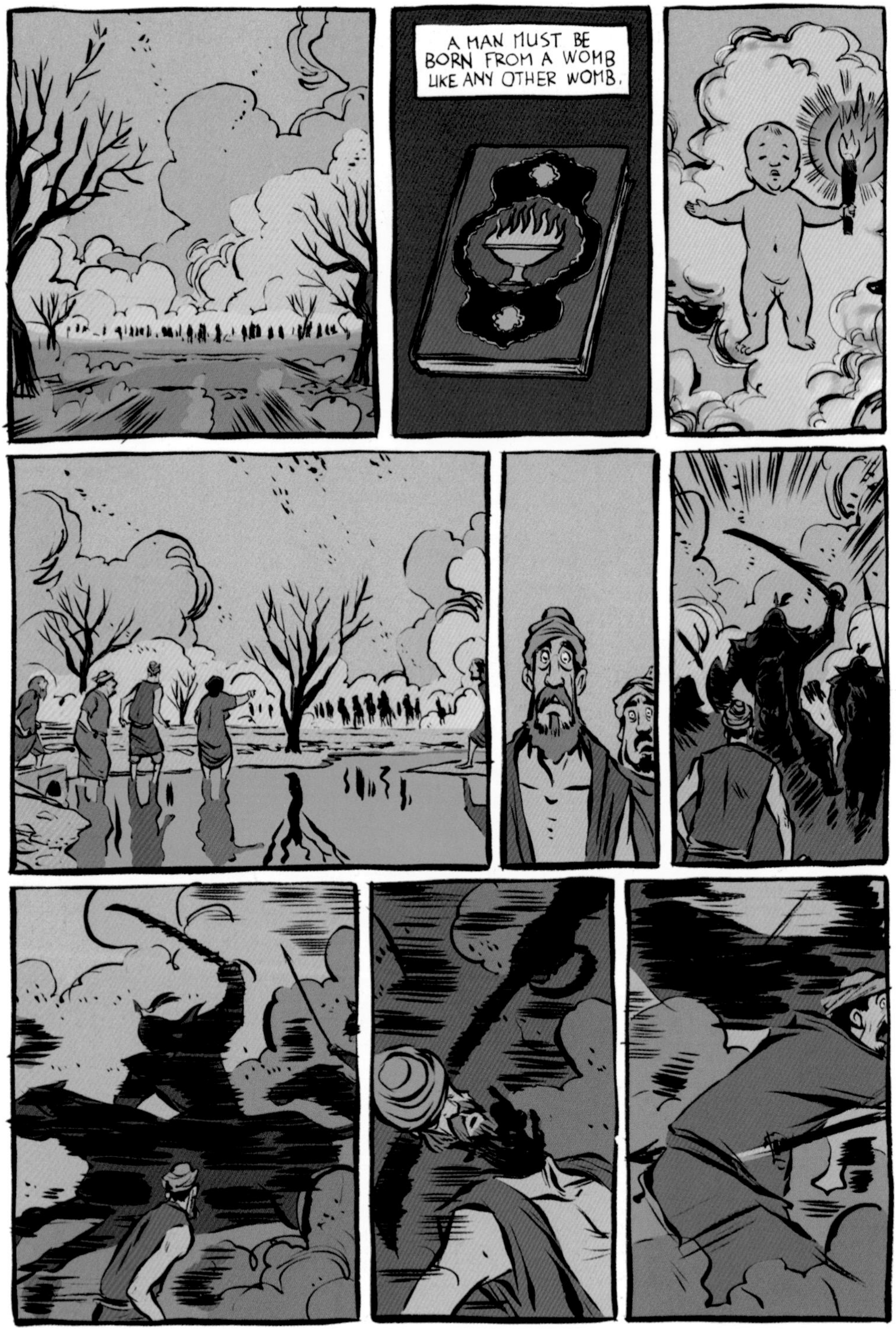
A MAN MUST BE BORN FROM A WOMB LIKE ANY OTHER WOMB.

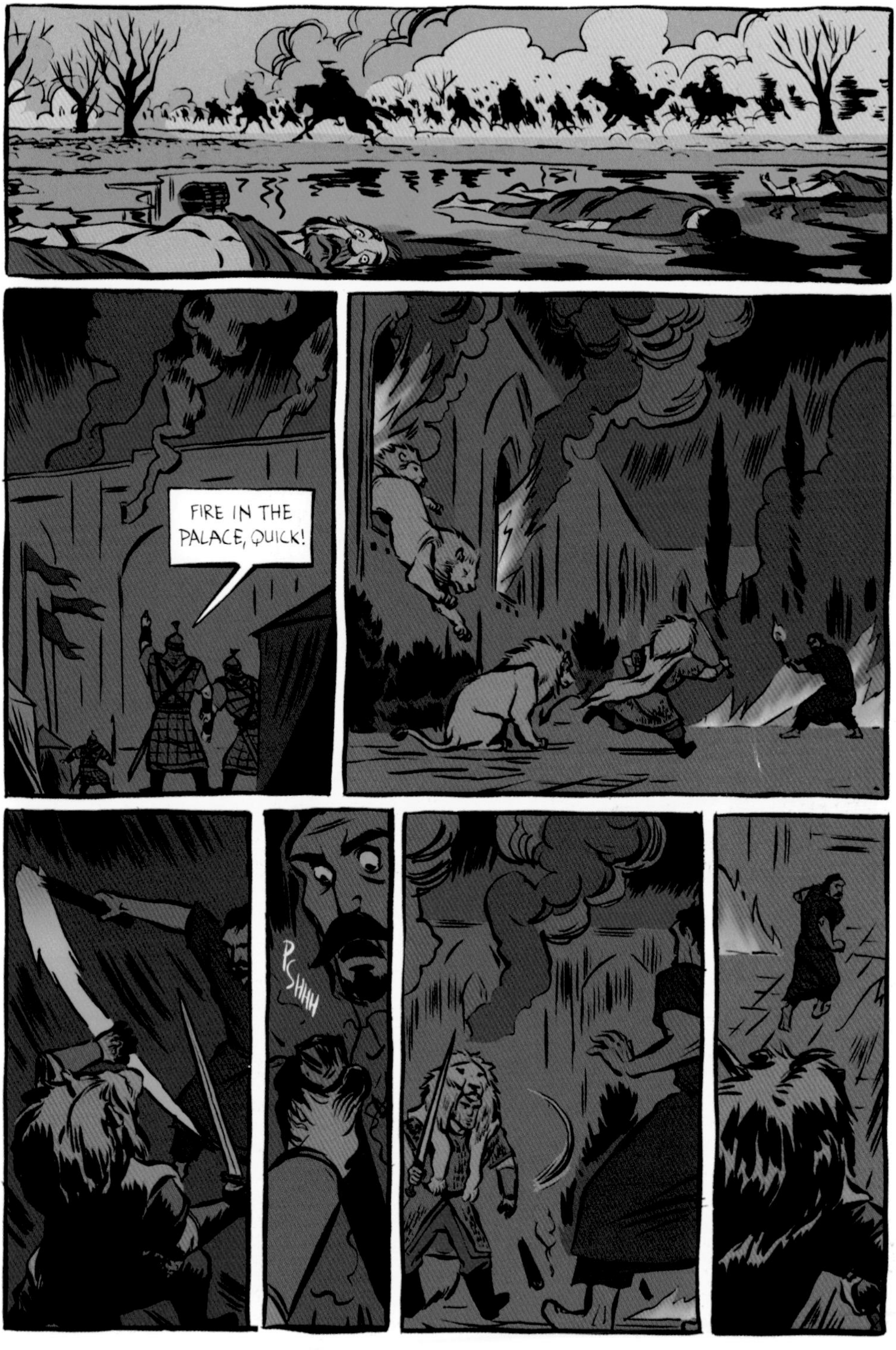
FIRE IN THE PALACE, QUICK!
PSHHH

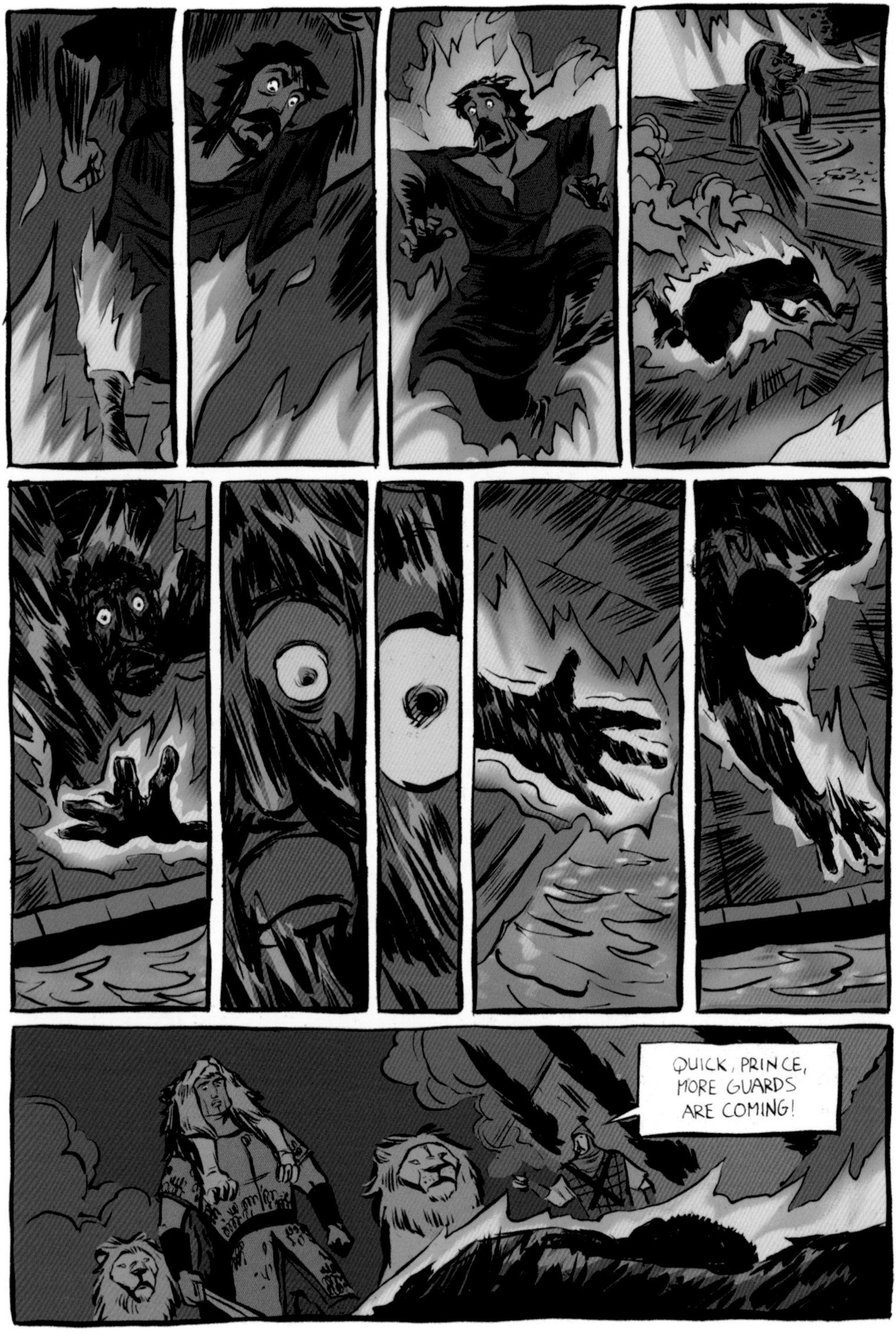
QUICK, PRINCE,
MORE GUARDS
ARE COMING!

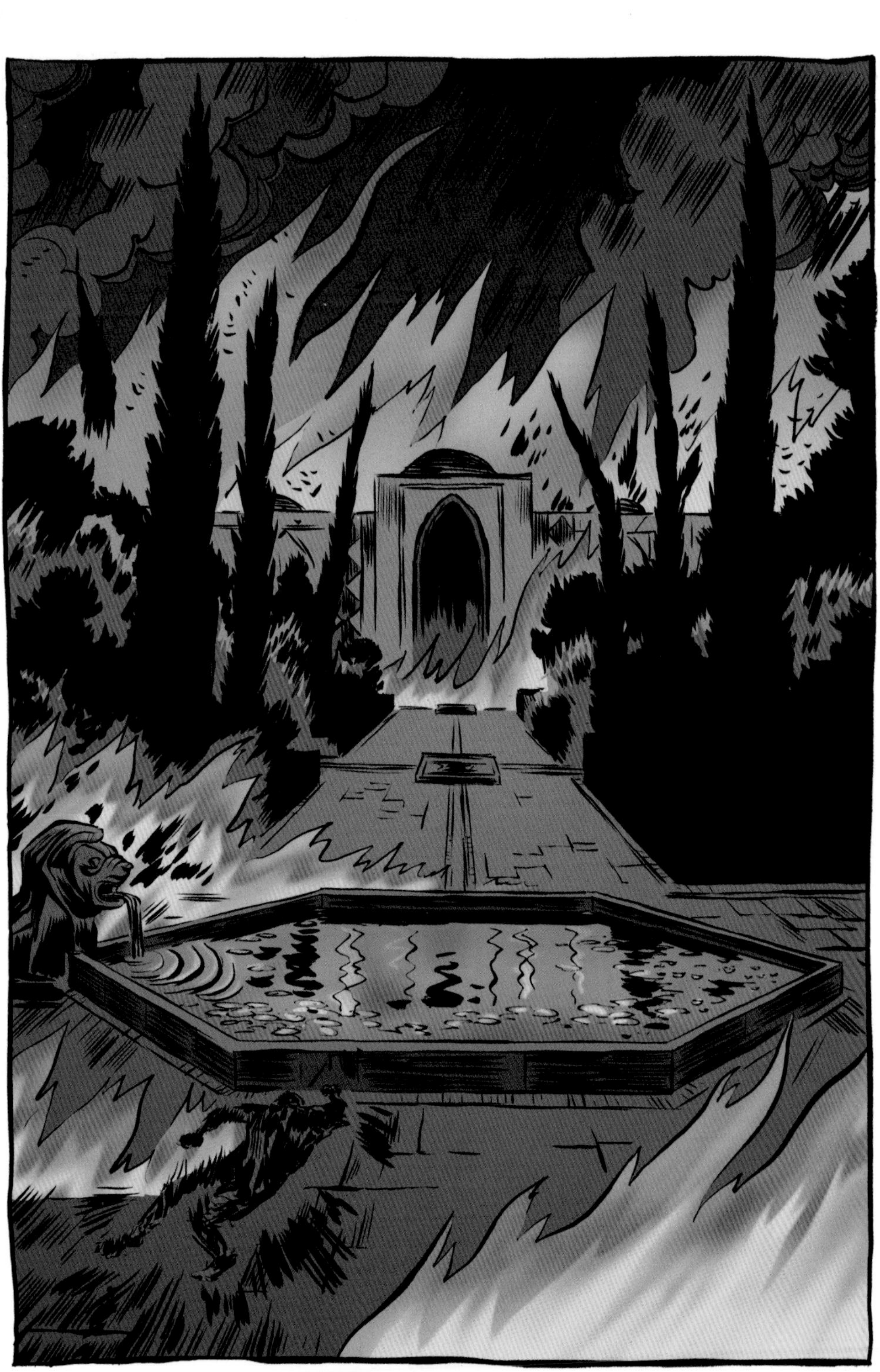

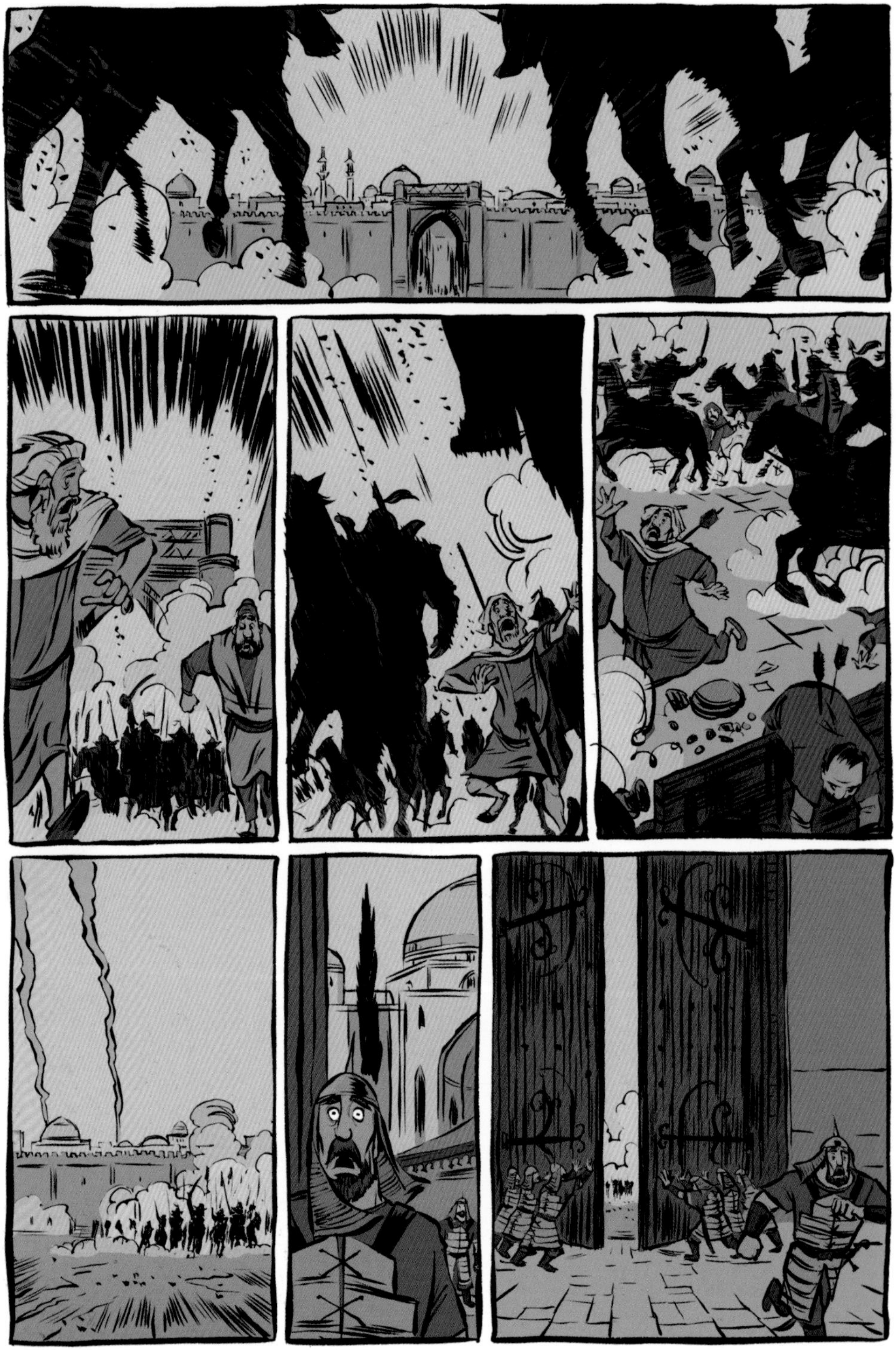

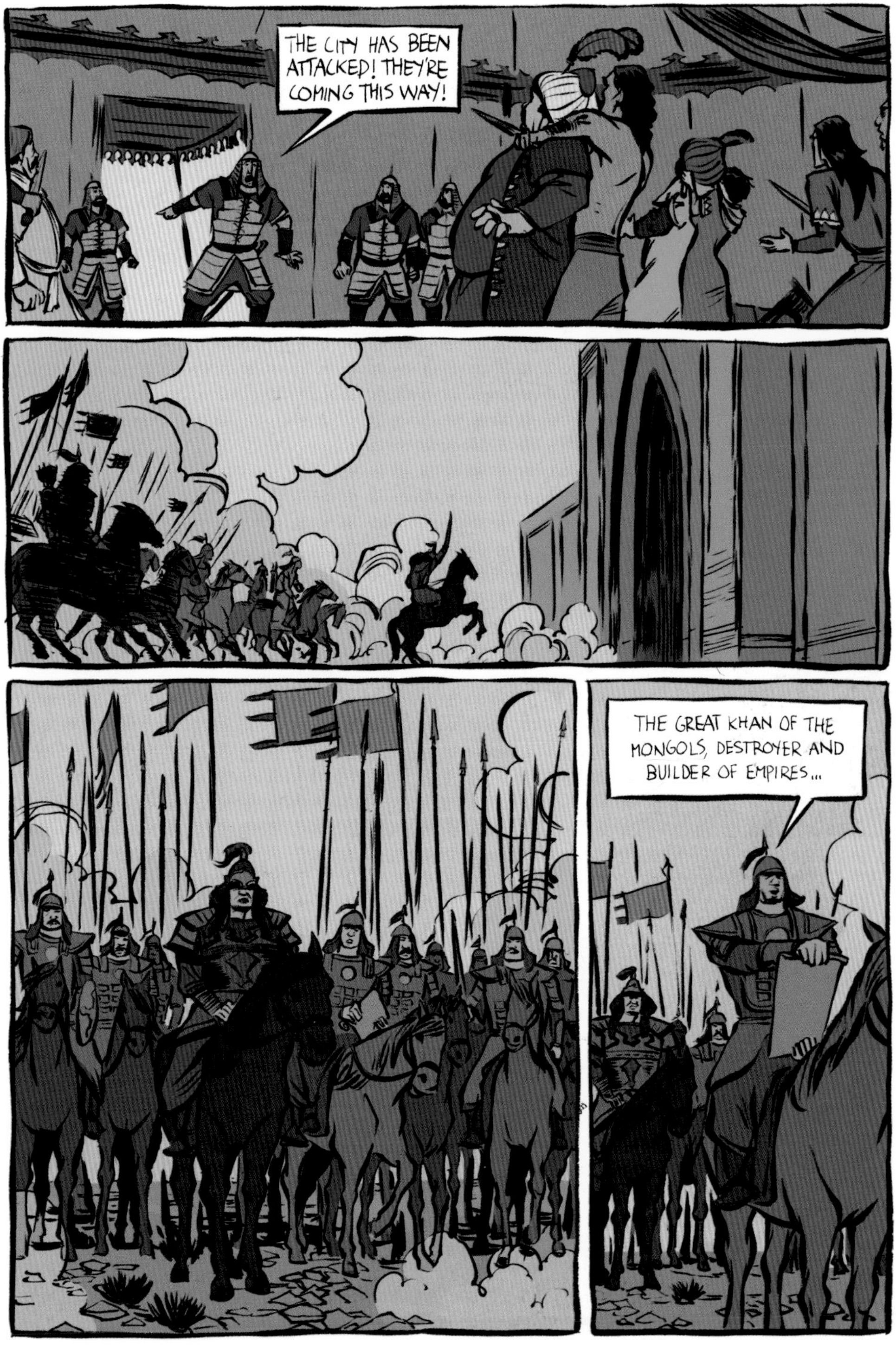
THE CITY HAS BEEN ATTACKED! THEY'RE COMING THIS WAY!
THE GREAT KHAN OF THE MONGOLS, DESTROYER AND BUILDER OF EMPIRES...

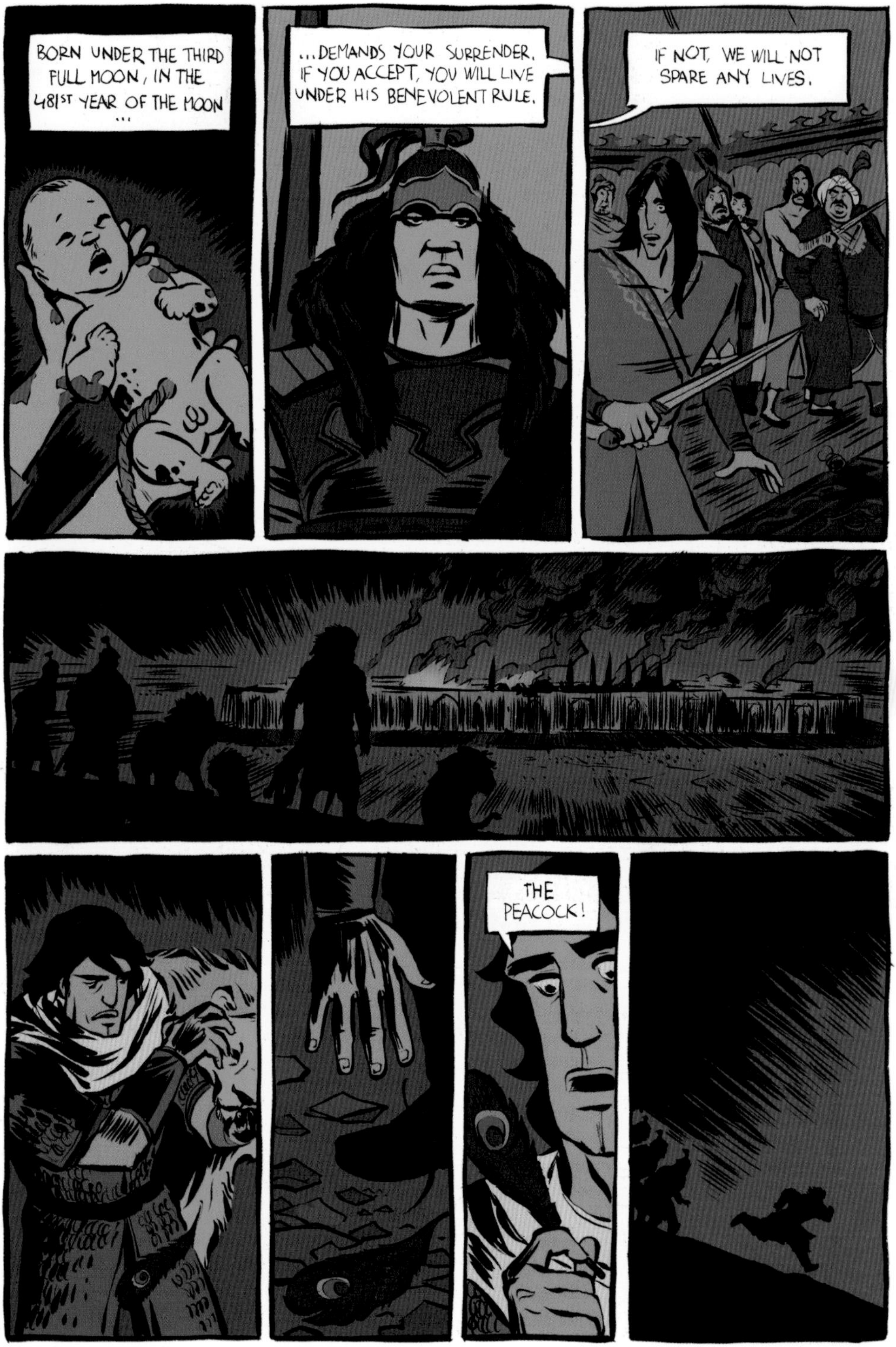
BORN UNDER THE THIRD FULL MOON, IN THE 481ST YEAR OF THE MOON ...
...DEMANDS YOUR SURRENDER. IF YOU ACCEPT, YOU WILL LIVE UNDER HIS BENEVOLENT RULE.
IF NOT, WE WILL NOT SPARE ANY LIVES.
THE PEACOCK!

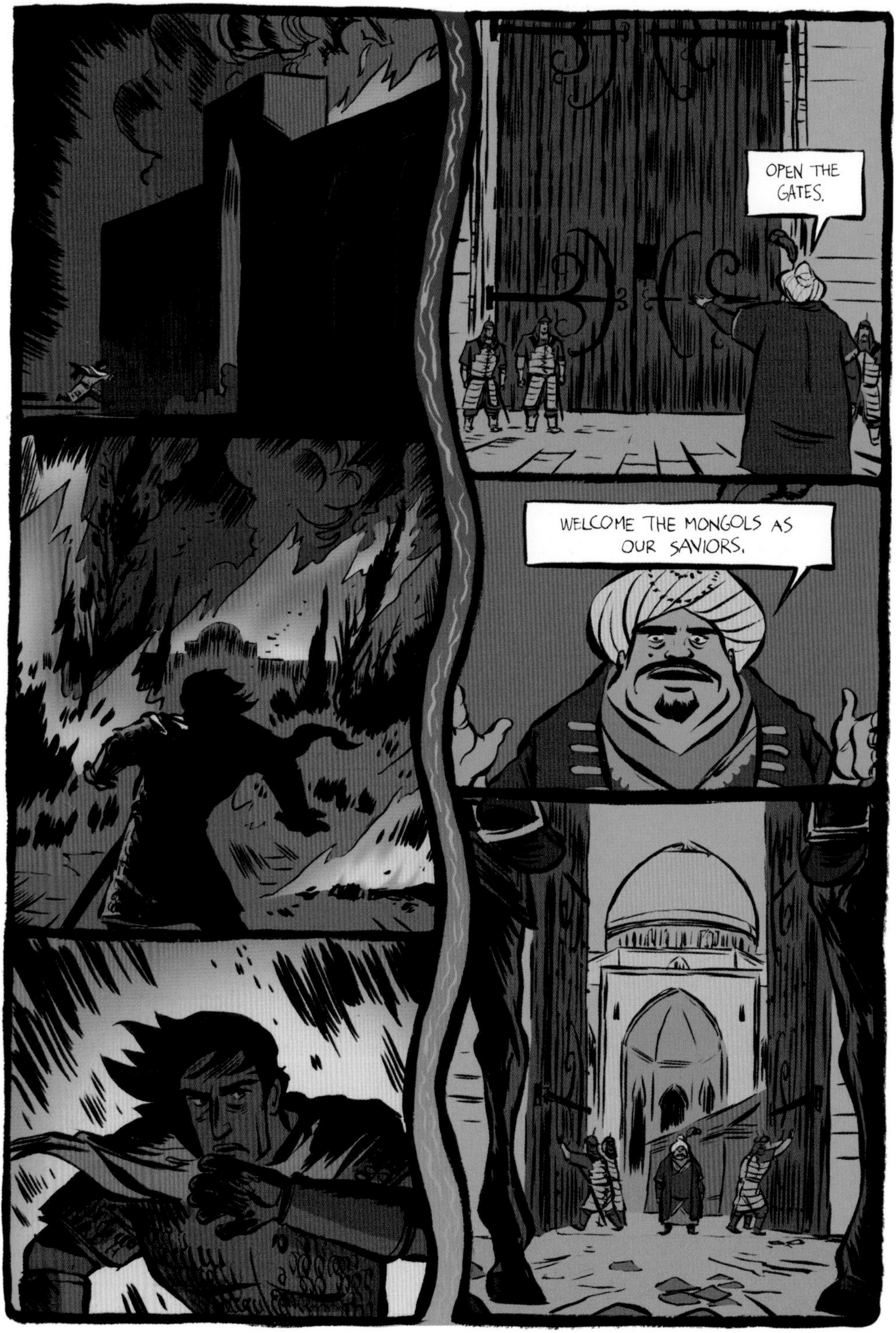
OPEN THE GATES.
WELCOME THE MONGOLS AS OUR SAVIORS.

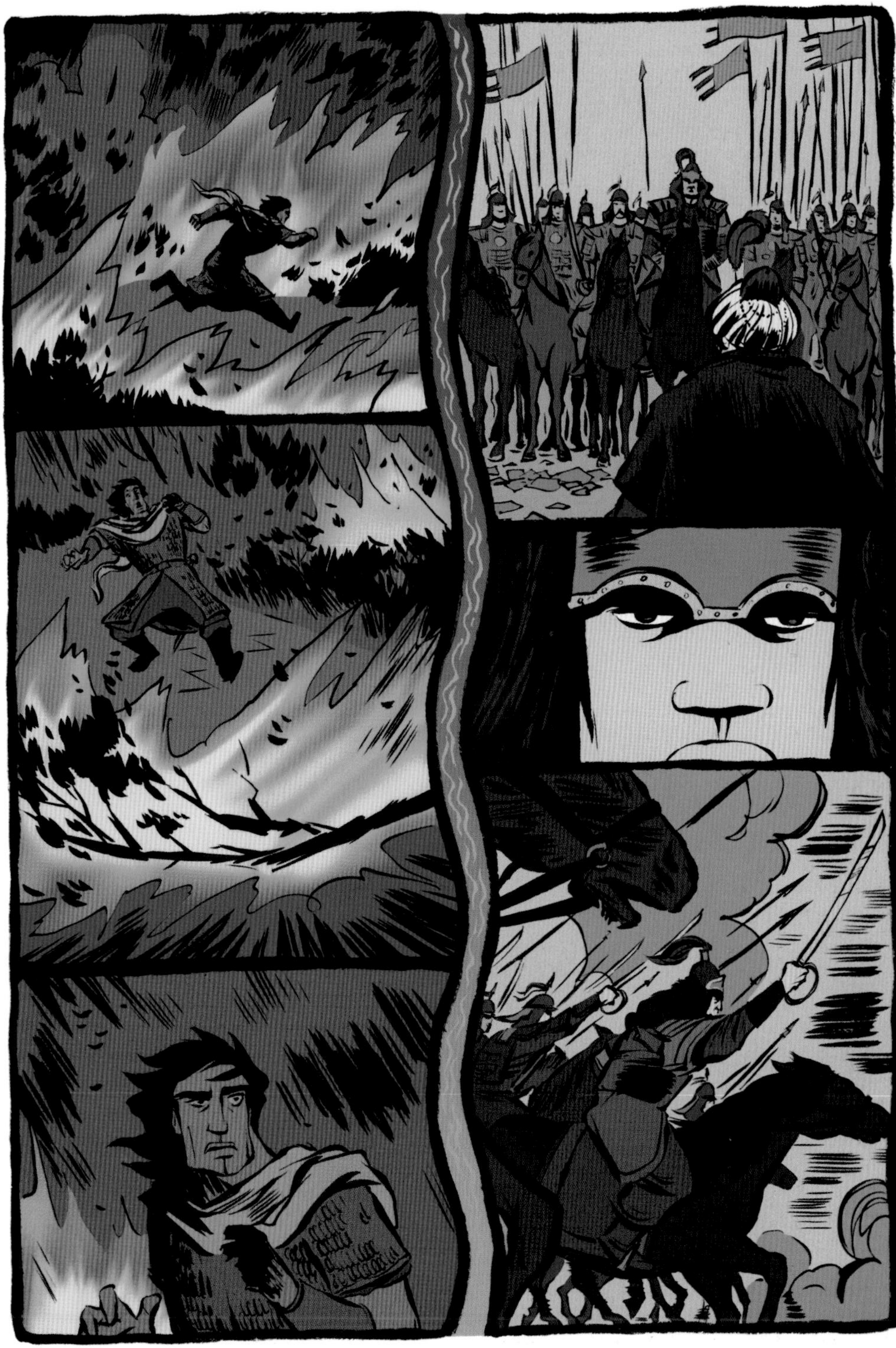

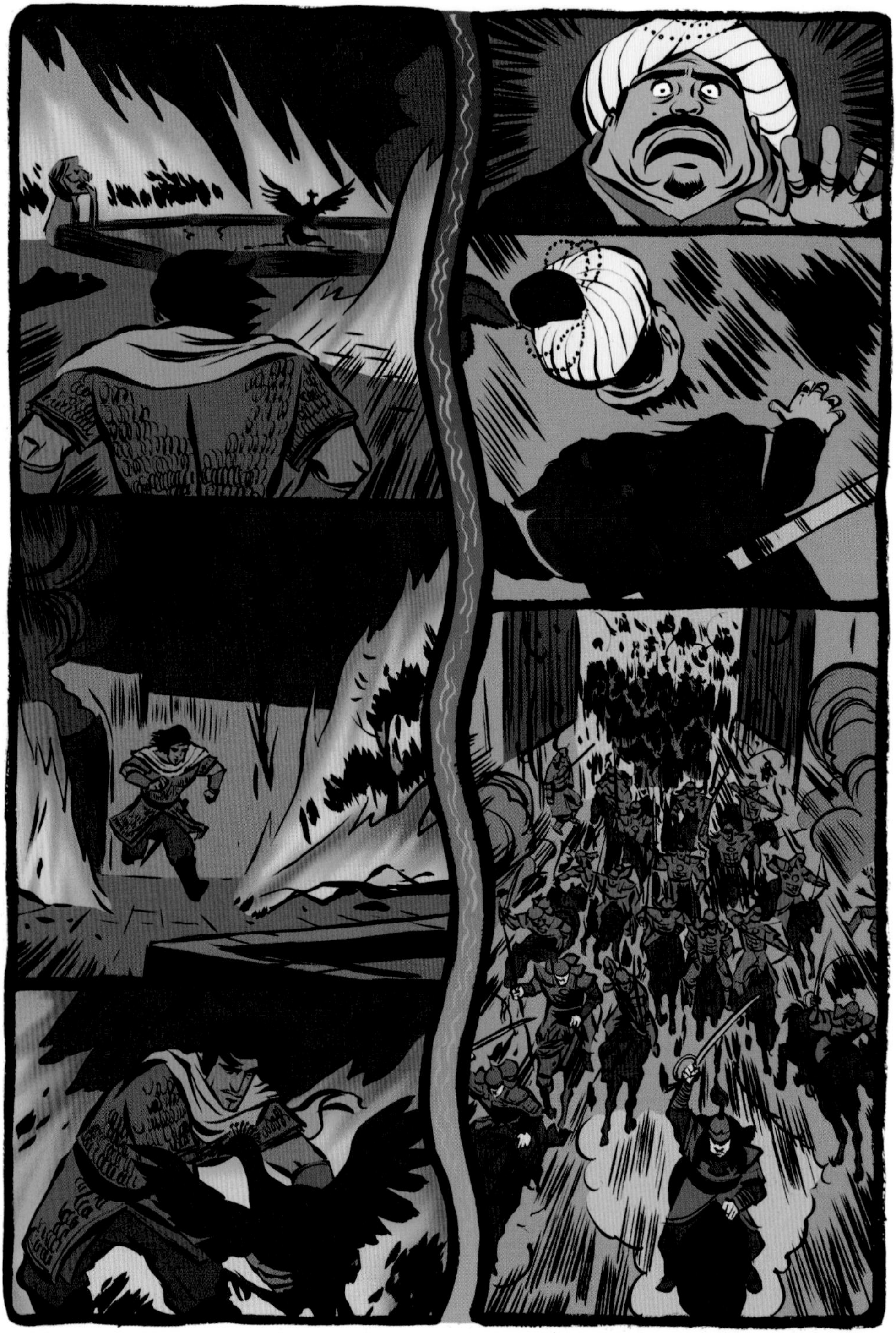

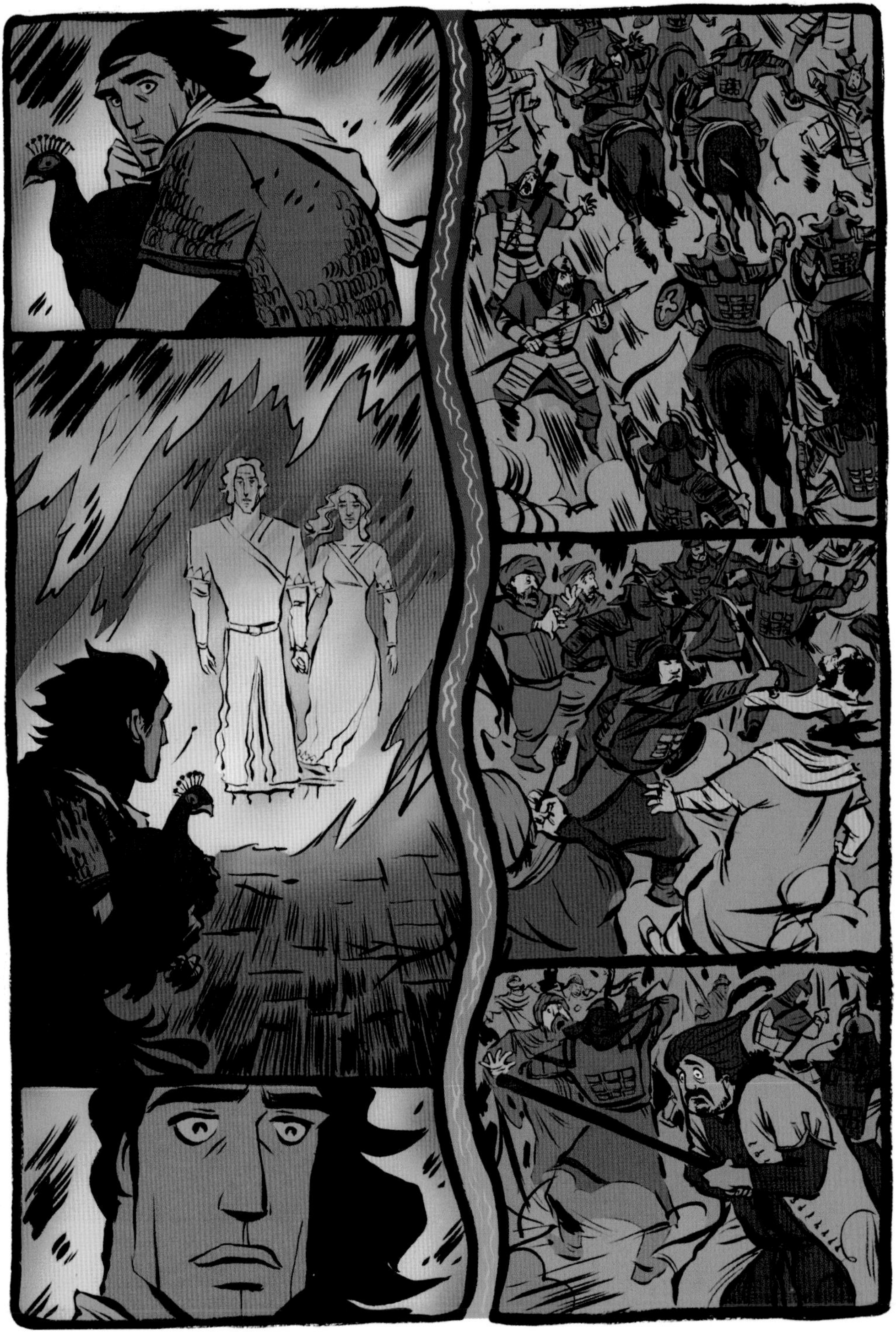

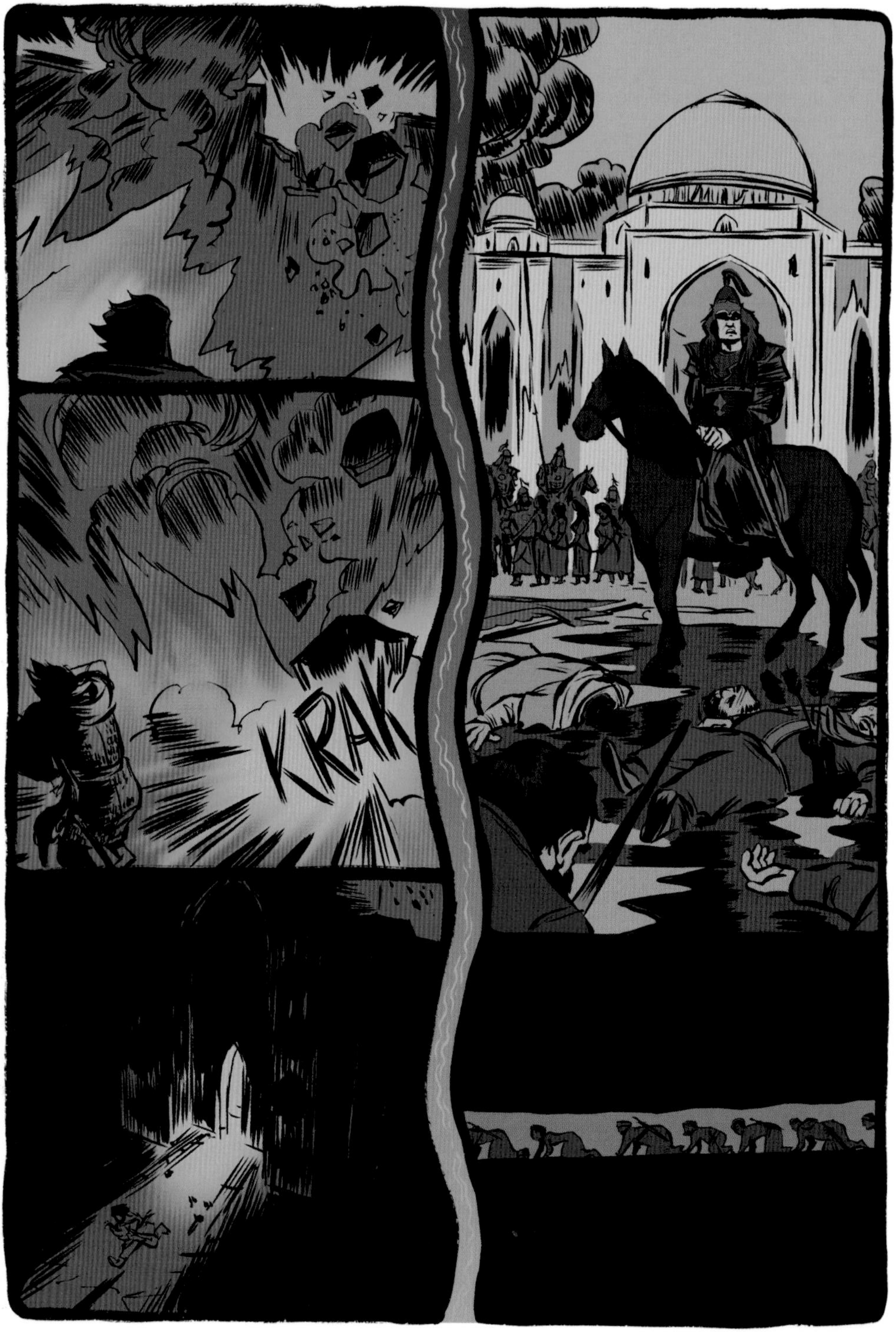
KRAK

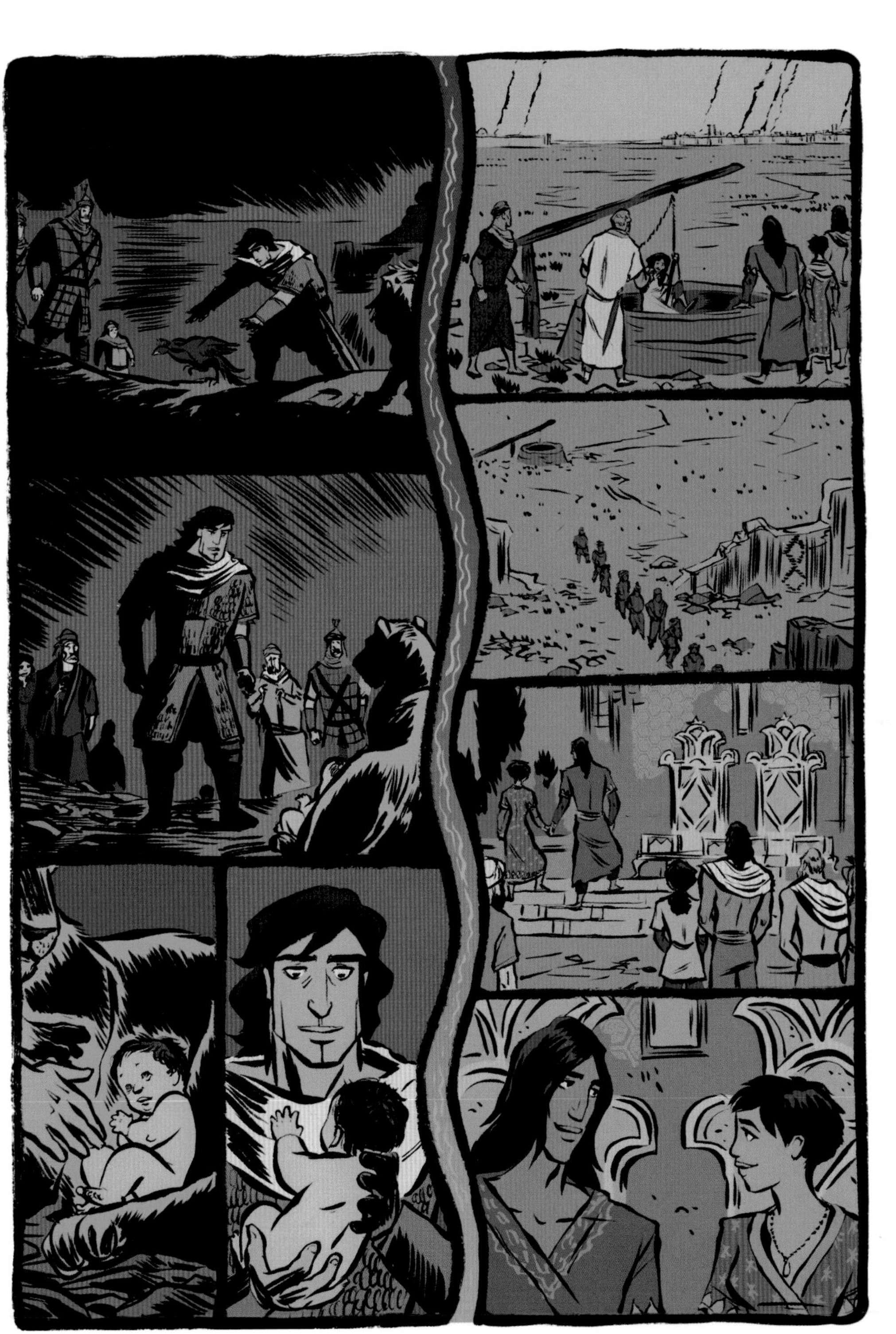

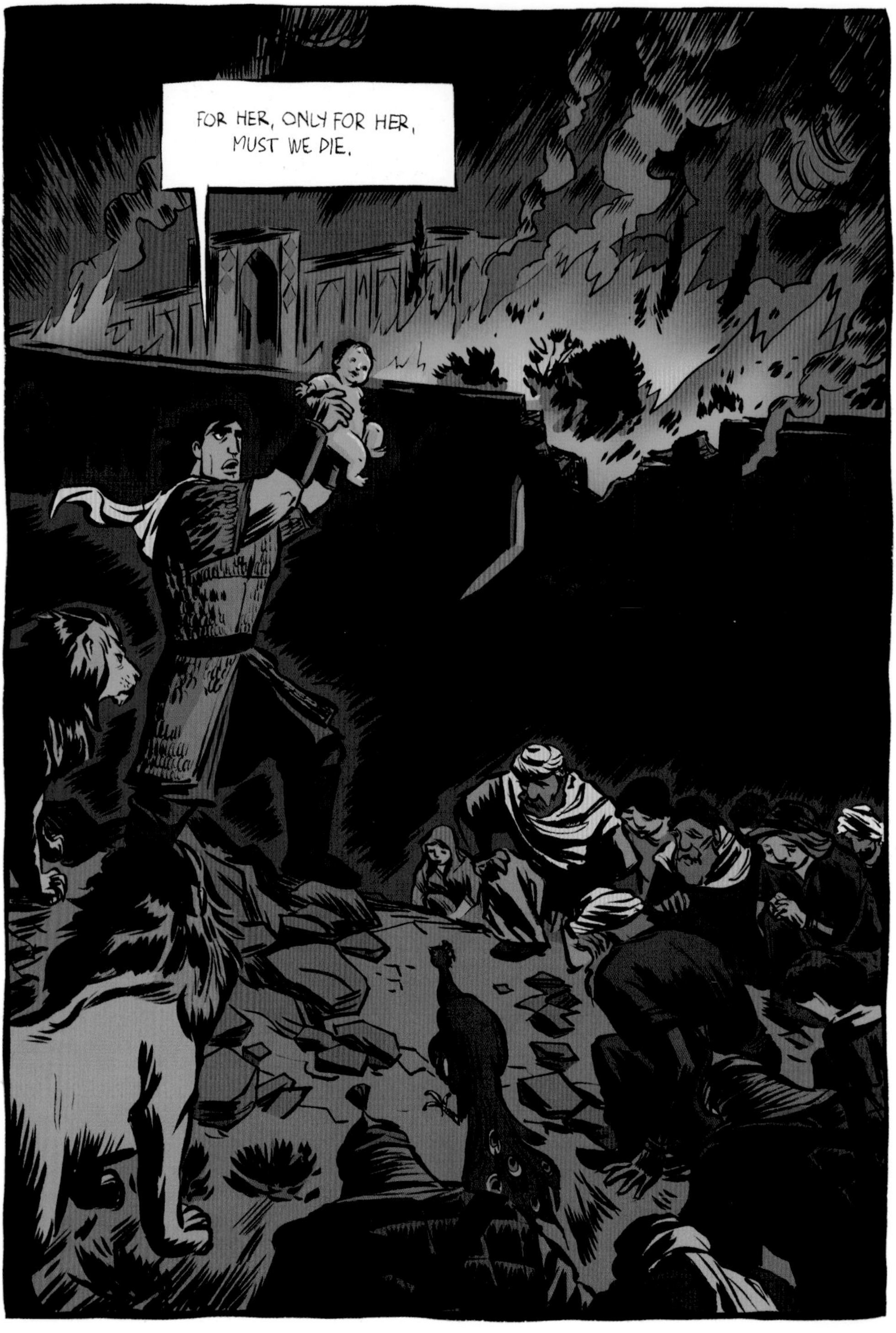
FOR HER, ONLY FOR HER, MUST WE DIE.

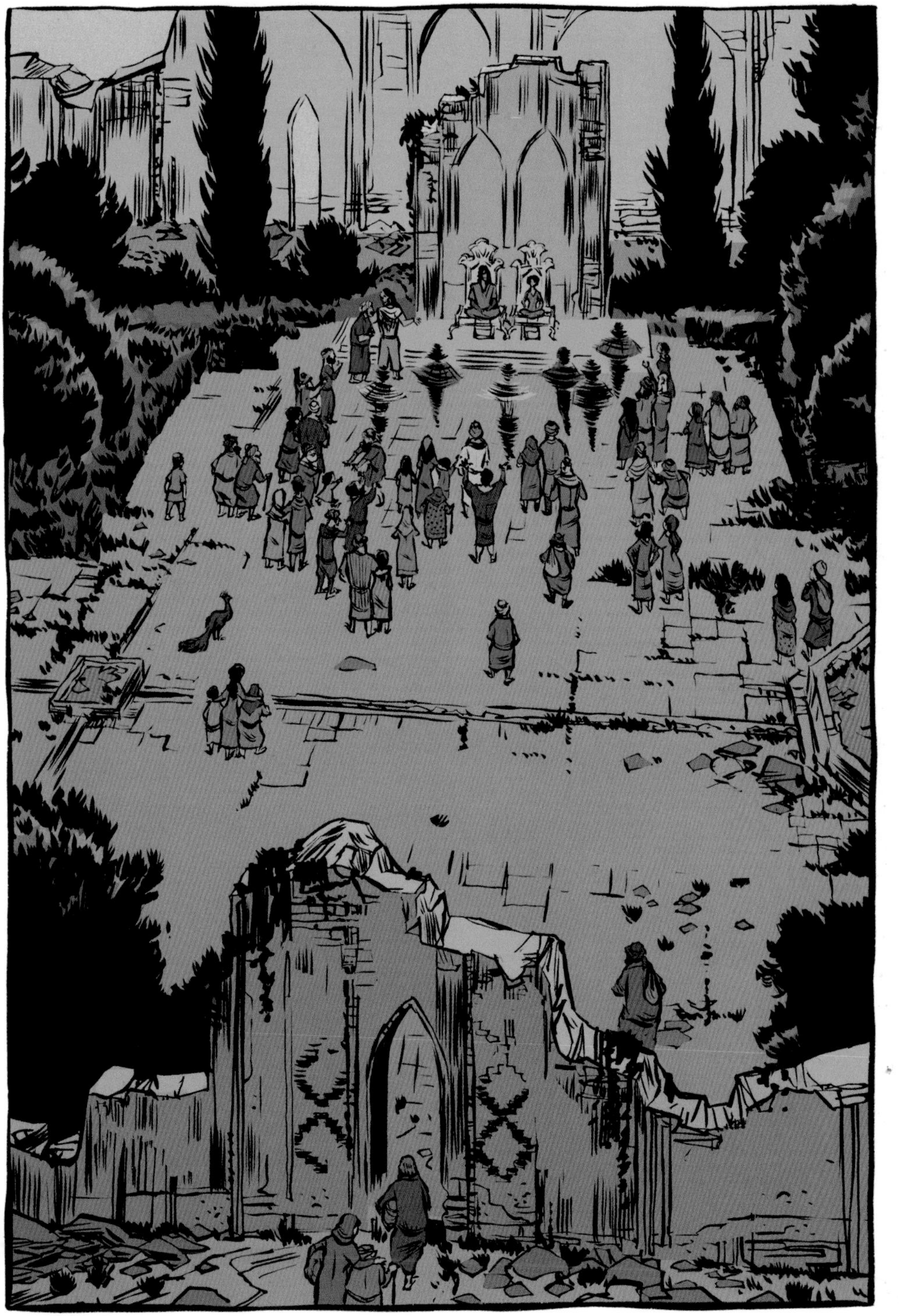

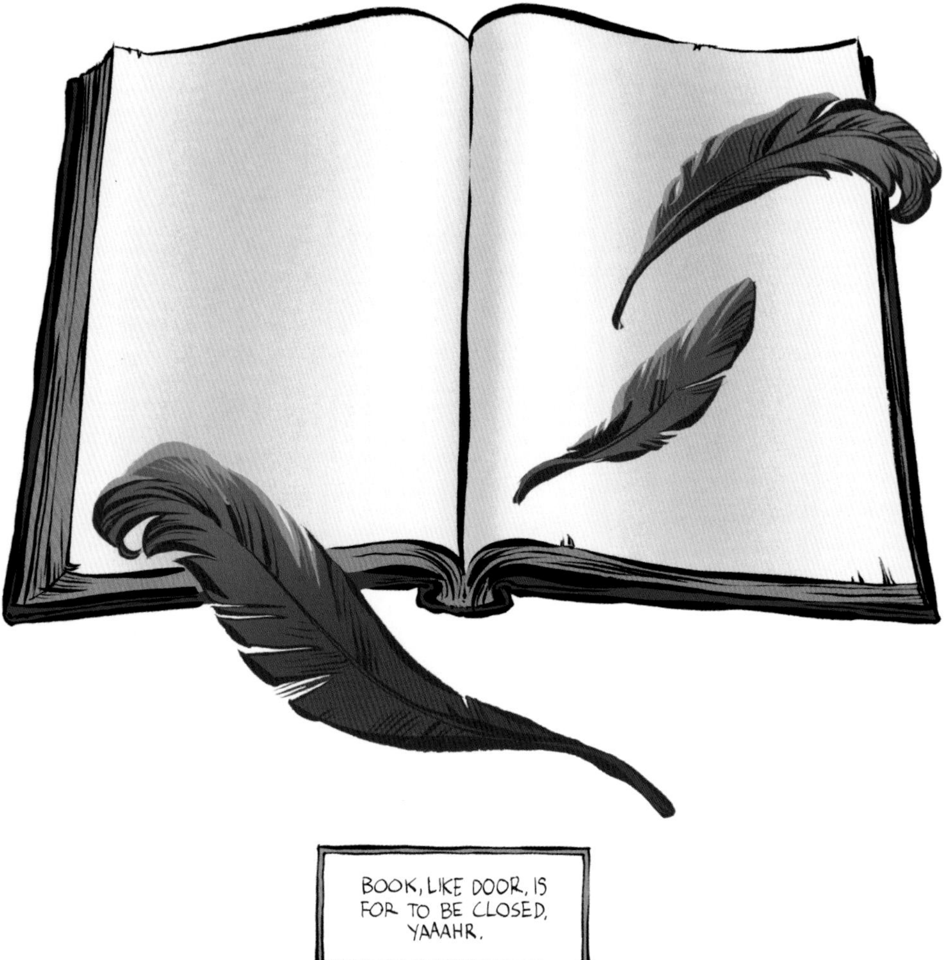
BOOK, LIKE DOOR, IS FOR TO BE CLOSED, YAAAHR.

For Jane and Ethan—J. M.

For Leo, our own little prince—L. P. & A. P.

"But helpless Pieces of the Game He plays

Upon this Chequer-board of Nights and Days;

Hither and thither moves, and checks, and slays,

And one by one back in the Closet lays."

—Omar Khayyam, Rubaiyat (trans. Fitzgerald, 1879)

WHO IS THE PRINCE?

❧

An Afterword by Jordan Mechner

Last year, while visiting UCLA's Powell Library, I saw a PlayStation 2 copy of *Prince of Persia: The Sands of Time* on display in a glass case alongside a 1903 edition of *The Arabian Nights*, a pack of Camel cigarettes, and a Las Vegas hotel ashtray with a picture of a harem girl. The title of the exhibition was "Seducing America: Selling the Middle Eastern Mystique."

It was an odd sensation finding my old familiar prince in such an unexpected place. I had lunch with the curator of the exhibit, an Israeli professor who collects twentieth century Orientalist pop-culture ephemera. I told him about the original *Prince of Persia* computer game, the one I'd programmed in the late 1980s. He was curious and asked where he might find a copy for his collection. You can download it for free, but what he really wanted was the box it came in.

BEGINNINGS

When I was twelve, I spent most of my free time drawing comics. I dreamed of a future with Bainbridge boards, T squares, and ink pen nibs.

Then the Apple II was invented.

A great thing about drawing comics is the intimacy of it. Hours vanish as you sit at your drawing board, absorbed in the characters and worlds you're creating. Comics were a perfect occupation for a kid inclined to daydreaming and solitude. So were computer games in the 1980s.

I found out quickly that I liked programming games and I liked animation—but what I loved was creating an imaginary universe that others could lose themselves in. The communion between game designer and player can be as personal as that between a novelist and reader. I wanted to create games that would not only challenge players but stir their emotions.

The Bainbridge boards went into the closet. I'd found a new obsession.

❧

It was 1985. I'd just graduated from college. I was in my old bedroom in the town where I'd grown up: eating my parents' food, playing video games, and thinking about a game I wanted to make and that I hoped Broderbund Software would publish. I knew the kind of running, jumping, puzzle-solving acrobatic game play I wanted. What I needed was a story.

It was Broderbund's Gene Portwood (a former Disney animator) who spoke the magic words: "What about Ali Baba; Sinbad?"

On that muggy, rainy August afternoon, in a single burst of creative energy, I wrote a two-page story about a boy who sets out to win a princess's love by stealing an amulet from the dungeons of an evil sultan. I didn't stop to think, much less do research. Ideas and vivid images poured out faster than I could write them down. It was as if the characters had been there all along, lying dormant, stored in a dream, and now sprang to life—animating themselves in my head, running, jumping, and even speaking.

Rotoscoped animation frames for *Prince of Persia* (1989)

I must have met them somewhere before, but where? Maybe in some illustrated storybook I'd read as a child. Or on late-night TV, in those days when movies were fascinating, elusive things you couldn't own, couldn't freeze in time, could only glimpse as they flitted past, having no idea when or if the opportunity to see them might come again.

Where do stories come from? All I know is that when they do come, it's smart to get out of their way.

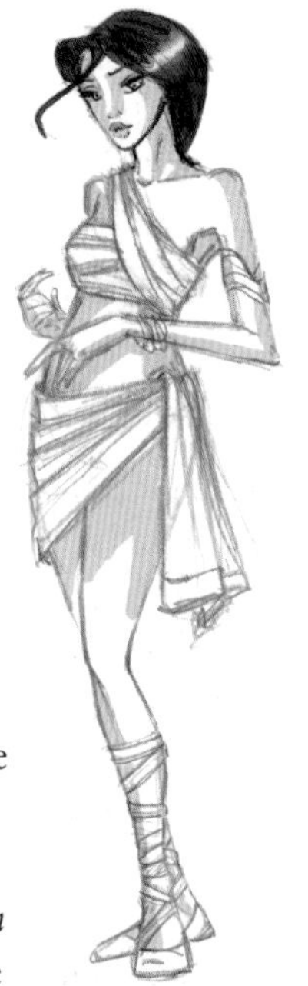

Concept art for Sands of Time (2003). Copyright © Ubisoft Entertainment. All rights reserved.

I moved to California and spent the next three years programming the game that would be *Prince of Persia*. The story line evolved, got tighter, streamlining and recombining elements. An evil sultan became a scheming vizier, a royal amulet was quietly dropped, a magic mirror was added.

One day I sat down at last and read *The Arabian Nights*. In those pages, I met my prince and princess, sultan and vizier, over and over in different guises. Shape-shifting, they peered out at me from behind different personas, like the broken fragments of a magic mirror.

Maybe the reason the land and characters of *The Arabian Nights* are so perfect for a video game is because they are themselves dreams. Peel away the layers of Western imaginings, the Hollywood harem girls and palm trees and, yes, video games that had fascinated my Israeli professor, and you find . . . more layers. Reading Husain Haddawy's excellent 1990 translation, I learned

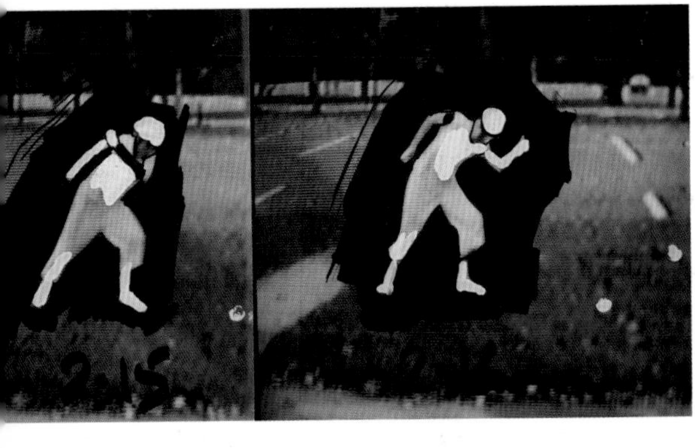

that what I'd believed were the original unexpurgated *Nights*, brought to the West by Galland, Lane, and Burton in the eighteenth and nineteenth centuries, are actually a hodgepodge of translation, invention, and outright forgery that medieval Arabic scholars are still trying to unravel. Even Haddawy's version, probably the truest available, is based on copies of copies of tales that, by the time they were first written down in the ninth or tenth century, were already older than anyone could remember.

I hadn't created the prince. I'd had the luck to tap into a deep, centuries-old well of other people's dreams.

In 1992 a Russian writer named Victor Pelevin wrote a short story about a Soviet government functionary who plays *Prince of Persia* so much that the game starts to merge with his reality. Set in the late 1980s, at a time when the American computers needed to play games such as *Prince of Persia* were still in short supply, the story made the game famous in Russia.

THE PRINCE ASSUMES A THOUSAND SHAPES

Given his slippery nature, it was inevitable that the prince would escape from my control. By 1992 *Prince of Persia* had become a worldwide best seller. Versions of the game were being sold on every computer and console platform I'd heard of and some I hadn't. Each new publisher and development team, in every country, put their own stamp on the graphics. The Super Nintendo prince didn't look quite like the Sega Genesis prince or the Sharp X68000 prince, the prince on the front of the box didn't look like the prince in the screen shots on the back, and some of them made me cringe.

I had no one to blame but myself. I'd chosen to present my story stripped down to its bare essentials, with characters that conveyed their personalities through gesture and action, not words. This left plenty of space for others to fill the void with their own imaginings.

Who is the prince? Does he have a name? How old is he? Is he a prince to start with, or does he become one by

"The little figure runs along the corridor. It is drawn with great affection, perhaps a little too sentimentally. If you press the <Up> key, it arches its back, and hangs in the air for a second, trying to catch hold of something above its head. If you press <Down> it squats and tries to pick something up from the ground under its feet. If you press <Right> it runs to the right, if you press <Left> it runs to the left. In fact you can use various keys to control it, but these four are the most important.

(. . .)

The final purpose is to reach the highest level, where the princess is waiting, but to do that you have to devote a lot of time to the game itself. In fact, to be successful, you have to forget that you're pressing keys and actually become the little figure— only then will it acquire the degree of agility required to fence, jump through the snapping body-scissors in the narrow stone corridors, leap over the stone shafts and run over the collapsing flagstones, each of which can only support the weight of a body for seconds—although the figure has no body, let alone any weight, and neither, if you think about it, do the tumbling slabs of stone, no matter how convincing the sound might be when they fall."

—Victor Pelevin, "Prince of Central Planning" (1992)

Prince of Persia in Japan: Super FamiCom *Prince of Persia* box (1992)

marrying the princess? What land is he from, who are his parents, what is the sultan a sultan of, and what century is it anyway?

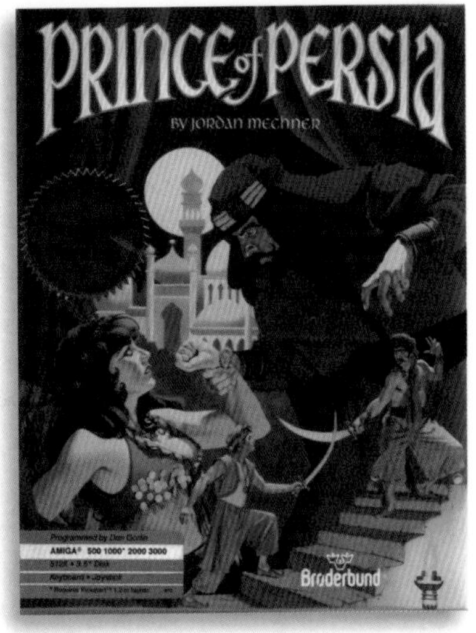
PRINCE of PERSIA
BY JORDAN MECHNER
Broderbund
Amiga *Prince of Persia* box (1990)

"Long ago in a certain city there lived a king . . ." *The Arabian Nights* tales rarely got more specific than that about time and place, and neither did 1980s video games. Baghdad or Samarkand, the ninth century or the twelfth—what did it matter so long as there was a scheming vizier, a beautiful princess, and a palace on a moonlit night? On the 280 x 192 screen of the Apple II, where the characters' faces were four pixels square, such details hardly seemed to matter.

But as the 1980s became the 1990s, as video-game technology improved, and teams of artists and engineers I would never meet began translating *Prince of Persia* to platforms with more memory and higher-resolution graphics, those questions I'd left unanswered started to chafe.

In 1993 Broderbund published the prince's second adventure, *The Shadow and the Flame*. Hoping to preempt the proliferation of princes and inconsistent backstories that my first game had spawned, I'd written up what I intended to be a definitive "bible" establishing the prince's past once and for all—as George Lucas had done for *Star Wars*, planting the seeds that would flower in future episodes.

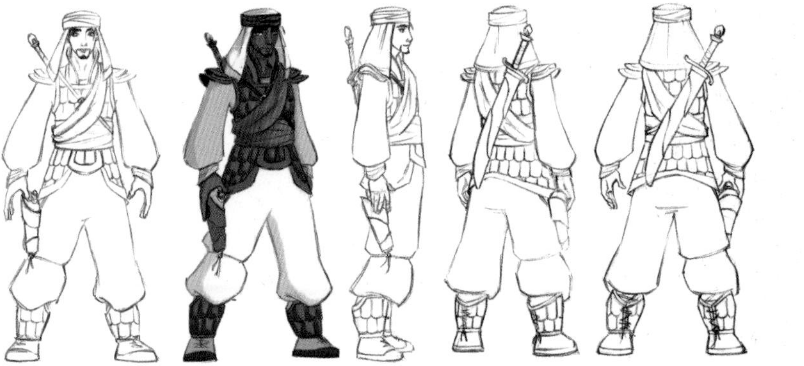
Concept art for *Sands of Time* (2003).

Even while I was writing it, I'd had a vague sense that it didn't feel quite right. In hindsight, I think my real problem was that in trying to force *Prince of Persia* into the Western, Nordic epic-trilogy-struggle-between-good-and-evil format that had worked for Lucas—and Tolkien and Wagner before him—I'd failed to take into account the prince's origins as an *Arabian Nights* character. Those were tales of wisps and dreams, whose nature was to spin and embroider themselves out of nothing, only to vanish again in the shimmering mist. In Wagner, everything is destiny. In the *Nights*, anything can happen.

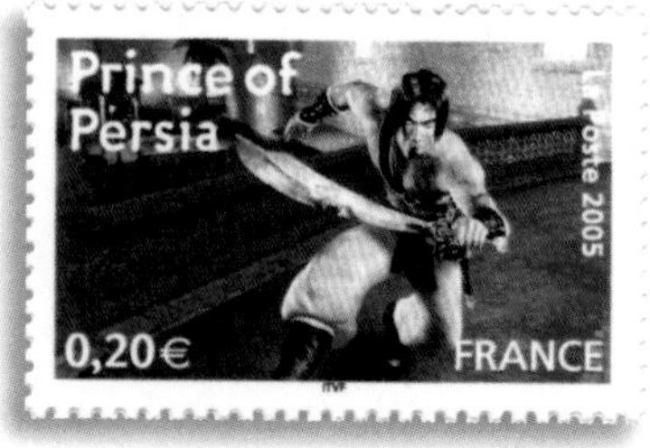
Prince of
Persia
Poste 2005
0,20€
FRANCE

As it turned out, I never got the chance to complete my epic trilogy. The big video-game sensation of 1993 was *Doom*, the first 3-D shooter. The public no longer wanted 2-D platformers; plans for a third *Prince of Persia* game were quietly shelved. Six years later, Broderbund tried to catch up by releasing *Prince of Persia 3D*, but the project was plagued by difficulties, and landed not with a bang but a whimper.

It seemed that the prince's adventures had run their course. And, I told myself, maybe that wasn't entirely a bad thing. He'd traveled so far from his origins, I hardly recognized him anymore.

In 2003, the prince got that rarest of things: a second chance.

When I joined Ubisoft Montreal as writer and game designer of the title we hoped would revive the all-but-dead *Prince of Persia* franchise, the team faced a daunting challenge. The best-remembered title in the series, the first one, was almost fourteen years old. In video-game years, that's an eternity.

Fittingly, the tale we chose to tell was about second chances. *Prince of Persia: The Sands of Time* is the story of a young warrior who is tricked by the villain into making a terrible mistake that threatens to destroy

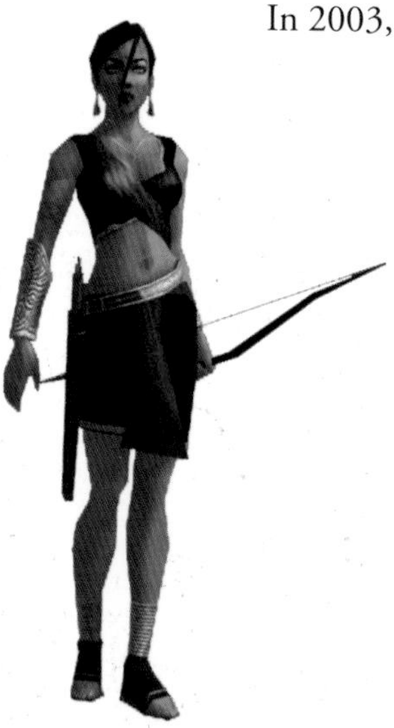

Character model for *Sands of Time* (2003). Copyright © Ubisoft Entertainment. All rights reserved.

not only his kingdom, but the fabric of reality itself. Only through heroic effort, helped by a princess he loves but is never quite sure whether to trust, can he set things right.

From the original game we took an hourglass; the basic triangle of prince, princess, and vizier; and a certain style of game play. The rest was new. The tremendous advance in graphics and sound technology meant that a team of talented artists could realize the prince's world with greater beauty and detail than ever before.

A decade and a half after he'd first run and jumped across an Apple II screen, the pixelly prince found his footing: ninth-century Persia—a time of warfare and intrigue, perfect for a tale of romance and adventure.

Doing research for *Sands of Time*, I picked up the *Shahnameh*, the Persian Book of Kings, set in verse a thousand years ago by the great poet Ferdosi. Reading the complete work for the first time, in an edition beautifully illustrated with sixteenth-century Persian miniatures, was a revelation to me.

The *Shahnameh* represents a different tradition from *The Arabian Nights*. Its epic tales of kings and heroes are to the East what Norse mythology is to northern Europe. A Persian prince like the one in *Sands of Time* would have grown up steeped in the oral tradition of the *Shahnameh*; he would have spoken about the strength of Rustam the way a 20-year-old soldier today might casually refer to Superman or the Hulk. (And, in *Sands of Time*, he does.) But as much as the prince aspires to resemble the noble warriors of the *Shahnameh*, doomed to fulfill their heroic destinies, he can't quite shed the basically happy-go-lucky nature of an *Arabian Nights* prince, stumbling from one adventure into the next. It's his inability to resolve this conflict that gives him his particular charm.

Ubisoft followed up *Sands of Time* with two sequels, *Warrior Within* and *The Two Thrones*, which gave the prince a more ruthless, violent edge. They're hard at work now in Montreal crafting his next adventure, which promises

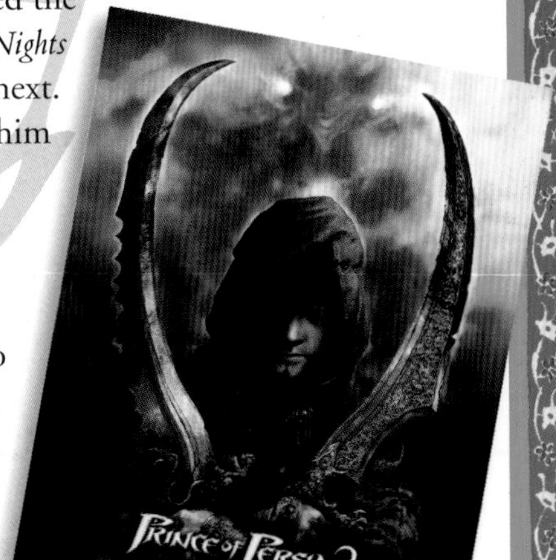
PRINCE OF PERSIA 2
NOVEMBER 2004
Poster for *Warrior Within* (2004). Copyright © Ubisoft Entertainment. All rights reserved.

Concept art for *The Two Thrones* (2005). Copyright © Ubisoft Entertainment. All rights reserved.

to feel closer in spirit to the romantic fantasy of *Sands of Time* and of the original game.

Jerry Bruckheimer and Walt Disney Pictures are making a *Prince of Persia* movie. I wrote the screenplay, but I won't be surprised if in his journey to the screen, the prince once again transforms into a somewhat different shape than I'd initially envisioned. This prince is a survivor. In the past two decades, he's shown himself more adaptable and resilient than I ever expected.

Will the actor who plays the prince in the movie become the real, definitive Prince of Persia? Will he supplant the prince in the video games? Can so many princes coexist peacefully?

Or are they all somehow the same person?

GAMES TO COMICS

In 2004 I got an e-mail from Mark Siegel, the editor of a new publishing imprint called First Second Books. He told me that *Prince of Persia* had had a special place in his heart since the early 1990s, when he'd first played it on a black-and-white Macintosh Classic. Would I be interested in developing it as a graphic novel?

He didn't know he was offering to fulfill one of my childhood dreams.

As Mark and I got to know each other, we found out that we had a lot in common—including a passion for the French hardcover graphic novels called *bandes dessinées*. I'd fallen in love with the work of Hugo Pratt, Enki Bilal, and François Schuiten in my twenties, when I spent a year in France. Their books had been a huge influence on my video-game writing, especially *The Last Express* and *Sands of Time*. When Mark told me that one of his missions for First Second is to foster European-quality graphic novels in the United States, I got even more excited.

And when artists LeUyen Pham and Alex Puvilland came on board, with their rich backgrounds in children's illustration and Dreamworks feature animation, we were more certain than ever that a graphic novel about the prince's adventures could be something special.

The question was, which prince?

The plucky Aladdin-like street urchin of the first game? The orphan-with-a-mythic-destiny of *The Shadow and the Flame*? The guilt-ridden young warrior of *Sands of Time*? The battle-hardened fugitive he became in *Warrior Within* and *The Two Thrones*? Or the prince of the *Sands of Time* movie—or

rather of the screenplay, which will have been rewritten many times over by the time cameras roll?

Which one is the true Prince of Persia? All of them. And none of them.

Our search for a writer who could encompass this paradox led us to the mysterious and reclusive A. B. Sina.

When A. B. asked us what we expected him to write, we said we weren't sure, exactly, but the connection to the video games should be deep below the surface, not evident at first glance. We didn't want an adaptation of any of the games or of the movie, but a new story that would tap into the deep wellspring of Persian myth, legend, and history from whence the prince had arisen.

A. B. thought about it for a bit, then remarked that in the tales of the East—from *The Arabian Nights* to Sufi stories—the characters' conflicts and relationships tend to be with the structure of reality itself, the structure of consciousness, rather than with individual psychological issues as we tend to focus on in the West. He pointed out that the struggle against destiny is the most universal of all struggles, that it fuels the American myths and the American dream, as well as Eastern ones.

We were off and running.

Playing video games is all about timing, so it's not too surprising that in every *Prince of Persia* story so far, time itself has been a central motif.

What is interesting is that with each iteration, the time frame seems to expand. The first game was confined to the hour it took for the sands in Jaffar's hourglass to run out. *Sands of Time* took place over several days, with the menace embodied by a different kind of hourglass. The *Sands of Time* movie screenplay paints a broader canvas and takes place over weeks. And the graphic novel spans centuries—specifically, two parallel stories unfolding four centuries apart.

A. B. has woven a delightfully subversive tale offering us not just one, but many Persian princes. All in their different ways fighting wild beasts and magical creatures, falling in love with princesses, and falling afoul of scheming viziers, as my prince had done for at least a thousand years before he ran and jumped through a late-summer rainstorm onto the Apple II computer screen.

One of the possible princes in A. B. Sina's story wonders if he is prophesying the future, or if the future is remembering him.

A sentiment the original Prince of Persia, wherever he is, must surely sympathize with.

Los Angeles
October 2007

Opposite: Concept art for the upcoming *Prince of Persia* video game.

Other Treasures from the First Second *Collection*

AMERICAN
BORN
CHINESE
Gene Luen Yang
FINALIST

★ AMERICAN BORN CHINESE

By Gene Yang

Winner of the
Michael L. Printz Award
A National Book Award
Finalist
"Gene Luen Yang has created that rare article: a youthful tale with something new to say about American youth."
– *New York Times*
★ *School Library Journal*, starred review

Christophe Blain
GUS

GUS

by Christophe Blain

Why become the sharpest sharp-shooter in the West? Why, for the women, of course! Gus is a whirlwind caper by one of the greatest talents in comics today.

THE FATE OF THE ARTIST

By Eddie Campbell

"Playful and wise, Campbell's latest report from the art front continues to demonstrate his mastery of the comics medium."
★ – *Booklist*, starred review
★ *Publishers Weekly*, starred review

EDDIE CAMPBELL
THE FATE of THE ARTIST

Notes for a War Story

NOTES FOR A WAR STORY

By Gipi

"[A] hard, human meditation on war and a society on the fringes of anomie."
– *Kirkus*, graphic novel spotlight

Three Shadows
Cyril Pedrosa

THREE SHADOWS

By Cyril Pedrosa

An affecting tale of a father's overwhelming love for his son and his struggle to protect him from a tragic fate.

EMMANUEL GUIBERT
ALAN'S WAR
THE MEMORIES OF G.I. ALAN COPE

ALAN'S WAR

By Emmanuel Guibert

The poignant graphic biography of World War II veteran Alan Cope.

JOANN SFAR
VAMPIRE LOVES

VAMPIRE LOVES

By Joann Sfar

"Sfar's artwork is effortlessly charming . . . a story that is funny and unpredictable."
– *Publishers Weekly*

KLEZMER

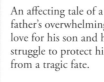

KLEZMER

By Joann Sfar

"Profane, messy, jagged and wildly enthusiastic, much like klezmer itself."
– *Publishers Weekly*

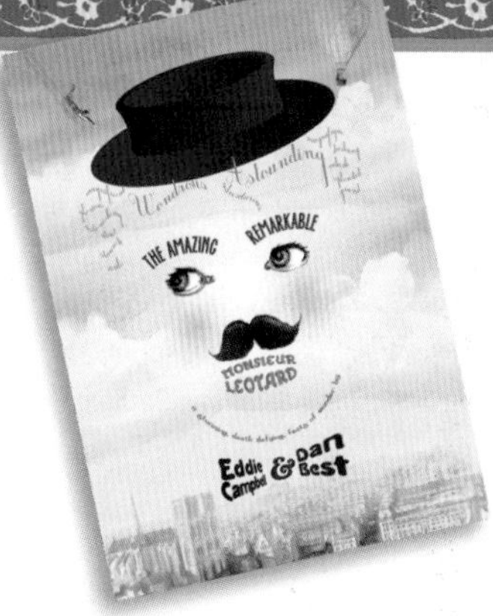
The Amazing Remarkable
Monsieur Leotard
Eddie Campbell & Dan Best

THE AMAZING REMARKABLE MONSIEUR LEOTARD

By Eddie Campbell & Dan Best

An adventure following the turn-of-the-century life of the amazing and remarkable Monsieur Leotard, Acrobat and Circus Manager, both before and after his tragic death by misadventure.

SLOW STORM

By Danica Novgorodoff

Tornado season in Kentucky brings together an illegal immigrant and a firefighter struggling with her job and family in this powerful American drama about homesickness, horses, storms, and saints.

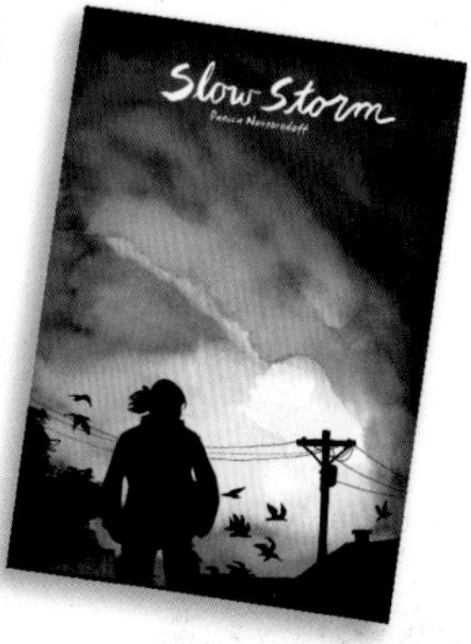
Slow Storm
Danica Novgorodoff

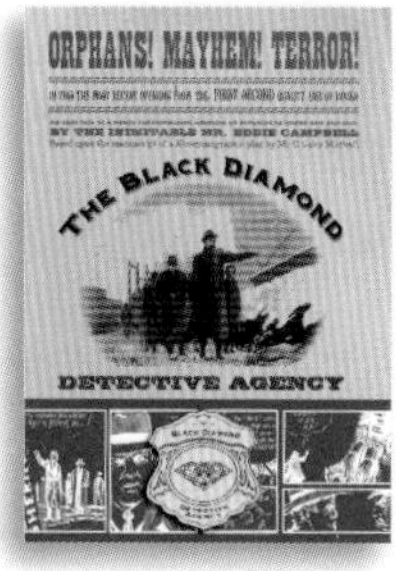
ORPHANS! MAYHEM! TERROR!
BY THE INIMITABLE MR. EDDIE CAMPBELL
THE BLACK DIAMOND
DETECTIVE AGENCY

THE BLACK DIAMOND DETECTIVE AGENCY

By Eddie Campbell

"A turn-of-the-century pulp thriller." – *Kirkus*

THE LOST COLONY

ANNJ 09SDRMNCFQ@RR BNMRОHQ@BX

By Grady Klein

"[A] witty, sophisticated, candy-colored adventure." – *Booklist*

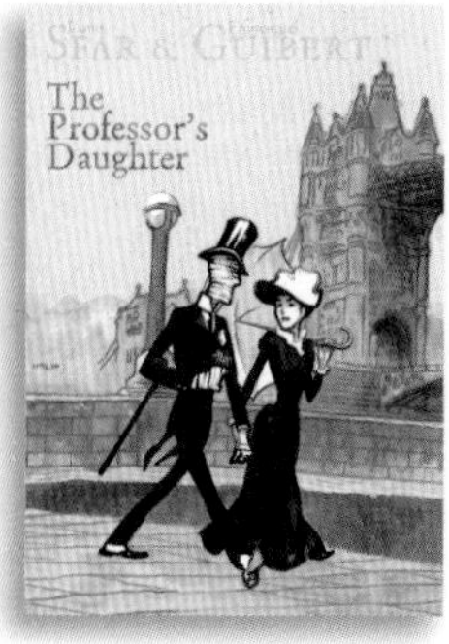
Sfar & Guibert
The Professor's Daughter

★ THE PROFESSOR'S DAUGHTER

By Emmanuel Guibert & Joann Sfar

"No glorified comic book, this graphic novel aspires to fine art."
★ – *Kirkus*, starred review
★ *BCCB*, starred review

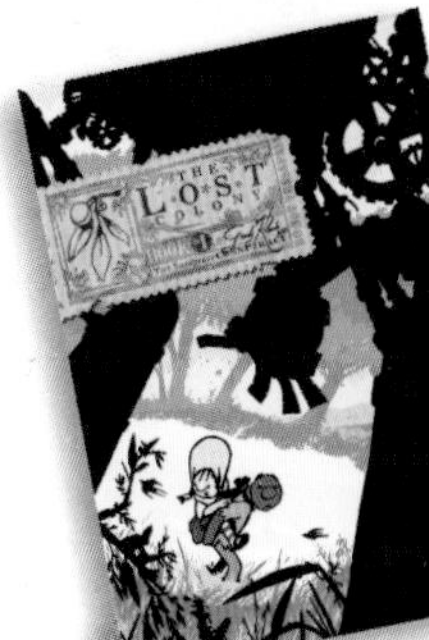
The Lost Colony

THE LOST COLONY

ANNJ 19SDQDC L DM@BD

By Grady Klein

"Insightful satire . . . willingness to suspend PC tsk-tsking comes in handy [for] enjoying . . . Klein's skewering re-enactment of the bad old days." – *Booklist*

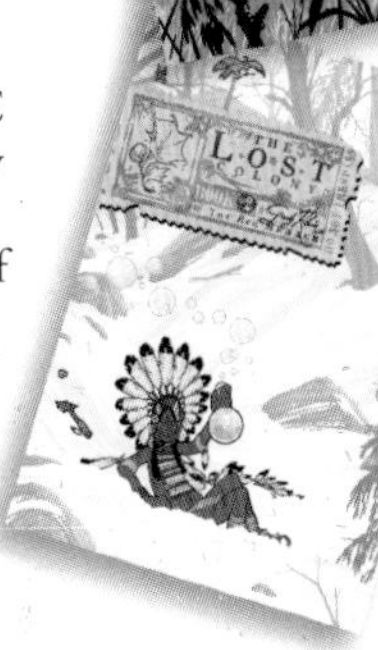
The Lost Colony

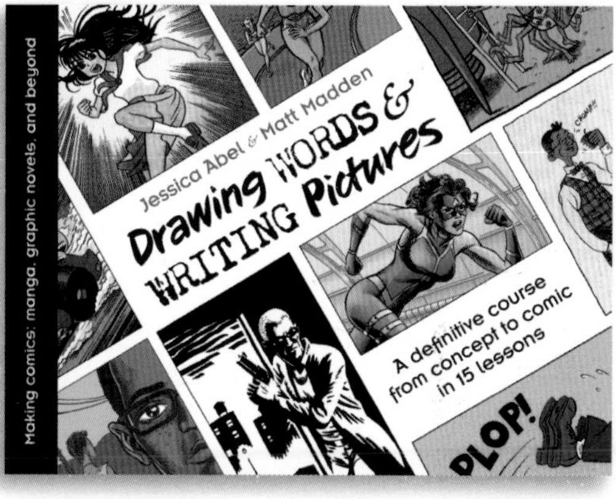
Making comics: manga, graphic novels, and beyond
Jessica Abel & Matt Madden
Drawing Words & Writing Pictures
A definitive course from concept to comic in 15 lessons
PLOP!

DRAWING WORDS & WRITING PICTURES

By Jessica Abel & Matt Madden

"A gold mine of essential information for every aspiring comics artist. Highly recommended." – Scott McCloud, author of *Understanding Comics*

Jessica ABEL
Gabe SORIA
Warren PLEECE
Life SUCKS

LIFE SUCKS

BY JESSICA ABEL, GABE SORIA, AND WARREN PLEECE

Life sucks for Dave Marshall – he hates his job, the girl he's in love with doesn't know he exists, and to top it all off, his boss just turned him into a vampire.

LAIKA
NICK ABADZIS

★ LAIKA

BY NICK ABADZIS

"A luminous masterpiece filled with pathos and poignancy."
★– *Kirkus*, STARRED REVIEW
★ *Publishers Weekly*, STARRED REVIEW

Garage Band

GARAGE BAND

BY GIPI

". . . real teens struggling to find their paths in life, sorting out what really matters to them." – *VOYA*

JOURNEY INTO MOHAWK COUNTRY

BY GEORGE O'CONNOR

"The book's quality ensures its place in studies of pre-Revolutionary America." – *Kirkus*

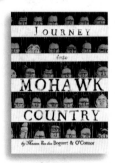

JOURNEY
into
MOHAWK
COUNTRY

A.L.I.E.E.E.N.
LEWIS TRONDHEIM

A.L.I.E.E.E.N.

BY LEWIS TRONDHEIM

"Readers will be delighted by this wordless tale with endearing, yet rascally alien characters." – *Kirkus*

★ Winner of the INTERNATIONAL HORROR GUILD'S AWARD for 'Best Illustrated Narrative.'

STASSEN
DEOGRATIAS
A TALE OF RWANDA

★ DEOGRATIAS A Tale of Rwanda

BY J.P. STASSEN

"The importance of the story and the heartbreaking beauty of its presentation make it an essential purchase."
★ – *Kirkus*, STARRED REVI

★ KAMPUNG BOY

BY LAT

"This companionable chronicle achieves that rare thing in an international title: making readers feel like they're hanging out with a friend halfway around the world."
★– *BCCB*, STARRED REVIEW
★ *Booklist*, STARRED REVIEW
★ *School Library Journal*, STARRED REVIEW

Kampung Boy

TOWN BOY

★ MISSOURI BOY

BY LELAND MYRICK

"The tenderness and intimacy of the spare words and pictures . . . set the book apart."
★ – *Booklist*, STARRED REVIEW

MISSOURI BOY
by Leland Myrick